Good Practice in

Play

3rd Edition

Paul Bonel
Jennie Lindon

Series Editor: Miranda Walker

Nelson Thornes

First published in 1996 as *Good Practice in Playwork* by Stanley Thornes
(Publishers) Ltd
Second edition 2000

This edition published in 2009 by:
Nelson Thornes Ltd
Delta Place
27 Bath Road
CHELTENHAM
GL53 7TH
United Kingdom

09   10   11   12   13   /   10   9   8   7   6   5   4   3   2   1

A catalogue record for this book is available from the British Library

ISBN 978 1 4085 0492 5

Front cover photograph © DigitalVision/Punchstock
Illustrations by Jane Bottomley
Page make-up by Columns Design Ltd

Printed and bound in Spain by GraphyCems

FOREWORD

My car once blew up on the M2. Our five children were on board and we all got out and stood on the verge waiting for the AA to turn up. The adults were fed up and anxious, and soon got irritable with each other.

But then I noticed the children. They had found a particular kind of grass which, if you whack it against another piece of grass, will lose its little head. They then devised some kind of knockout tournament in grass-whacking . . . It was a wonderful example of how children will, if given the chance, go into play mode. But what *is* children's play?

I think play is a way of dealing with – experimenting with – the surrounding world, or parts of it. It is a way of exposing yourself, and your surrounding world, to chance, trial and error – and seeing what happens. Maybe that's a pompous way of describing children mucking around with bits of grass. But I do think such a description lends dignity and seriousness to play, which is, after all, central to effective learning.

Many people think that learning has something to do with someone barking facts at 30 children sitting in a classroom. In fact, learning nearly always involves some element of trial and error. It is vital for children to grow up having safe places where they can work with trusted and experienced people, to experiment with aspects of their world in a spirit of trial and error.

Paul Bonel and Jennie Lindon's book is especially welcome for the way it embraces this philosophy whilst offering a thorough and rigorous course for students to follow.

Michael Rosen

DEDICATIONS

To Felicity, Rachel and Finn; and to Lance, Drew and Tanith.

CONTENTS

ABOUT THE AUTHORS

Paul Bonel is Playwork Development Manager with the National Training Organisation for Sport, Recreation and Allied Occupations (SPRITO). He originally joined SPRITO on a secondment from the National Centre for Playwork Education – London to set up a Playwork Unit dedicated to education and training. The Unit is pioneering work on peer-led endorsement for the Playwork sector. Paul also writes poetry and plays.

Jennie Lindon is a Child Psychologist who has specialised in working with children, young people and the services for them and their families. She runs her own business as a consultant, trainer and writer. She has published many books and articles, some written for workers with children and young people, and some for parents.

Miranda Walker has worked with children from birth to 16 years in a range of settings, including her own day nursery and out of school clubs. She has inspected nursery provision for OFSTED, and worked at East Devon College as an Early Years and Playwork lecturer and NVQ assessor and internal verifier. She is a regular contributor to industry magazines and an established author.

ACKNOWLEDGEMENTS

We would like to thank the workers and children from the projects who feature in many of the photographs: these are the Notting Hill Adventure Playground, Battersea Adventure Playground, Ashburnham Adventure Playground, Angell Town Adventure Playground and Loughborough Play Centre.

Thank you to Caroline Kerslake who took all the photographs in the book with the exception of those credited separately below.

Thank you to the following organisations for permission to reproduce material:
- Kidsactive for the photograph on page 227, taken by Tilly Odell.
- Play on the Estates in Hackney for the photograph on page 16.
- The Asthma UK for the Asthma Attack card on page 211.
- The Health and Safety Executive for the F2508 notice on page 208.

We would also like to thank the following people for advice and information during the writing of the book:
- Anna Lubelska, who introduced us and first suggested the idea of this book.
- Maureen McCree and Betty Campbell for access to their NVQ portfolios.
- Liz Leicester – the London Borough of Camden.
- Mick Conway – Hackney Play Association.
- Paul Durr – Pooles Park Playcentre, London Borough of Islington.
- Steven Derby – St John's Wood Adventure Playground, London Borough of Westminster.
- Steve Flynn – The Log Cabin, Ealing.
- Glynis Knight – Brent Children's Services.
- Mary Miles and Fiona Mitchell – Miles and Mitchell Training.
- Dave Wainwright – Hayward Adventure Playground, Islington.
- The National Centre for Playwork Education – London for building Paul's writing on the first edition into the National Centre – London work programme.

Crown copyright © material is reproduced under Class Licence No. CO1 W0000195 with the permission of the Controller of HMSO and the Queen's Printer for Scotland.

The National Centre for Playwork Education – London is developing education and training opportunities at both a regional and national level. In cooperation with partners in London and the South East, the centre works on innovative training and assessment projects for playworkers, managers and volunteers. Through publications, discussion groups and seminars, the centre also contributes to the expanding skills and knowledge base of playwork. One of four centres in England, the National Centre – London is based in Islington and managed by a consortium of people from play and play training.

INTRODUCTION

Good practice

Playwork goes on in a wide range of play settings, which have evolved from vary-ing traditions in provision, or responses to the perceived local needs. Yet, all play-workers have in common their wish to provide the best for those children and young people who use their play facility. Playwork is in a new phase of change and those who work in the area have needed to look carefully at their key values and the details of what leads to good quality work.

This book has been written with the aim of bringing together important themes within good practice, but with full recognition of the knowledge and understanding which needs to underpin any practice. Discussion and debate are still continuing for the many aspects to playwork in all the different settings. There will never be complete agreement on all issues, and this is equally true of other areas of work with children and young people.

Communication with others as well as personal reflection and review are essential to good practice. However, playworkers faced with children and young people cannot postpone interesting activities for the users in favour of lengthy debates. Activity and review have to go hand in hand. It was with this realism in mind that we have written a book that blends practice and principle.

All the chapters are based in the realities of undertaking playwork with chil-dren and young people. The ideas and any suggestions are grounded in exam-ples which have been taken from real people and places, only the names, of children and play settings, have been changed for confidentiality.

USING THE BOOK

This book will be useful to you in whatever play setting you work currently, since the basic tenets of good practice apply to all the different settings and the book draws on examples from the full range. The content will support you in extend-ing your skills and reflecting on your work, whether you are relatively new to the area of playwork or are more experienced, perhaps at the stage of now guiding others as they gain their own experience.

Some readers of the book will be attending, or planning to attend, a course in playwork. This may well be a course that underpins the system of Scottish or National Vocational Qualifications (the S/NVQs). The content of this book has been designed to support most of the units for levels 2 and 3 of the S/NVQ com-petencies. The revised and extended edition of the book takes account of the changes in the Playwork S/NVQs. The chapters have been arranged so that you can easily select the material in the order that is best for your own study.

Appendix B will help you if you wish to find material that is relevant to particular S/NVQ units activities relevant to particular key skills.

Some of the suggested activities can be followed without additional help. However, part of improving your own playwork practice will be taking opportunities to talk over what you have observed or discovered with colleagues, or with your supervisor on a course.

In most courses of study you will be developing your own portfolio of work. The examples and activities in the book provide many suggestions for exploring aspects to the work. Some of the activities will ask you not only to do something – find out information or obtain details on how your work setting deals with an issue – but also to think over the implications of what you have found, or the new questions that now arise. Appendix A will help you to plan an effective portfolio.

Continuing development of good playwork practice has emphasised the importance of thought and discussion about completed activities and events, as well as a valuable focus on what is actually done day-by-day. The idea of the *reflective practitioner* in playwork is that playworkers new to the profession develop a habit of reflection and that even experienced playworkers do not abandon this aspect of practice. The reflective practitioner in playwork is someone who is able and willing to:

■ think over what has happened as well as become closely involved in activities with children and young people. This does not mean considerable amounts of time spent in deep thought! It is about a willingness and enthusiasm to think sometimes as well as do

■ consider issues and events from more than one perspective, from that of the children, or the parents, as well as the playwork team

■ acknowledge and recognise feelings: your own, those of the children and of other adults (colleagues and parents)

■ plan ahead, whilst being flexible for the possibilities of the moment and children's interests

■ review activities and approaches and realise that finding scope for improvement is not necessarily a criticism of what has gone before

■ be open-minded and willing to continue to learn, no matter how many years of experience you have had.

Two NVQ units, A53 in level 2 and A55 in level 3, are especially linked to the effort to develop as a reflective practitioner within your playwork. You need to learn how to evaluate your own practice, to learn from constructive feedback from others (colleagues, the children, parents) and to give useful feedback in your turn. Some sections within Chapter 9 are specifically relevant to giving and receiving feedback and learning within your play setting. However, all the other chapters give plenty of opportunities to develop aspects of being a reflective practitioner in different areas of playwork.

Good practice in playwork, as in any other area of work with children and young people, does not require that playworkers lose their individuality. Part of being an effective playworker in any setting is that children and young people can see that you are a real person, with ideas, interests and feelings. This book will support you in developing your playwork practice and in being a genuine support to the children and young people who come to your play setting with the wish to enjoy their play.

1 *THE TRADITION OF PLAYWORK*

The development of playwork

Playwork is a relatively young profession. In England the origins of play centres can be traced back to early 1900 and adventure play to 1943 – both explored later. Recognition of playwork as an occupational area is even more recent and it was only in 1992 that it at last gained its own national vocational qualification. The National Vocational Qualification (SVQ in Scotland), through its description of the playworker's tasks and underpinning knowledge, has shown the complex and sophisticated nature of the playworker's job. In the four nations of England, Wales, Scotland and Northern Ireland, playworkers are operating in a rich variety of settings. Despite this the playwork field is still a fragmented one and it is only in recent years that attempts have been made on coordination in England and between the four nations.

GOOD PRACTICE

Playworkers need to gain an understanding of the tradition of playwork. Placing what you do now in the context of where it has come from can give a fuller and firmer base to your work. It can also be instructive to consider the way in which playwork has evolved over the years and how it has consistently changed and grown in its scope and professionalism.

SORENSON AND THE JUNK PLAYGROUND

It was in 1931 that the Danish architect C Th. Sorenson first mentioned his idea of a 'sort of junk playground in which children could create and shape, dream and imagine, and make dreams and imagination a reality'. In 1943 Sorenson's own dream became a reality when the first playground opened in Emdrup Weg, on a huge new housing project close to the centre of Copenhagen. Dedicated to the freedom of exploration that Sorenson believed in it was no more than a

Children constructing a den

large open space surrounded by an earth bank. The children were free to come and go as they wished and Sorenson was fortunate in that his first playleader, John Bertelsen, fully shared his vision and imagination. All sorts of materials and equipment were shipped onto the site to facilitate the children in digging, building and generally creating their own environment. Bertelsen's philosophy was to be a helpful and enthusiastic guide and assistant to the children but to generally intervene as little as possible. Like Sorenson he saw it as the children's space in which they should be empowered to shape it in their own way as long as it wasn't going to endanger themselves or others. From accounts of the early days and months of this project the playground literally exploded into life. Here is a recollection of Bertelsen himself from 1943.

> At 10.45 am today the playground opened. The weather was cool and the sky overcast. In spite of this, by 9.30 the children were already pushing at the door to the promised land. Due to a slight misunderstanding I didn't have the key until 10.15 and was unable to open up until fifteen minutes later than planned.
>
> By this time some fifty to seventy-five children, together with a few mothers and grandmothers, had gathered. Grumbling dissatisfaction at the still-locked door increased each minute, as did the number of children, and the situation was beginning to look almost threatening.

> *Then at last the company's carpenter arrived with the key, the door was opened and the children burst through, completely taking over the playground, appropriating wheelbarrows and everything.*
>
> *We began by moving all the building material in the open shed. Bricks, boards, firposts and cement pillars were moved to the left alongside the entrance, where building and digging started right away. The work was done by children aged 4 to 17. It went on at full speed and all the workers were in high spirits; dust, sweat, warning shouts and a few scratches all created just the right atmosphere. The children's play- and work-ground had opened, and they knew how to take full advantage of it.*
>
> *When I eventually closed the door at 6.15pm, approximately 900 children had visited the playground.*

The level of activity was staggering and with the building of camps, dens and gardens as some of the principal occupations the site soon developed into a huge network of dwellings. This tradition continued and Emdrup today is like a children's village. Some of the 'dwellings' are quite sophisticated and everywhere there are the results of the children's planting including mature trees that have grown over more than fifty years since the playground was established. The idea caught on and the junk playground movement took off in Denmark and neighbouring countries. It also inspired people in England who were similarly interested in the notion of children's freedom to play, particularly in the urban areas of Britain after the war.

JUNK PLAY TO ADVENTURE PLAY

It was Lady Allen of Hurtwood, an active campaigner for children's rights, who took on the idea of junk playgrounds after a visit to Copenhagen in the late 1940s. Following her visit she wrote enthusiastically about the idea and set up an 'Under 14s Council' to campaign for the establishment of junk playgrounds in this country. Her vision was to enable local communities to set up projects using unused or waste ground along the lines of the Danish experiment. Between 1948 and 1953 several pilot projects were set up, the first being in Camberwell, South London. They all came into being by the enthusiasm and commitment of volunteers. It wasn't until the mid 1950s however that the idea began to take on some permanence with the interest and financial support of the National Playing Fields Association (NPFA) and the London County Council (LCC). The shortage of funds to pay permanent staff and keep the playgrounds supplied with materials and equipment had meant that the early projects, despite the good will involved, proved unsustainable. The model of the voluntary managed playground, however, with grant aid and employed staff – but run by local people – continues today. Of course many playgrounds have also over the years been set up and run by local authorities.

In 1953 a conference was organised to discuss the junk play experiment and in the following few years the first NPFA funded projects were set up in

Liverpool, Grimsby, Bristol and London. It was also at this conference that the term 'adventure' playground was first used in a public forum considering what was then still a 'junk' playground movement. It is not clear why the term 'adventure' rather than 'junk' was used except perhaps for its inherent acceptability in some quarters. However, in his book *Grounds for Play*, Joe Benjamin, one of the early pioneer playworkers and the first to document the movement's evolution, recognised the significance of such a change. He quotes John Bertelsen: 'The junk playground should be characterised by signs of wear and tear. It should be a safety valve to children whose town existence otherwise keeps them nice and well ordered. I think by calling these playgrounds by other names something very important is excluded – the margin that keeps room for destruction and junk play.'

It is difficult to judge how much the change of title from 'junk' to 'adventure' influenced the evolution of these forms of provision. What is clear is that the junk play idea has been complemented by the more permanent constructions such as timber swings and platforms seen on many adventure playgrounds today.

Throughout the 1960s, 1970s and even into the early 1980s adventure playgrounds continued to grow. In the voluntary sector the London Adventure Playground Association (LAPA) and the Handicapped Adventure Playground Association (HAPA) provided inspiration and support. It is only in recent years that the growth of play provision has shifted from the adventure play to the playcare model, though its origins are in fact somewhat earlier.

MARY WARD AND THE PASSMORE EDWARDS SETTLEMENT

Mary Ward was one of the founders of the settlement movement in Victorian Britain. Her involvement in settlements led directly to setting up what became the first play centres for children of working mothers. It was also through her initiative that the first schools for children with disabilities were established and the idea of organised play provision for children in the school holidays was first entertained.

The settlement movement took off in the 1860s amongst growing concern in some quarters of Victorian England about the socially disadvantaged. The central idea was that the middle classes should not only work with, but also reside among, the poor they were endeavouring to help. In 1883 the movement began to crystallise through a series of memorial lectures for Arnold Toynbee the economist and promoter of 'active citizenship' and, later, in 1885, the opening of Toynbee Hall in St Judes, Whitechapel.

In his book *Mrs Humphrey Ward*, John Sutherland describes the residents of Toynbee Hall as being a mixture of: 'Middle class intellectuals, writers, social workers, aspiring clergymen, rabbis and politicians ... ' all under the wardenship of the parish priest Canon Samuel Barnett. Canon Barnett's wife ran a children's Country Holiday Fund giving thousands of children from deprived families their first experience of the countryside.

Mary Ward could have become involved with Toynbee Hall or its sister organisation Oxford House, also in the East End, but instead chose to start up her own. She founded a number of settlements, the second of which, the Passmore Edwards Settlement, opened in 1897 on a corner of Tavistock Square in Bloomsbury. With its aim to be free of overt Christian or other ideological doctrines and its programme of concerts, lectures, clubs, classes, debates and sporting activities it was more accessible and useful to the adult working classes and those in need in the area.

However, it was with children that the settlement made such an important and lasting impact. Janet Ward, Mary Ward's daughter, recorded in her diary: 'there were at least 120 children to deal with. We also had to give each child a pair of list slippers to put on over its own boots, and this was a tremendous business and took over half an hour. Miss Neal made them a little speech before we began the games, and then we all formed rings and played Looby Loo and others of that stamp for nearly an hour or more.'

Although the first of these occasions was 'perfect pandemonium' they soon became better organised until by 1902 no fewer than 1200 children were being provided for, the maximum that the new building could accommodate with safety. The Saturday mornings were supplemented by weekday evening sessions and Mary Ward also persuaded schools in the area to follow the example. Staffed by teachers aided by voluntary helpers these school play centres were so popular that by 1914 attendances of 1.5 million were recorded in the London area. So great were the demands that the management of the system was handed over to the London County Council in 1942. As well as the establishment of the play centre idea after school and on Saturday mornings, the Passmore Edwards settlement also offered a holiday 'Vacation School' for children during the school holidays – an idea that was similarly taken up by agencies and organisations across the country.

FROM SETTLEMENT TO KIDS' CLUBS

It is no accident that Kids' Clubs Network, formerly the National Out of School Alliance, was until recently a tenant of Oxford House, one of the original settlements in London. The organisation's formation in 1981 was a direct result of a research project carried out by the British Association of Settlements and Social Action Centre (BASSAC). Set up to promote and develop the concept of after school provision, Kids' Clubs Network (KCN) has been part of a growing demand in the last decades of the twentieth century for play facilities that will also provide a care service for the parents and guardians of the children who use them. In 1990 KCN carried out a research programme called Patchwork Provision and found that of the 350 after school clubs identified the majority were in the voluntary sector and under funded. Since then the number of clubs has grown enormously, aided by government support from both the Department of Health and the Department of Employment.

The Department of Employment initiative which made 45 million pounds available over three years from December 1992 through Training and

Enterprise Councils (TECs) in England and Wales has resulted in the establishment of around 1700 new clubs, and in Northern Ireland a similar initiative is being explored. Despite this recent spurt of growth KCN recognise that many more clubs are needed to provide adequate provision across the UK and are actively campaigning both for this and the long term sustainability of all these new projects.

NATIONAL CHILDCARE STRATEGY

In the late 1990s the Labour Party, in their first term in office, invested further in childcare. For the first time children themselves were brought into focus rather than just the childcare needs of their parents. The child's experience in pre-school and out-of-school provision was brought to the fore and the issue of children's development through quality play was put on the agenda. The National Childcare Strategy was a much broader and more ambitious plan for children and their families than under the previous administration.

Through the application of a Working Family Tax Credit and access for community groups to a New Opportunities Lottery Fund, the government greatly increased the numbers of places available to children. To meet this demand, new workers were given access to a much wider range of education and training and qualification opportunities which were incorporated within a nationally recognised Framework of Training and Qualifications.

Responsibility for the main thrust of this initiative for new places, new workers and better training and qualifications was given to the 150 Early Years Development and Childcare Partnerships (EYDCPs) in England and similar partnership grouping in Wales, Scotland and Northern Ireland.

TEN YEAR CHILDCARE STRATEGY

Building on the National Childcare Strategy, in 2004 the Government published the *Ten Year Childcare Strategy: Choice for parents, the best start for children*. Its key themes are:
- *Choice and Flexibility* – greater choice for parents in how they balance their work commitments and family life through enhanced parental leave and easy access to Sure Start children's centres for all (not just families who experience social disadvantage. See page 8).
- *Availability* – flexible childcare for all families with children aged up to 14 who need it; and 15 hours a week free early education for all 3 and 4 year olds for 38 weeks a year, with 20 hours as a goal.
- *Quality* – high quality provision delivered by a skilled workforce, with full daycare settings professionally led and a strengthened qualification and career structure.
- *Affordability* – affordable provision appropriate to their needs with substantial increases in tax credit support.

THE CHILDCARE ACT 2006

This Act takes forward some of the key commitments of the Ten Year Childcare Strategy. It introduces the Early Years Foundation Stage (see page 24) and aims to support settings in providing high quality, integrated care and education for all children aged 0-5 years. It gives local authorities the responsibility to improve outcomes for **all** children under five. Since April 2008, local authorities have also had a duty to provide information, advice and assistance to parents and prospective parents of children and young people up to age 20.

EVERY CHILD MATTERS

Every Child Matters is the government agenda which focuses on bringing together services to support children and families, including schools, childcare settings, play settings, hospitals and the police. The government describe it as "a new approach to the well-being of children and young people from birth to age 19." The aim is for every child, whatever their background or their circumstances, to have the support they need to:

- Be healthy
- Stay safe
- Enjoy and achieve
- Make a positive contribution
- Achieve economic well-being.

The government tells us that:

> Organisations...will be teaming up in new ways, sharing information and working together, to protect children and young people from harm and help them achieve what they want in life. Children and young people will have far more say about issues that affect them as individuals and collectively.
>
> Over the next few years, every local authority will be working with its partners, through children's trusts, to find out what works best for children and young people in its area and act on it. They will need to involve children and young people in this process, and when inspectors assess how local areas are doing, they will listen especially to the views of children and young people themselves.
>
> In March 2005, the first Children's Commissioner for England was appointed, to give children and young people a voice in government and in public life. The Commissioner will pay particular attention to gathering and putting forward the views of the most vulnerable children and young people in society, and will promote their involvement in the work of organisations whose decisions and actions affect them.
>
> In addition, the Children's Fund was launched in November 2000 to tackle disadvantage among children and young people. The programme aims to identify at an early stage children and young people at risk of social exclusion, and make sure they receive the help and support they need to achieve their potential.

You can find out more at www.everychildmatters.gov.uk.

QUALITY TRAINING, QUALITY PLAY

SkillsActive works across the UK in partnership with nine regional playwork centres, leading the development of playwork education and training for all those working with children and young people. To ensure that playworkers and employers are consulted and involved in the development of playwork, they carry out an important playwork survey each year.

They have launched a playwork strategy *Quality Training, Quality Play*. Described as "the first ever playwork strategy to have a UK focus whilst accommodating the diverse needs of each of the UK nations," it sets out a ten year vision and a five year plan for the development of playwork education and skills. You can read the full strategy at www.skillsactive.com/resources/publications/FINAL_UK_play.pdf.

THE CHILDREN'S PLAN

In 2007, the Government published the "Children's Plan" which sets out ambitious new goals for 2020. The Plan is intended to:

- strengthen support for all families during the formative early years of their children's lives
- take the next steps in achieving world class schools and an excellent education for every child
- involve parents fully in their children's learning
- help to make sure that young people have interesting and exciting things to do outside of school
- provide more places for children to play safely.

There will be regular reports on the progress the Government is making. For more information, visit www.dfes.gov.uk/publications/childrensplan/.

SURE START

Sure Start is the Government's programme to deliver the best start in life for every child by bringing together early education, childcare, health and family support. Some Sure Start initiatives apply universally, while others only apply in targeted local areas and/or to disadvantaged groups in England.

Responsibility for Sure Start lies with The Early Years, Extended Schools and Special Needs Group, which belongs to the Department for Children, Schools and Families. Sure Start tells us the following about their service:

Services

Sure Start covers children from conception through to age 14, and up to age 16 for those with special educational needs and disabilities. It also aims to help parents and communities across the country.

There are a wide range of services currently available, from Children's Centres and early support programmes to information and advice on health and financial matters. We are helping set and maintain childcare standards.

Sure Start is the cornerstone of the Government's drive to tackle child poverty and social exclusion working with parents-to-be, parents/carers and children to promote the physical, intellectual and social development of babies and young children so that they can flourish at home and when they get to school.

All Sure Start local programmes have become children's centres. Local authorities are responsible for Sure Start children's centres, and the services on offer may vary from area to area.

How do our services work?

Our services bring together universal, free, early education and more and better childcare. Sure Start does this with greater support where there is greater need through children's tax credit, children's centres and Sure Start local programmes.

Integrated Early Years Services

For some time we have been encouraging the delivery of childcare alongside early education and other health and family services.

Sure Start Children's Centres

Sure Start Children's Centres are building on existing successful initiatives like Sure Start Local Programmes, Neighbourhood Nurseries and Early Excellence Centres, and bringing high-quality integrated early years services to the heart of communities.

Our target of 2,500 children's centres was reached in early March 2008, and 2,914 centres have now been established (October 2008), offering services to over 2.3 million young children and their families.

By 2010, the number of children's centres will increase to 3,500 – so every family has easy access to high-quality integrated services in their community and the benefits of Sure Start can be felt nationwide.

Early Education

All 3- and 4-year-olds are now guaranteed a free, part-time ($12\frac{1}{2}$ hours per week, 38 weeks per year, increasing to 15 hours per week in 2010), early-education place. There are over 37,000 settings delivering free, Government-funded, early education in the maintained, private, voluntary and independent sectors.

Childcare

In June 2008, the stock of registered childcare stood at approaching 1.3 million places (more than double the 1997 level).

There will be a childcare place for all children aged between 3 and 14, between the hours of 8am and 6pm each weekday by 2010, when there will be over 2 million sustainable childcare places for children up to 14.

Different playwork settings

There are many different settings in which playwork occurs. On the next page is a description of the key defining factors that distinguish one setting from another.

ADVENTURE PLAYGROUNDS

The adventure playground grew out of a movement dedicated to children's freedom of expression in an outdoor environment (see above) and the children's involvement in using tools and materials to adapt and construct on the outdoor space remains an important feature. Building camps, cooking on open fires, digging gardens, tending animals and generally playing with, and in, the outdoor space are all typical activities. The adventure playground is now also associated with play equipment, known as play structures, built from timber such as telegraph poles, joists and planking along with cable, tyres, nets and ropes. Because of the size and technical competence involved, these structures require adults to take the lead in their design and construction. However, children and young people can also be involved wherever it is appropriate.

The indoor provision may be fairly basic, e.g. a hut or cabin of a temporary or portable nature, or may be quite sophisticated with special rooms for arts, crafts and games, e.g. a purpose-built brick or timber building. There may also be sheds and storage cabins for tools and equipment on site and an outside storage area for timber. All kinds of activities may take place within the adventure playground building depending on its size and the scope of its resources. As a provision dedicated to children's use the elements of choice and spontaneity are as equally applicable to the indoor space as to the outdoor.

Adventure playgrounds are either managed by a voluntary management committee or by the local authority and staffed by one or more full-time workers complemented by part-time and voluntary help.

The majority of adventure playgrounds are open access, i.e. children are free to come and go as they please, and many cater for children from 5 to 15 years of age. Although the tradition of the adventure playground is towards children of this, and a wider age range, some now work only with children from 5 to 12 years of age.

PLAY CENTRES

These play facilities may be voluntary managed or run by the local authority or district council. They often operate in a shared-use building such as a community centre, church hall or sports centre, but some may be fortunate in having a building for their own use. School-based play centres are described separately under the next heading.

The bulk of the playworkers are part time and team sizes vary according to the size of the facility and the numbers of children. A senior worker or coordinator will normally lead the team. There are some projects with permanent full-time staff. Whilst many play centres have outdoor provision, some of which may also include equipment of the adventure playground type, e.g. rope swings and climbing apparatus, they do not have the full scope of the adventure playground. Consequently the emphasis of the centre or club is on indoor activities. Arts, crafts, games, drama, cooking, writing, discussion and reading are some of the typical activities that take place in the after school play centre.

Play centres may be either open access or 'closed door' schemes, i.e. parents and carers must register their children with the centre and the children are signed in and out of the play session and not allowed to leave except under these conditions. Some play centres not only provide registration but also escort children from their school to the club either on foot or by mini-bus.

Although there are always exceptions to the rule the age range of play centres is usually not as wide as for the adventure playground, 4–12 or 5–12 being typical. Similarly the length of play sessions is often shorter, e.g. 3.30–6pm during school term time.

SCHOOL PLAY CENTRES

Many of the features above also typify the school play centre. However, school play centres tend to be established by education authorities and are seen as an extended service to the children using the school in which they operate. In recent years some of these centres have passed from the responsibility of education to other local authority departments.

The school play centre by definition operates within a shared-use environment, although within the school it may have its own designated room and storage space. School play centres have access to the school playground and often to school facilities such as hall, gym, library, kitchen and craft room. In this respect one could argue that they are well provided for. Unfortunately, and this is true of other forms of shared-use provision, it is not an environment dedicated to children's play and this imposes some constraints on, and considerable challenges to, the playworker. Where there is a designated play area messy activities can take place

has been proven. They operate in a wide variety of play environments depending on their location, the resources available and, often, the dedication, imagination and ingenuity of the planners and organisers. Holiday playschemes run in streets, on estates, in parks, in church halls and community centres, in fields, in recreation grounds and in the gardens of parents. Those planners and organisers, who may range from a local authority social services department to a group of local parents, are as much event managers as play providers.

In established play settings the term-time provision is often extended to provide a service during the school holidays. These periods, particular at Easter and summer, are often a special marker and focus in the year for many projects. The full-day sessions, the longer spells of fine weather and the potential influx of new children all contribute to it being the high spot of the year for both the children and the playworkers. It is true that most projects recruit extra workers and volunteers in this period but this is often more than compensated for by increased numbers of children, particularly in the open access type of provision.

MOBILE PLAY PROVISION

Mobile play is a unique provision that uses buses and community mobiles – specially adapted vans – to take play opportunities directly to children in their communities. They are literally play buildings on wheels and some, such as the Hackney Play on the Estates vans in London, have innovations like inflatable marquees to extend the scope of the play space. Their mobility allows them to provide a service for families most in need both in the rural and urban environment.

RESIDENTIAL HOLIDAYS

There are a number of organisations running residential holiday schemes for children who may visit with their family, their youth or play project, or unaccompanied. The settings are usually rural and may be situated in areas that provide opportunities for outdoor pursuits such as climbing, orienteering, sailing and archery. Although playwork as it occurs in the main settings in this book may not be the priority for residential holiday workers there are crossovers in the areas of competence.

SCRAP STORES

There are a number of organisations which specialise in providing re-cycled and scrap materials for use by play projects. They are run rather like 'cash and carry' supermarkets. Projects can either join a membership scheme or buy off the shelf. Workers in these projects sometimes engage in direct face to face playwork by introducing children to using the junk materials through on-site or outreach craft workshops.

PLAYWORK IN HOSPITALS

Playwork in hospitals occurs either through playworkers – sometimes called play specialists in the hospital environment – visiting children on the wards and engaging them in play, or through the children visiting a special playroom or playground. These are often smaller versions of full-time play provision with children having access to many play opportunities. The hospital play profession is somewhat unique in having its own qualification and endorsement structure.

If you would like further information on any of the above play settings there are some reading materials and a number of addresses you can follow up in Appendices D and E respectively.

INCLUSION

Disabled children have a right to be included in society and to participate within it. All playworkers should promote inclusion, and do what they can to make their setting as inclusive as possible. See page 90 for further information about this and specialist play settings.

The Playwork Principles

When work on defining the National Occupational Standards for Playwork got under way in 1989 many people involved in playwork were concerned that a description of what a playworker needs to do to be competent wouldn't necessarily embrace the principles and values of the playwork tradition. Even though

underpinning knowledge is also required in assessing a playworker as competent within the S/NVQ system, these areas of knowledge are linked directly to the functions of the playworker rather than any value base. It was therefore decided to complement the playwork standards with a number of statements that would:

- make a definition of children's play
- define the role of the adult in children's play
- set out a number of value statements about good practice in playwork.

In 2002 Play Wales was funded to conduct a UK review and consultation on the Assumptions and Values. This led the establishment of the Playwork Principles, which were endorsed by SkillsActive in 2004 as a replacement for the Assumptions and Values. They are currently being incorporated into the Playwork National Occupational Standards.

PERSONAL EXPERIENCE

Unlike workers in many other occupational areas you have the distinct advantage of having a direct line of experience to underpin your work – namely your own play as a child. Whatever theories may abound on children's play you will always be able to compare them with your own experience. An exploration of these childhood experiences, and the sharing of your findings with friends and colleagues, are invaluable in constructing the principles and values that will underpin your work.

THE NATURE OF PLAY AND PLAYWORK

There is a distinction to be made between play and playwork. Play is something that children engage in of their own free will. It is in no way essential for adults to be part of children's play and, often, children's play goes on to the total exclusion of adults. However, for play to take place in a free and spontaneous way the conditions have to be right. Looking at the child in the home environment is a useful way of examining the role that the playworker takes in the supervised play setting. Invariably what the parent does is to run the home in a way that offers the child safety and security. She or he will also provide the child with a range of play materials. Although these will include bought toys, many parents have an intuitive understanding that children enjoy playing with ad-hoc and found materials. Parents may interact and play with their children but often their role is to maintain a presence whereby the child can engage the parent as they choose.

Playworkers fulfil a similar role in the supervised play setting. They manage the play environment and provide the resources which enable children's play. In common with the parent the playworker may at times play with children, intervene when there is a need for direct supervision and generally ensure that there is an atmosphere of safety and security. The difference for playworkers is that they operate within an environment that is dedicated to children's play. The playworker is expected to have an understanding of the process of play leading to a wider range of quality experiences.

KEY POINT

Play is the natural activity of children. Playwork is the involvement of adults who wish to support and help children's play.

PLAYWORK PRINCIPLES:

These Principles establish the professional and ethical framework for playwork and as such must be regarded as a whole.

They describe what is unique about play and playwork, and provide the playwork perspective for working with children and young people.

They are based on the recognition that children and young people's capacity for positive development will be enhanced if given access to the broadest range of environments and play opportunities.

1 All children and young people need to play. The impulse to play is innate *(built in)*. Play is a biological, psychological and social necessity, and is fundamental to the healthy development and well-being of individuals and communities.

2 Play is a process that is freely chosen, personally directed and intrinsically motivated. That is, children and young people determine and control the content and intent of their play, by following their own instincts, ideas and interests, in their own way for their own reasons.

3 The prime focus and essence of playwork is to support and facilitate the play process and this should inform the development of play policy, strategy, training and education.
4 For playworkers, the play process takes precedence and playworkers act as advocates for play when engaging with adult led agendas.
5 The role of the playworker is to support all children and young people in the creation of a space in which they can play.
6 The playworker's response to children and young people playing is based on a sound up to date knowledge of the play process, and reflective practice.
7 Playworkers recognise their own impact on the play space and also the impact of children and young people's play on the playworker.

Playworkers choose an intervention style that enables children and young people to extend their play. All playworker intervention must balance risk with the developmental benefit and well-being of children.

KEY POINT

The Playwork S/NVQ uses the term 'child centred'. Throughout this book there is reference to both children and young people, and in recognition of this the book uses the term 'user centred' rather than 'child centred'.

Relevant legislation

THE HEALTH AND SAFETY AT WORK ACT 1974

This Act, for the first time, put a responsibility on all employers for the health and safety of both their employees and members of the public. The Act states: 'An Act to make further provision for securing the health, safety and welfare of persons at work, for protecting others against risk to health or safety in connection with activities of persons at work, ... and for connected purposes' (31 July 1974). As a playworker your employer, whether voluntary management committee, local authority or commercial company, is legally bound to ensure that you are not put at risk whilst at work. They have a duty to ensure:

■ that the workplace itself and the materials and equipment are in a safe condition and present no risk to health
■ that the handling, storage and transporting of substances and articles present no risk to health
■ that there is provision of adequate welfare facilities and a safe working environment
■ that there is provision of information, instruction, training and supervision.

As an employee you too have a duty, and that is:

■ to cooperate with your employer in ensuring that the employer's legal duty on health and safety is carried out
■ to take reasonable care for the health and safety of yourself and others who may be affected by your actions, i.e. your colleagues, the children, their parents and carers, and others who may use or visit your project
■ not intentionally or recklessly to interfere with or misuse anything provided in the interests of health, safety and welfare.

The daily playwork tasks and responsibilities relating to health and safety are covered in Chapter 8 and there is further help and advice identified in Appendices D and E. However, there will always be occasions when you will need to think on your feet and consider a completely new challenge. The London Adventure Playground Association, now PLAYLINK, employed a useful tool to help think through these situations when training new playworkers. It came out of the recognition that responsibilities under the Act are described in terms of what is 'reasonably practicable'. This phrase is open to interpretation and, in many circumstances, acceptable conduct in accordance with the Act will only be established following precedents determined by case law. Wherever there is doubt the risk must be measured against the cost or sacrifice. Wherever the risk outweighs the cost, remedial or prohibitive action must be taken. The tool was called The Reasonable Practometer – see illustration. In one side of the scales goes the risk and in the other goes the cost.

The reasonable practometer

An example of where action would have to be taken would be if there was broken glass on the playground. The risk is high: children could pick it up or fall on it, the cost is low: a playworker puts on a pair of gloves and clears it up. An example of where action would not be practicable would be in removing all play equipment because a child has fallen off a swing. The risk is low: children do sometimes fall from play equipment but with sound design and maintenance will not hurt themselves badly; the cost is high: the denial of play opportunities that are both fun and developmental.

As a playworker you should be able to:

■ respond to situations of accident or emergency, e.g. apply first aid, give comfort, inform colleagues or managers
■ protect against hazardous situations, e.g. plan and run activities safely, carry out regular checks and inspections, intervene before a situation becomes dangerous
■ keep yourself informed, e.g. know the project's Health and Safety Policy, read the relevant books and documents, take up training.

THE CHILDREN ACT 1989

This Act brought together the many different laws affecting children in England and Wales into one single Act of Parliament. It is very wide ranging and requires local authorities to review and amend their child care policies, procedures and provision. Key features of the Act include the focus on children as individuals, services for children and inspection and registration.

The focus on children as individuals

- A key principle of the Act is that the welfare of the child must be the paramount consideration of any court.
- There is a duty to ascertain the wishes and feelings of a child in any proceedings or decisions.
- Part of a child's individuality is racial origin, and cultural and linguistic background – and these factors must be taken into consideration.
- The Act introduced the concept of 'parental responsibility' rather than rights over children.
- Families are considered to be the best place to raise children and local authorities should intervene only to safeguard the child.

Children Act 2004

In January 2003, the Laming Report, looking at the death of Victoria Climbie, found that health, police and social services missed 12 opportunities to save her. As a result, the Children Act 2004 was passed to implemented the recommendations of the green paper *Every Child Matters*:

1 Children's commissioners are appointed in England, Wales, Scotland and Northern Ireland. The commissioners' job is to raise awareness of the best interests of children and young people and report annually to Parliament.
2 Local authorities have a duty to make arrangements to promote co-operation between agencies (social services, health, education and the justice system) in order to improve children's well-being. Key partners will have a duty to take part in these arrangements.
3 Key agencies that work with children have a duty to put in place arrangements to make sure that they take account of the need to safeguard and promote the welfare of children when doing their jobs.
4 Databases that contain basic information on young people to help professionals in working together to provide early support to children, young people and their families.
5 Local authorities required to set up statutory Local Safeguarding Children Boards and ensure that key partners take part.
6 Local authorities required to put in place a director of children's services and lead member to be responsible for, as a minimum, education and children's social services functions.
7 An integrated inspection framework and provision for regular joint area reviews to be carried out to look at how children's services as a whole operate across each local authority area.

REGISTRATION AND INSPECTION

All daycare providers in England caring for children under the age of eight years are registered and inspected by the Early Years Directorate within the Office for Standards in Education (Ofsted). There are two registers, the *Childcare Register* and the *Early Years Register*.

CHILDCARE REGISTER

This is a register of providers who are registered by Ofsted to care for children from birth to 17 years. The register has two parts:

■ **the voluntary part**
Providers who are not eligible for compulsory registration may choose to register here. These are mainly people looking after children aged eight and over, or providing care in the child's home (e.g. nannies).
■ **the compulsory part**
Providers must register if they care for one or more children following their fifth birthdays until they reach their eighth birthdays.

Registered settings must meet the Requirements of the Childcare Register at all times. Ofsted will carry out periodic inspections of settings to assess the standard of the provision, and will publish a public report which will be available to families using, or wishing to use, the provision. The Requirements fall into the categories below. An example of the content of each category is given here. You can see the requirements in full in the document *The Guide to Registration on the Childcare Register*, available on the Ofsted website (www.ofsted.gov.uk).

WELFARE OF THE CHILDREN BEING CARED FOR

Example content of this category:
■ Children receiving childcare are kept safe from harm
■ There must be a ratio of 1 adult to every 8 children

Arrangements for safeguarding children
■ There must be written child protection procedures
■ No one unsuitable to work with children has unsupervised access to a child

Suitability of persons to care for, or be in regular contact with children
■ There must be effective systems to ensure that those in contact with children are suitable to work with them

Qualifications and training
■ At least half of all persons caring for children have successfully completed a relevant qualification at a minimum of level 2
■ The manager has a relevant qualification at a minimum of level 3

Suitability and safety of premises and equipment
■ Premises and equipment used are safe and suitable for childcare

How the childcare provision is organised
■ Where older and younger children are together, the behaviour of children over the age of eight years does not have a negative effect on the younger children
■ Childcare is accessible and inclusive by taking all reasonable steps to ensure that the needs of each child are met

Procedures for dealing with complaints
■ Each complaint must be fully investigated

Records to be kept
■ Certain records must be kept and retained for a period of two years (see page 26)

Providing information to parents
■ Information about the activities the children will undertake is given
■ copies of safeguarding procedures and complaints procedures are available

Providing information to Ofsted
■ Ofsted must be informed of changes of circumstance as soon as possible

Changes to premises and provision
■ Settings must inform Ofsted of a change to the address of the premises where they are providing childcare

Changes to people
■ The registered person must inform Ofsted of a change to their name, address or telephone number

Matters affecting the welfare of children
■ Ofsted must be informed of certain events, including incidents of food poisoning and any serious accidents or injuries to children

Insurance
■ The setting must be covered by insurance for death, injury, public liability, damage or other loss

Certificate of registration
■ The certificate of registration must be displayed

All childcare providers must also comply with other relevant legislation including that covering health and safety, disability discrimination, food hygiene, fire and planning requirements.

Early Years Register

In addition, since 2008, all childcarers providing for children from birth to the 31 August following their fifth birthday must register on the Early Years Register and deliver the Early Years Foundation Stage (EYFS), which is a curriculum framework. This is a big change for play settings, and we will look at the implications on page 25.

The Early Years Foundation Stage

Since September 2008 *The Early Years Foundation Stage* (EYFS) has been mandatory for:

■ all schools
■ all early years providers in Ofsted registered settings (including nurseries, pre-schools, childminders and out-of-school clubs caring for young children)

It applies to children from birth to the end of the academic year in which the child has their fifth birthday.

In the *Statutory Framework for the Early Years Foundation Stage* the Department for Education and Skills tells us that:

> Every child deserves the best possible start in life and support to fulfil their potential. A child's experience in the early years has a major impact on their future life chances. A secure, safe and happy childhood is important in its own right, and it provides the foundation for children to make the most of their abilities and talents as they grow up. When parents choose to use early years services they want to know that provision will keep their children safe and help them to thrive. The Early Years Foundation Stage (EYFS) is the framework that provides that assurance. The overarching aim of the EYFS is to help young children achieve the five *Every Child Matters* outcomes...

Every Child Matters is the government agenda which focuses on bringing together services to support children and families. It sets out five major outcomes for children:

■ being healthy
■ staying safe
■ enjoying and achieving
■ making a positive contribution
■ economic well-being

The EYFS aims to meet the *Every Child Matters* outcomes by:

■ **Setting standards** for the learning, development and care young children should experience when they attend a setting outside their family home. Every child should make progress, with no children left behind.
■ **Providing equality of opportunity and anti-discriminatory practice**. Ensuring that every child is included and not disadvantaged because of ethnicity, culture, religion, home language, family background, learning difficulties or disabilities, gender or ability.

- **Creating a framework for partnership working between parents and professionals**, and between all the settings that the child attends.
- **Improving quality and consistency in the early years** through standards that apply to all settings. This provides the basis for the inspection and regulation regime carried out by Ofsted.
- **Laying a secure foundation for future learning** through learning and development that is planned around the individual needs and interests of the child. This is informed by the use of on-going observational assessment.

All settings following the EYFS must have regard to the Special Educational Needs Code of Practice 2002.

THE EARLY YEARS FOUNDATION STAGE WELFARE REQUIREMENTS

Settings to which the EYFS applies must also meet the Early Years Foundation Stage welfare requirements. These fall into the following five categories:

Safeguarding and promoting children's welfare
- The provider must take necessary steps to safeguard and promote the welfare of children.
- The provider must promote the good health of the children, take necessary steps to prevent the spread of infection, and take appropriate action when they are ill.
- Children's behaviour must be managed effectively and in a manner appropriate for their stage of development and particular individual needs.

Suitable people
- Providers must ensure that adults looking after children, or having unsupervised access to them, are suitable to do so.
- Adults looking after children must have appropriate qualifications, training, skills and knowledge.
- Staffing arrangements must be organised to ensure safety and to meet the needs of the children.

Suitable premises, environment and equipment
- Outdoor and indoor spaces, furniture, equipment and toys must be safe and suitable for their purpose.

Organisation
- Providers must plan and organise their systems to ensure that every child receives an enjoyable and challenging learning and development experience that is tailored to meet their individual needs.

Documentation

■ Providers must maintain records, policies and procedures required for the safe and efficient management of the settings and to meet the needs of the children.

THEMES, PRINCIPLES AND COMMITMENTS

The EYFS is based around four **Themes**. Each theme is linked to a **Principle**. Each Principle is supported by four **Commitments**. The Commitments describe how their Principle can be put into action. The Themes, Principles and Commitments are shown in the table below.

Theme	Principle	Commitments
1.A Unique Child	Every child is a competent learner from birth who can be resilient, capable, confident and self-assured.	1.1 Child development 1.2 Inclusive practice 1.3 Keeping safe 1.4 Health and well-being
2.Positive Relationships	Children learn to be strong and independent from a base of loving and secure relationships with parents and/or a key person.	2.1 Respecting each other 2.2 Parents as partners 2.3 Supporting learning 2.4 Key person
3.Enabling Environments	The environment plays a key role in supporting and extending children's development and learning.	3.1 Observation, assessment and planning 3.2 Supporting every child 3.3 The learning environment 3.4 The wider context
4.Learning and Development	Children develop and learn in different ways and at different rates. All areas of learning and development are equally important and interconnected.	4.1 Play and exploration 4.2 Active learning 4.3 Creativity and critical thinking 4.4 Areas of learning and development

Additional statements are provided within the EYFS to explain each Commitment in more detail.

AREAS OF LEARNING AND DEVELOPMENT

Theme 4, Learning and Development, also contains six **Areas of Learning and Development**:

- Personal, social and emotional development
- Communication, language and literacy
- Problem solving, reasoning and numeracy
- Knowledge and understanding of the world
- Physical development
- Creative development

Each Area of Learning and Development is divided up into **Aspects**. You can see these on Department for Education and Skill's Learning and Development card, reproduced below. Together, the six areas of Learning and Development make up the skills, knowledge and experiences appropriate for babies and children as they grow, learn and develop. Although these are presented as separate areas, it's important to remember that for children everything links and nothing is compartmentalised. All areas of Learning and Development are connected to one another and are equally important. They are underpinned by the principles of the EYFS. Each Area of Learning also has a list of **early learning goals** (elgs). The aim is for children to reach the goals by the end of their Reception year.

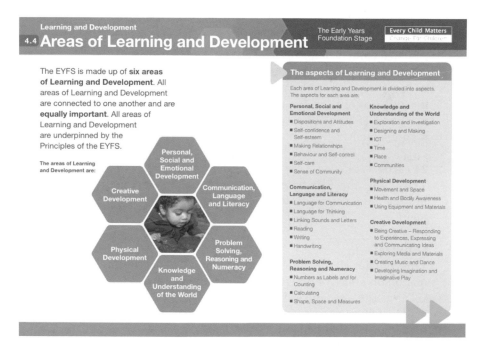

Department for Education and Skill's Learning and Development card extract

IN SUMMARY

Childcarers working in settings following the EYFS need to meet the standards for learning, development and care. Their responsibilities include:

- planning a range of play and learning experiences that promote all of the Aspects within all of the Areas of Learning
- Assessing and monitoring individual children's progress through observational assessments
- Using the findings of observational assessments to inform the planning of play and learning experiences
- Ensuring that children's individual interests and abilities are promoted within the play and learning experiences

EYFS RESOURCES FOR CHILDCARERS

The EYFS pack of resources for providers includes:

The Statutory Framework for the Early Years Foundation Stage
This booklet sets out:

- The welfare requirements
  You can find out more about the welfare requirements on page 25.
- The learning and development requirements
  Which set out providers' duties under each of the six areas of Learning and Development.

Practice Guidance for the Early Years Foundation Stage
This booklet provides further guidance on:

- legal requirements
- the areas of Learning and Development
- the EYFS principles
- assessment

24 cards
These give the Principles and Commitments at a glance, with guidance on putting the principles into practice. They include an overview of child development.

CD-ROM
This contains all the information from the booklets and cards. It includes information on effective practice, research and resources. This can also be accessed via a website – see the web link section at the end of the Unit.

The following websites are also valuable resources:

- www.standards.dcsf.gov.uk/eyfs/
- www.everychildmatters.gov.uk
- www.skillsactive.com/playwork/early-years-foundation-stage

IMPLICATIONS OF THE EYFS FOR PLAY SETTINGS

Most playwork settings will only have a small number of children following the EYFS at any one time, and some playworkers are concerned that the delivery of the EYFS will have an adverse affect on the delivery of the freely chosen playwork opportunities they provide for a wide age-range of children. There have also been concerns over whether playworkers will be required to formally assess the children's progress at the end of the EYFS, which involves completing an assessment scales document known as the EYFS Profile. SkillsActive have been working with the Department of Children, Schools and Families (DCSF) on the implementation of the EYFS, and at the time of writing tell us that:

The DCSF assures us that as long as Playworkers are adhering to the Playwork Principles they will be in a good position to meet the EYFS requirements.

In addition, the following should be noted:

The assessment scales (appendix 1 of the Statutory Framework for the Early Years Foundation Stage – SFEYFS) will be completed by the primary setting where the child spends the majority of their time between 8am to 6pm. Given that play settings operate before and after school and during the holidays, they are **not** going to be the primary setting.

In respect of holiday play schemes, although for a number of weeks children may be spending a large proportion of their time there, taking into consideration the whole year, they still wouldn't be the primary setting.

SkillsActive believe that, given this scenario, there is no need for Playwork practitioners to engage in any further training over and above that required for their usual Playwork practice or general information about the introduction of the EYFS."

For further details visit www.skillsactive.com/playwork/early-years-foundation-stage.

THE UNITED NATIONS CONVENTION ON THE RIGHTS OF THE CHILD

The UN Convention has not had the direct impact on play provision that the above legislation has had, at least not yet, but it has already been both a great morale booster and a powerful campaigning tool. As an international treaty that has been ratified by both our and many other governments in the United Nations Assembly its influence should in time prove far reaching and long lasting.

Adopted on 20 November 1989, it came into force on 2 September 1990. Broadly, governments who ratify the Convention commit themselves to ensuring that:

- the child's basic needs are met
- the child is protected from cruelty and exploitation
- parents are in a position to care properly and to the best of their ability for their children's needs
- particularly vulnerable children, including those who cannot be with their families, for whatever reason, receive the best possible care
- children are given appropriate opportunities to play an active role in society and to have a say in their own lives.

Specifically, in terms of children's play, the Convention states in Article 31 that:

1   Parties recognise the rights of the child to rest and to leisure, to engage in play and recreational activities appropriate to the age of the child and to participate freely in cultural life and the arts.
2   Parties shall respect and promote the right of the child to participate fully in cultural and artistic life and shall encourage the provision of appropriate and equal opportunities for cultural, artistic, recreational and leisure activity.

Playday, a coordinated day of play activities across the UK, has regularly campaigned for the rights of the child through the promotion of Article 31. PLAY-TRAIN, a well-known and respected playwork training agency in Birmingham, runs the 'Article 31 Network' dedicated to raising awareness about, and promoting work on, the rights of the child to play. The Article 31 Network includes children and young people in its membership.

In conclusion

This chapter has covered a little of the history of playwork, the settings in which playwork takes place, and the assumptions and values of playwork, and has concluded with a brief look at a treaty and some of the laws and policies that now have a bearing on children's play provision. In 1897 when Mary Ward opened her Passmore Edwards Settlement she was motivated by good will a nd moral instinct, and had a talent for raising money but no legal, philosophical or occupational framework in respect of the children she wished to help. For you as playworker today it's a different story and a mark of how far the tradition of playwork has travelled in the last hundred years.

KEY TERMS

You need to know what these words and phrases mean. Go back through the chapter to make sure that you understand.

National Occupational Standards
National Vocational Qualification
Equal opportunities
Child centred
User centred
Playcare
Shared-use environment

Voluntary sector
Commercial sector
Disabilities
Junk playground
Adventure playground
The settlement movement

2 WORKING WITH CHILDREN AND YOUNG PEOPLE

> **This chapter covers:**
> - **Development from childhood towards adulthood**
> - **Physical skills and interests**
> - **Communication**
> - **Thinking and reasoning**
> - **Social relationships and feelings**
> - **Self-reliance and social skills**

Development from childhood towards adulthood

Playwork facilities are offered to users as young as children of 4 or 5 years old through to young people of 15 years. Every play setting will not necessarily cater to this wide range of ages, although some will. Open access adventure playgrounds, in particular, can be enthusiastically used by the full age range. In recent years it has become increasingly common for play facilities to offer wrap-around childcare to children from four years of age. It has also become more common for early years providers, such as day nurseries and children's centres, to offer their own wrap-around care which extends to children of primary school age. So, any playworker needs a sound understanding of the patterns of development from the boundary of the early years of childhood right through to the brink of young adulthood.

GOOD PRACTICE

Your own play setting may have to decide on the minimum age of child users and 5 years of age is not always the simple choice. Children in Northern Ireland start school at 4 years. In England and Wales, compulsory education starts the term after the child's fifth birthday. However, many four year olds are admitted early to full-time primary education. An after-school club or holiday scheme could therefore be approached by parents who reasonably argue that their four year old is in primary school, and so should be allowed to attend the club or scheme.

SOCIAL AND CULTURAL INFLUENCES

Development through childhood only really makes sense when you recognise that children grow and develop whilst living in a particular social and cultural group. The direction of children's development will always be shaped, to some

The youngest children may still get tired or easily distressed

Activity   **2.1**

Until anyone stands back from his or her own childhood, those experiences are taken as the yardstick for 'ordinary' life. But, of course, your own childhood will have been shaped by social and cultural traditions just as much as childhoods that seem unusual or exotic to you. All playworkers need to gain some perspective, whatever their own cultural identity.

Discuss this issue within your team, sharing what seems 'normal' to each of you.

extent, by the power of their individual temperament. But the opportunities they energetically pursue and those which they ignore, or never encounter, are shaped by their families, and by other adults and children who pass on through their behaviour the social and cultural traditions.

CHALLENGE TO TRADITIONS

Traditions about childhood and how to treat children can, and do, change over time. Some are challenged, either from within a given culture, or by people who hold to a different set of traditions. Two important issues of good practice in playwork – and in other areas of work with children – have emerged from a relatively recent challenge to beliefs about what is normal and right in behaviour of adults towards children.

Hitting children

Physical punishment of children has a long history in Britain. The traditional view was that effective discipline in the family and in institutions, such as schools, should include hitting with the hand or with implements like canes. Since then, opinions have changed, and the rights of children and young people have been protected by legislation. Playworkers must NEVER physically punish, frighten or humiliate a child or young person – it is illegal. Sadly, many adults still believe strongly that children cannot be taught 'good' behaviour unless their 'bad' can be punished by hitting. (The preferred word is 'smack' – perhaps because that sounds less serious.)

GOOD PRACTICE

As a playworker, you need to understand that some parents equate discipline with the right to hit children. They will need reassurance that you are not going to let the children run wild, nor will you and your colleagues take any kind of nonsense from young people who are keen to push the limits. (Chapter 6 covers a positive approach to dealing with children's behaviour.)

Treatment of boys and girls

Social traditions in most, perhaps all, cultures address whether childhood should be different for boys and girls. The treatment of the two sexes during childhood is directly related to the expectations of how men and women are expected to behave. The social history of British society demonstrates strong views about appropriate games, toys and hobbies for the play of boys and girls.

Good practice in playwork, child care and education has developed along the lines of promoting equal opportunities for boys and girls through play and learning. However, this practice is a direct challenge to tradition – not just for some cultural groups and religious faiths who have settled in Britain in recent decades, but also to British cultural traditions stretching back many more decades. (See also page 59 for more on equal opportunities on the basis of gender.)

KEY POINT

It is only by recognising existing traditions, and people's feelings and beliefs, that you will be able to implement good practice that forms a challenge to some traditions about children.

WHAT IS DEVELOPMENT?

The years of childhood are inevitably a time of change. Whatever else may be happening around children, whether their immediate social world is fairly stable or undergoing upheaval, the children themselves will be experiencing change through the unfolding of their development.

KEY POINT

Development is the term used to cover the changes that can be observed in children as they pass through the years from birth to young adulthood. Study of development has included not only what happens, but also how and why it happens.

Individuality and development

There are some common patterns in how children and young people develop and the skills that they are able to learn. However, they are all individuals, and so it is impossible to make exact predictions about how children will react, or at what age they will gain a new physical or intellectual skill. A great deal depends on their experiences.

Ability and motivation

With very young children the issue is often one of ability. Have they yet learned how to do something? With older children and young people the issue becomes just as much one of 'Will they – won't they?' as that of 'Can they – can't they?' Children and young people may choose not to try an activity that they could most likely manage. Their reluctance may be a mix of emotion and reasoning and the behaviour of adults may tip them one way or another.

GOOD PRACTICE

Children and young people can have a number of reasons for their actions, or inaction. These are not always immediately obvious to adults, including playworkers. Underlying reasons will not become any clearer unless you talk with and listen to children and young people. On occasion, the reasons will seem neither sensible nor 'good enough'. Yet genuinely helpful and supportive playworkers have to be willing to consider seriously the perspective of the child or young person.

DIFFERENT ASPECTS TO DEVELOPMENT

Of course, different areas of development do not operate as if they were completely separate channels. Children's lives unfold as they progress, or become temporarily blocked, in all the different areas of their development at the same time. What happens for children in one area can affect, positively or negatively, how they are developing in another.

Examples

Eight-year-old Liam is having serious difficulties in school with his reading. However, Liam has been interested in books from his early childhood and has a broad general knowledge. He is getting by so far with shrewd guesses of what the words most probably say. He is confident in talking with adults and is developing an effective strategy of distracting his teacher through conversation when he is seriously stuck. However, Liam is aware that he cannot read, as some of his friends are able to, and his underlying worry about this is coming out at home and in his after-school club where he bosses his younger sister unmercifully.

Thirteen-year-old Maryam has been an enthusiastic swimmer. Her ability in swimming and diving has been a major source of self-confidence to her so far. This year, however, she has become very friendly with a group of girls who are uninterested in any kind of physical activity. Maryam is torn between her friends from the swimming club and her new group. She is also uncertain about what will make her an interesting and attractive person, if she discounts her swimming talents.

THE DEVELOPMENT OF GIRLS AND BOYS

Careful study of the development of boys and girls does suggest that there may be some patterns on which the sexes differ within their development other than the different physical patterns of the two sexes during puberty. However, any differences are averages, that emerge from study of large groups of children and young people. Even when the differences are fairly clear, as they are for instance with boys' greater average level of aggressiveness, the actual size of the difference is normally quite small. On most of the average differences found between the sexes, you will find the full range of ability or behaviour in both boys and girls. So, for instance, although boys emerge, on average, better at tasks that involve mathematical reasoning and girls on verbal reasoning, you will find many girls who are very adept at maths and boys who are effective in working with words.

It is not sexist to acknowledge average differences between boys and girls in some areas of their development. However, interpretations of the data become sexist if the differences are presented as part of an argument that one sex is better than the other, or that some abilities are of more value than others. For example, it would be taking a sexist line to argue that boys', on average, greater dominance is evidence of their positive qualities of leadership, but that girls', on average, better verbal abilities only go to show that females waste their time talking.

So, if girls and boys develop along different pathways, there will be a number of factors, which interact with one another:

- Inherited differences as part of the biological sex differences.
- Social pressures on boys and girls about appropriate behaviour for the sexes, including cultural traditions.
- The patterns of encouragement and discouragement that shape children's learning.
- The process of modelling – children copy adults and later their friends and respected figures from music or the television.
- The messages passed on through books, films and play materials.

(See also page 89 on a positive approach to playwork with boys and girls.)

Activity 2.5

Over the next few weeks collect some examples of how expectations and beliefs appear to be shaping how boys and girls behave. Your examples might be from within your play setting; perhaps a boy tells a girl, 'No, you can't be in the team. Everyone knows girls are hopeless at cricket.' Or perhaps you notice an example outside your play setting, for instance, a parent in front of you in the supermarket check-out telling a young boy off with, 'Don't snivel. Big boys don't cry.'

Make a short presentation to your team or write up your observations as a brief report.

CHILDREN WITH DISABILITIES

All children will have some difficulties to overcome or to accept within their own development. For some children, disabilities or continued ill-health can have an impact, perhaps serious, on how their development unfolds. However, their opportunities for play and learning are also shaped by the adults responsible in different parts of their life – home, school and play settings.

The most common source of disability for children and young people is the variety of learning disabilities. Physical and sensory disabilities are less frequent in comparison. Some children and young people are significantly affected by medical conditions, for example by the impact of cystic fibrosis or cardiac problems.

You can only work well for children with disabilities when you have some understanding of how their individual pattern of disability affects their physical movement, communication skills, capacity to take care of themselves and so on. Children and young people who have been diagnosed as experiencing the same syndrome or illness may yet have many differences in the severity of the condition. Additionally, there will be the differences in temperament and family experience that all children and young people bring to your play setting.

GOOD PRACTICE

Children with disabilities need the support that acknowledges the consequences of their physical or learning disability, or health conditions. But they will not benefit from any play setting if their play is restricted unnecessarily or they are protected more than is crucial for their safety.

Activity   2.6
Read some of the relevant suggested resources about disabled children from page 291, or contact one or two relevant organisations from page 293.
  Summarise your findings.

PROGRESS CHECK

1 What children can do is affected by their age – but what else may influence the abilities that they show?
2 In what ways do you need to be cautious in making sense of apparent differences between boys and girls in their development?
3 Describe two ways in which good practice in playwork may clash with cultural tradition, and therefore with some parents' wishes.

Physical skills and interests

PHYSICAL GROWTH AND PUBERTY

Some of the visually most obvious developments occur in the first five years, as children's physical appearance continues to change from the largely helpless, head-heavy baby to the walking, talking and differently proportioned five year old. Yet, children continue to grow through the years of middle childhood and they change steadily in body shape and their facial appearance.

The second set of significant events happens at the onset of puberty, with both internal and external changes for boys and girls. The changes involved in the whole process of puberty do spread over several years and there is variation in when puberty starts for different individuals. Some girls or boys may start as early as 9 or 10 years; others do not start the shift until 13 or 14 years.

These changes are not just physical events for boys or girls. For most, the moves towards maturity bring a sense of pleasure that they are growing up. However, there is usually also a time of getting used to their still changing bodies, even some level of discomfort with some of the changes, and doubts over whether they are shaping up acceptably in comparison with others. Many young people passing through puberty are convinced that nobody else has ever been as worried about their appearance as they are now.

Examples

Katie had her growth spurt when she was 10. She started her periods in the last year of primary school. She felt pleased to be more grown up than most of her peers. But Katie felt uncomfortable that she had become the tallest in the class and was always anxious about her period because the school had no proper facilities in the toilets.

Kashif started his growth spurt when he was 13 and spent a very uncomfortable time feeling that he had become clumsy overnight. He was very relieved that his voice got steadily deeper without embarrassing squeaks, but is still battling with spots on his face. Kashif is convinced that no girl will ever find him attractive.

Activity 2.7
1 As a playworker, in what ways might you be involved appropriately in conversation with young people about the events of puberty?
2 Are there issues or questions to which you should reply, 'I'd suggest you talk with your parents about that'?
3 Write up your thoughts in a short report and present it to a team meeting.

Young people become more sexually aware and at some point they will have serious attachments. For the majority of young people, such partnerships will be with the opposite sex, but some will develop a sexual orientation that is gay, lesbian or bisexual.

PHYSICAL ABILITIES

Five and six year olds can have an impressive array of abilities on which to build. They will have learned a range of whole body movements and, for example, will be able to:

- Run – often quite fast and with sudden changes of direction.
- Climb – fairly safely, up equipment and trees.
- Enjoy simple gymnastics involving the movement of their whole body.
- Jump and hop about – often for the sheer joy of it.
- Control wheeled vehicles such as bikes or trolleys.
- Join in simple team games.
- Use their physical abilities expressively, for instance in dance and simple drama.

Children are also learning to coordinate their physical abilities with their senses, especially sight and touch. Five year olds can be adept at:

- Drawing and painting in a variety of artwork.
- Making models with a range of materials.
- Needlecraft under careful supervision.
- Using tools for simple crafts.
- Building indoor and outdoor structures with different kinds of material.
- The coordination required for self-help skills in eating, dressing and managing in the toilet without help.
- Helping out in everyday domestic routines.

Children can develop and extend their physical abilities but a great deal depends now on their experiences. What types of activities are they offered? How much help are children given as they learn? For instance, children can have become adept swimmers well before their teenage years, but only if they have regular access to a safe area of water and receive good coaching. Children can learn a wide variety of arts and crafts, but again, they need access to materials and, almost certainly, some guidance on technique.

Children with disabilities do not usually need a different range of physical play activities, but, depending on the kind of disability, children may benefit from specialist equipment to ensure safe and involved play. Children with learning disabilities may be physically very capable but some will need more careful guidance in craft activities and perhaps more finely graded steps towards a particular skill.

MAKING CHOICES

Perhaps you are puzzled by the reluctance of some children or young people to get involved. You know there is a wide range of activities and you feel confident that you work hard to be encouraging as children learn, yet you are getting nowhere with some users of your play setting. You may then be facing the other major issue that affects the physical development of 5–15 year olds, namely the attitudes that children have learned. For instance:

- Some children may have taken on board the belief that only certain kinds of boys, or girls, get involved in active sports.
- Others may have become very disheartened because they have been subjected to deadly serious, competitive games and can't see that there will be any fun.
- Older children and young people might have decided that there is no point in continuing with art, crafts or music activities unless they have a real talent in that area.
- Both boys and girls are affected by the beliefs about appropriate activities for their sex. There may be pressure from families on children and young people but, at least as likely is the power of views expressed by friends.

Some physical skills will only be learned through special opportunities

To think about   **2.8**

Of course many children and young people have very positive attitudes towards extending their physical skills and improving their abilities as much as they are able. As a playworker, you can be in a strong position to:
■ create an encouraging atmosphere
■ model how activities can be enjoyed regardless of level of talent
■ intervene, sensitively, to ensure that users of your play setting get their chance to join in or to practise. (See, for example the case study on page 102.)
How might you achieve any of the above?

KEY POINT

By middle childhood, boys and girls have developed attitudes that affect their outlook on physical activities and therefore the direction of their physical development.

Communication

ABILITIES IN COMMUNICATION

The younger children whom you meet through your playwork will have a broad range of abilities in communication. These will include:
■ Fluency in their spoken language. Some children can be fluent in more than one language by five years of age.
■ The ability to express themselves and to understand what is said to them. Difficulties now will tend to be that they cannot follow the ideas you are expressing or they lack vital information that you have failed to say.
■ Being alert to all the messages that come without words – the body language of adults and children – although they will probably not realise.
■ Children now have such a large working vocabulary that they will recognise words that are new to them. Confident children will ask you the meaning of a new word.
■ An awareness of the broader social rules about communication in their group. They will have learned through copying and guidance from adults about the balance between talking and shouting, whether to listen, do you interrupt, is it worth expressing an opinion?
■ The ability to use their words in a wide range of different uses of language. They can talk about 'what I did … ' but also about 'what I would like to do … ' or 'what I'll have to sort out before I can do … ' They can use their language skills to explain or justify, to ask questions or to speculate, to think out loud and to express opinions.

Children's abilities and awareness in communication can continue to develop. A great deal will depend on the opportunities that are available from 5–15 years, and a substantial part of these arise through the behaviour of adults in their communication. Obviously, children's continued development in communication is affected by their school and family experiences. However, the playwork setting offers many possibilities – see, for example, pages 71 and 99.

If children have a disability that affects communication, there may be different ways in which their ability to communicate can be affected. Some children's difficulties may be focused on the forming of words and what they express may be hard for others to understand, unless additional channels of communication are used, for instance, sign language or written notes. Other disabilities may slow down the process of learning to communicate, or effectively scramble the messages that are reaching the child's brain.

GOOD PRACTICE

If some of the users of your play setting have disabilities, then you need sound advice to guide you in how best to communicate. Children's parents can help, as can professionals with appropriate expertise. The most important aim is to find, and learn, the ways in which you can communicate directly with the child.

BODY LANGUAGE

Very young children are dependent on body language and context to make sense of communication, because they understand only a few of the actual words. Fluent children and young people are still influenced by the messages of body language, and so are you. We are all aware of facial expression, the wide range of gestures and the messages we read from someone's posture and general body stance.

There can be misinterpretations of body language, just as there are misunderstandings of what people have said.

CASE STUDY 2.9

In Willow Tree adventure playground Janet feels that Adrian's loud volume and 'macho' swagger are evidence of a troublemaker who will need watching. In fact, the loud words and large movements are more Adrian's way of covering up his relatively low self-confidence, and it is how all his friends behave.

In his turn, Adrian has decided that Janet is a shut-down, disapproving kind of playworker. He has formed this impression by noticing that Janet has spent most of the first session of the half-term playscheme with her arms tightly folded against her chest. She, on the other hand, is simply very cold, having forgotten to bring a thick jumper against the cold autumn wind.

Question
Think over your first impressions of some of the users of your setting. How many of your impressions have been established before the user said a single word? Discuss the issues with some of your colleagues.

Neither playworkers nor children talk just with words

KEY POINT

Studies of body language, sometimes called non-verbal communication, estimate that at least two-thirds of the full meaning of any communication is transmitted without words. When anyone – child, young person or adult – senses a mismatch between the words and a person's facial expression, stance or gestures, then it is practically always the non-verbal message that is believed, although not always acted on.

Thinking and reasoning

Sometimes both children and adults think about intellectual development as falling completely within the territory of school. Undoubtedly, if the school years go well, children and young people should make great strides in how they apply and extend their intellectual abilities. However, children are also thinking and reasoning outside the school gates.

THE SKILLS OF THINKING

Intellectual development is more than grasping a particular area of knowledge or learning specific techniques, such as how to conduct a scientific experiment. Intellectual development covers the whole span of thinking about a topic and thinking through a problem.
- How children make sense of the world around them, how things work, why people behave as they do.
- Why is this happening and why don't I understand it?

- How much do I know about this topic or problem? How reliable is my information?
- If I don't know something, how might I find out?
- Why did this go wrong – what can I do next time?
- If I don't know the way to approach this problem, do I know something similar that could guide me?

Children with physical disabilities can be frustrated and angry, with some justification, if other children or adults assume that a physical disability inevitably means difficulties in thinking and reasoning. Children who have learning disabilities are a very varied group. Some may have specific difficulties, for instance, with the written word. Other children may have more extensive learning disabilities which mean that adults, and other children, will have to adjust their communication and perhaps the way that play opportunities are presented.

FACTS AND A FRAMEWORK FOR IDEAS

Children are taking on board a massive array of facts. In addition, the framework which they use to make sense of the facts is continuously changing. Five and six year olds know a great deal, compared with a two year old, and the older children have developed powers of reasoning. But children, just like adults, can only think through an issue on the basis of the knowledge that they have gained to date and the way that they think the world works. So children may reach a logical conclusion that is wrong, but perfectly sensible from their information base.

WHAT IS IT LIKE NOT TO KNOW?

Ideas that are obvious to you, or ways of approaching a problem, can be far from obvious to children. Helpful adults – playworkers, teachers or parents – make the effort to look through the children's eyes when something is not clear and to offer a clear explanation in answer to children's questions. If you look back over the section on communication, you will be able to see how closely these two areas of development can be related – both in what children are learning and in the skills on which helpful adults have to draw.

Kieran is in charge of the Willow Tree Adventure Playground outing. After lunch he spots eight-year-old Gaven edging down the steep incline of the bank to a fast-flowing river. Frightened for Gaven's safety, Kieran yells at him and pulls him sharply back up to the towpath. Kieran confronts Gaven with, 'You thoughtless idiot! What on earth do you think you were doing! I told you all to be careful!' Gaven is angry in turn with Kieran, 'I can swim! You know I can swim! And I was going down really carefully.'

When he calms down, Kieran has a longer conversation with Gaven and it emerges that Gaven had thought through his action. In his terms he was being careful, but Gaven did not yet understand that even good swimmers can be swept away by the current and did not know that much of the slope to the river was greasy with algae.

Kieran apologised for yelling and then listened properly to what Gaven had to say. The eight year old learned something practical about safety around water. Just as important, he learned, because Kieran was honest with him, that adults who are frightened by what children are doing often express this as anger. Gaven also learned that Kieran, at least, was prepared to apologise when he had been unfair.

Question

Have you experienced incidents with children or young people where you realised, perhaps afterwards, that they were missing vital pieces of information or had generalised wrongly from other experiences?

Try writing up some of these incidents using visuals (line drawings or cartoons) to illustrate the points. Present this to your team as a short talk.

Activity   2.12

This is a selection of questions put to the authors by children ranging from 6–11 years. They illustrate how children are keen to understand and know more. They also demonstrate that answering their questions fully can make you think.
How would you have replied to each of the queries?

- 'I know you're looking at the street map to find out how we get to Joe's house. But I don't understand why it helps. The map is all lines, there's no houses on it.'
- 'I don't know why the boys keep on winding me up. I was crying today, they could see they had upset me, but they didn't stop.'
- 'Why do I go all crinkly after I've been in the swimming pool?'
- 'How do aeroplanes stay up when they're so heavy?'
- 'What makes a double rainbow?'

We did not know the answers in every instance. Sometimes the best thing to say is, 'Let's find out.' Children then learn as you consult a reference book or ask someone who does know. Discuss your thoughts with colleagues.

Playworkers in hospitals are dealing with children who may be confused or worried about what is happening to them. Children may be facing treatments or operations that are outside their current understanding. Alternatively, children's previous experience, for example of injections, may be the main source of their upset. Part of the role of hospital playworker has been to use play and friendly contact to help children to grasp what will be happening and to express their anxieties.

PROGRESS CHECK

1 In what ways could children and young people's attitudes affect the physical activities that they will try?
2 List five ways in which ten year olds might use their abilities to communicate.
3 Why might a child understand every word you have said but still not grasp your meaning?

Social relationships and feelings

By five years of age children have a level of personal awareness. You have to take care not to lay adult concepts over young minds. However, by the age that children start to use your play setting they will have developed a sense of personal identity, a level of self-esteem and an awareness of their own feelings, as well as those of others.

Young people may come to your play setting to meet each other

DEVELOPING PERSONAL IDENTITY

Five and six year olds have the beginnings of a sense of themselves as unique individuals, with a name, a sex, an age and a sense of belonging to a social or cultural group. For most children, their family will be a source of identity, including their position in the family. They will also be drawing on other sources of a personal identity as they compare themselves with others – on skin colour, style of dress, language and accent, perhaps religion or diet and on a pattern of abilities and possible disabilities. These other sources of identity are not value-free because of the prejudiced attitudes that exist in society.

Children's personal identity develops within a social framework in which some aspects to identity may be valued more positively than others. Children become aware of this evaluation and can think less of themselves because of the prejudices of others. Alternatively some children may come to believe – again because of social learning – that they are automatically a better person because they are white rather than black, a boy rather than a girl, or that they have no visible disabilities.

KEY POINT

It is not inevitable that a positive sense of identity has to go hand in hand with an arrogant sense of superiority over particular other individuals or groups. Yet children are fast learners and they easily take on pride intermingled with prejudice from adults and other children.

To think about   2.13
Some play settings will have users who vary in skin colour or other visible indicators of racial and cultural diversity. Good practice will never be to claim 'not to notice' these differences or to stress that you 'treat the children all the same'. Children are not all the same, so the point is to treat all children with equal fairness, which includes a positive acknowledgement of their personal identity.

Activity   2.14
1 Try making the 'I don't notice' kind of claim about differences in sex, age or height in a group of children. Do your words sound sincere or sensible?
2 What might be the reasons why some adults feel it is appropriate to say that they do not notice differences in skin colour? What else might they really be saying?
3 Discuss this sensitive issue with colleagues.

RELATIONSHIPS AND FRIENDSHIPS

Children choose their friends from neighbouring families in the area and from their contacts at school or other social groups. Friendships between boys and girls often develop without incident in the first six or seven years of

childhood. Then it becomes increasingly difficult, although not impossible, for boy-girl friendships to continue because of the level of teasing, as with, 'You love her!' and 'He's your boyfriend!', delivered with mocking noises or laughter. Group games are often single sex – but not always. A great deal depends on the confidence of the children involved, both the boys and the girls, and on how adults behave.

Children's friendships may also cross social, cultural and religious boundaries when families live in mixed neighbourhoods. Children learn the attitudes of those around them and, if these are rejecting of people who are judged to be different, or less acceptable, then children's friendships will begin to conform. On the other hand, children whose families hold to a strong value of taking others as individuals may well form lasting friendships with boys and girls who differ from them in skin colour, religious outlook or other, varied indicators to some type of group membership.

GOOD PRACTICE

Children have the right to make their own friends. As a playworker you will be working to create a friendly atmosphere in which children, and young people, can get to know one another. However, they will make the choice over whom they wish to be their more regular companions. You will make an exception to leaving choices entirely up to children if one or more of the users of your play setting are being ignored or deliberately excluded, apparently because of their race or gender, or because of a disability.

From five or six years onwards, children's friends are becoming an influence on how they behave. Through the years of childhood, boys and girls come to place greater importance on what their peers – the children who are of a similar age to them – say and do. Young people can be very influenced by their friends, but not always in a negative direction. Yet, children and young people remain willing to listen to parents, playworkers or teachers who pay them the respect of listening in their turn.

DEVELOPMENT OF SELF-ESTEEM

Children's self-esteem is related to their image of themselves, which is built up through the experiences of their young lives and especially the prevailing pattern of those experiences. Children can have a high level of self-esteem when experience has taught them that they are valued and liked for what they are – not what adults think they ought to be or insist on claiming they are.

KEY POINT

Self-esteem is built through a sense of worth and acceptance of both how you are at the moment and your capacity to continue to develop.
High self-esteem, for children or adults, is not an inflated and unrealistic view of yourself or your capabilities. On the contrary, it is a realistic outlook that you are worthy and worthwhile – even on your off days.

Children can be very forgiving and can bounce back from upsetting events or the cross word of a loved adult, so long as they are experiencing an overall message that important adults in their life accept and care about them. Children's resilience is chipped away by experiences that continue to give messages that undermine – you are not lovable, you should be different, or you are a bad child. The material in Chapter 6, on dealing positively with children's behaviour, is based on the importance of building children's self-esteem whilst holding to limits on acceptable and unacceptable behaviour.

Activity   2.15
Look back at the case study on page 46, which describes the incident between Kieran and Gaven. Draft a few sentences of what Kieran could have said in his apology to Gaven.
   Explain why the apology, and the conversation about the incident, were important in order to support Gaven's self-esteem.
   What might have resulted if Kieran had taken the uncompromising line that Gaven 'ought to have known better'? What are your views on the opinion that adults only look weak if they apologise to children?
   Discuss your thoughts with colleagues.

AWARENESS OF EMOTIONS

Children under four or five years undoubtedly have feelings, some of them very strong. They take time to learn about the range of emotions they feel and that others, children and adults, also experience these kinds of feelings.

Children of five and six can have learned to recognise their emotions as they well up inside and to direct the means of expressing stronger feelings, but only up to a point. For instance, five and six year olds are very unlikely to fling themselves on the ground, kicking and wailing, as is quite frequent with two and three year olds. However, without sensitive adult direction, angry or frustrated children – and young people – are very likely to express this emotion with energy. It may be a loud expression by shouting, some physical action such as banging something or stamping, or all of these at the same time.

Children's ability to express and deal with their emotions is closely linked to their development in the skills of communication. This, in turn, will have been strongly influenced by the important adults in their early years. In your playwork, you will meet some nine and ten year olds who still have very limited vocabulary to help them to express their feelings and little conviction that there is any point in making the effort. On the other hand, you will meet some six and seven year olds who have been encouraged by adults to talk about what they are feeling. These children will have the words to say 'I'm so cross with you because … ' or perhaps, 'I'm sad, but I don't know why.'

Activity   2.16

Over a period of a week, try to keep alert to the feelings of children, or young people, in your play setting. Note down the different ways in which you think that individuals are expressing their feelings. For instance, you might have noted something like this:

■ Kashif tells me in words. He seems to use the same phrase, 'fed up', to cover mild frustration, crossness and boredom.

■ I think that Eva deals with her angry feelings by stomping out into the yard. She seems to calm herself down by energetic wild swinging on the tyre. Once this week Eva started to cry, but it looked as if she didn't want anyone to see.

■ I am not sure what Dai is feeling. He seems stand-offish, then I wondered if it's his way of acting cool. Now, I'm wondering if he just isn't confident in starting up a conversation with anyone. Needs more thought!

Discuss your findings with colleagues, in a confidential setting.

The activity above raises three important points about making observations of users of your play setting.

1 Keep a clear distinction between what you observe in the children's behaviour and the interpretation that you make of it. That is why the examples use words like 'seems' and 'I think'. You are making shrewd guesses; you don't know for certain.

2 Don't leave your notes lying around. Other children may wind up the one whom you have been observing. Your notes should be kept confidential.

3 Take the opportunity to talk afterwards, in general, about your observations with the children. They may give you an opening by asking what you are writing down. This time, you might answer something like, 'I'm doing a project on how people express their feelings. It's interesting – take four of you when you're angry and you'll all show it in different ways.' Don't talk about

what you noticed about individuals except with the child in question, if she or he asks.

GOOD PRACTICE

It would be neither practical, nor useful, for playworkers to attempt a continuous analysis of what might or might not be going on inside the heads of users of the play setting. The point of raising your awareness of emotional development is that you are ready to look beyond the apparently obvious and that you recognise that children's feelings and expectations are relevant. And so, of course, are yours.

Children can experience strong emotions

Self-reliance and social skills

The point was made on page 32 that childhood unfolds within a particular social and cultural setting. Children's development in self-reliance, and adults' attitudes and behaviour towards this development, can be an area that is especially revealing about society itself.

EARLY SELF-HELP SKILLS

Boys and girls who are entering school will usually have learned some basic skills that enable them to take care of themselves in everyday tasks. For instance, five-year-olds can be capable of feeding themselves, dealing with their indoor and outdoor clothes and going to the toilet. What children also need is enough self-confidence and the communication skills to ask for assistance when they need it. This outlook relates, of course, to their previous experiences. These may lead children to believe that adults, on the whole, will help and share skills that enable you to manage better next time. Alternatively, children may have learned to avoid adults and cover up what they cannot manage because experience tells them that adults either mock your difficulties or tell you impatiently 'just get on with it!'

Older children with disabilities can become acutely aware that they cannot manage everyday self-help skills unless adults provide help, and in some cases, specialised equipment to enable the children to operate independently. Well meaning, but thoughtless, adults can make matters worse for children if they fail to offer the help with discretion, or if they insist on a speed that the children or young people cannot manage.

GOOD PRACTICE

At the outset, you need to talk with children with disabilities, and with their parents, to get the most appropriate answer to the question, 'How would you like me to help you?'

DEALING WITH CHANGES AND NEW SITUATIONS

The generations of children who grew up in Britain before the 1960s and 1970s usually entered primary school with their first five years of experience focused on their family and neighbourhood. In the more recent decades, many under fives have experienced different pre-school settings, such as playgroups, nursery classes and drop-in facilities for young children and their parents. Children whose parent or parents hold a job will have experienced some kind of child care, perhaps outside their home.

In terms of their development, five year olds have almost certainly gained experience of:
- Different settings outside their family – with variety in equipment, usual activities and timetables.
- Staying in a pre-school or child care setting without a parent.
- Getting used to somewhere new – the people and the place, and later moving on.
- How not all adults behave in the same way towards children, or have the same expectations.

Of course, children's previous experience of changes does not mean that they sail through any new situation, and nor does it mean that they will not benefit from a proper welcome and settling-in process. (See pages 62–65 on what this can mean for the playwork setting.)

Becoming self-reliant

Children are expected to continue in their development of self-help and social
skills beyond doing up their own shoes and getting down their dinner with minimal mess. However their development beyond these daily basics can be more
difficult than it need be. Adults often disagree amongst themselves about the
appropriate age for expecting children, or young people, to be able to, allowed
to or trusted to do particular things. Consequently, children can be faced with
mixed messages.

    Play facilities can offer many opportunities for children and young people to
learn skills in relative safety. There will always be some level of risk, however
careful adults try to be. (See the discussion on page 101 about risk as part of
learning.) With the support of observant playworkers they can also be learning
the more mature social skills that accompany greater self-reliance. They learn
to:

■ Handle conflicting expectations from different settings, adults, their friends
   and pressure from different groups of friends.

- Weigh up their wants with those of others.
- Face new situations with reasonable confidence and recognise what they already know that could be of help.
- Manage their time and assess priorities.
- Take care of themselves and sometimes of others as well.
- Resolve difficulties with other people – usually without reaching screaming pitch or fisticuffs.

To think about   2.18

Adults find some of these social skills very difficult, so it is perhaps not surprising that children and young people sometimes complain that they could do with more help.

Think about the kinds of situations in your play setting in which you, or your colleagues, are able to support children and young people in the kinds of learning listed above.

Note down your ideas and discuss them with other team members.

KEY POINT

A great deal of discussion, and argument, about 'how old should children be before you let them … ' overlooks the most important point. It is not that there are absolutely correct, or safe ages at which children can be trusted to walk to school unaccompanied or be left alone at home. The much more important point for children's development is what do they need to have learned, and so what do adults need to have taught them, before the children are ready to try it on their own?

To think about   2.19

Whatever the children's age, you also need to watch out that you are not expecting standards of behaviour from the users of your play setting that you would not realistically expect from a group of adults. So-called 'grown-ups' can behave in less than impressive ways when it comes to waiting for their turn, taking care of equipment, considering the perspective of others and keeping their promises.

PROGRESS CHECK

1 Why would it be bad practice to claim that you did not notice racial or cultural differences in the users of your play setting?
2 Describe two circumstances in which you might intervene over users' choice of play companions.
3 List four ways in which you might observe children learning to be more self-reliant in your play setting. How might you help?
4 Describe two ways in which physical or learning disabilities could affect a child's development.

KEY TERMS

You need to know what these words and phrases mean. Go back through the chapter to make sure that you understand.

Development

Culture

Modelling

Disabilities

Puberty

Communication

Body language

Personal identity

Self-esteem

3 POSITIVE RELATIONSHIPS WITH CHILDREN AND YOUNG PEOPLE

> **This chapter covers:**
> - Anti-discriminatory practice
> - Developing relationships with children and young people
> - Communication in playwork
> - Learning and playwork settings

Anti-discriminatory practice

PRINCIPLES INTO DAILY PRACTICE

In services for children, young people and their families, the term 'anti-discriminatory practice' has come to mean several, linked aspects to good practice:
- to establish a consistent team outlook of acknowledging and being positive about differences between individuals – children, team members and parents or other carers
- a determined effort to challenge and to change any procedures and practices that have a consequence of discrimination against any group. It does not matter whether anyone had the intention to discriminate. If that is the result, then the situation needs to be addressed
- to promote equal opportunities for children and families, and the equalising of uneven opportunities, actively within the service and through ease of access for individuals from all groups
- to counter the development of prejudiced attitudes and discriminatory behaviour as children learn their outlook on life and how to behave.

These aspects to good practice are usually applied within the following broad areas:
- ethnic group and cultural background, including language and, where appropriate, religious faith
- gender and, as it becomes appropriate with young people, sexual orientation (in terms of heterosexual, gay and lesbian or bisexual identity)
- disability and continuing health conditions.

KEY POINT

Everyone has an ethnic identity, culture, a language including accent and a social background. Sometimes, the details of your own past and present only come into sharper focus through differences with others. Supporting children to have a positive sense of their own identity can have the unexpected and favourable consequence of helping you to find satisfaction in the sources of your own personal identity.

REFLECTIVE PRACTITIONERS – REFLECTIVE TEAMS

Depending on where you work, some aspects of diversity may appear to be more locally applicable than others. It is important to keep an open mind within your team and to avoid dismissing whole areas of practice as 'not relevant for us here'. For instance, in areas with considerable cultural diversity, it can seem very obvious that your play and celebratory activities should draw from the local community and their resources. Yet, in an area with very little apparent ethnic and cultural diversity, your sensitive use of play materials and conversation may be the only balanced source of information for the children. You will have an important role in helping children and young people to look beyond their own backyard. Some areas of the UK, that are visibly almost completely white, nevertheless have traveller communities who can experience considerable discrimination.

Undoubtedly, in some parts of the UK specific issues arise because of the composition of the local community and past history. Anti-discriminatory practice in Northern Ireland has to take account of the deep-rooted hostilities between two branches of the Christian faith: Catholic and Protestant. Anti-sectarianism is central to good practice in this part of the UK and includes the need for playworkers to consider, sometimes painfully, their own experience and attitudes, as well as working to make a difference to the current younger generation.

Throughout the book, not only this chapter, you will find many examples to help you make anti-discriminatory practice come alive in your playwork. A few general points are made here, to give you and your colleagues food for thought.

Positives, not just negatives
Anti-discriminatory practice needs to be promoted in a positive way. It may seem easier at first to highlight all the unacceptable actions and words. However, good playwork practice, and support for children and the team, can only go forward with a clear idea of what you want, and not just a long list of what you wish to stop. Anti-discriminatory practice will fail if it overrides principles of good practice in dealing with behaviour. (Look especially at some of the approaches within Chapter 6.)

Show, don't just tell
Neither children nor adults usually respond well to being told or 'told off'. The success of anti-discriminatory practice in your setting depends upon the application of good communication skills, as in all the rest of your work. (See especially the ideas within Chapter 9.) You need to discuss in your team the details of what an anti-discriminatory approach will be like in practice. For instance, how do ordinary children behave when they have taken on board an anti-sexist approach? What is realistic and what is not? How can the adults set a good example?

Putting words in their place
Part of anti-discriminatory practice has to be dealing with offensive language between individuals from any group (see also Chapters 6 and 7). However, good

practice will get bogged down if the adults focus excessively on the 'right' words or phrases to use. Team discussions will be unhelpful if they slide into point scoring and even recrimination. Any discussion on 'how do we talk appropriately about this issue or this group of people?' has to be closely tied to what it all means in practice and 'what are we actually going to do that will directly benefit the children and families?'.

Be realistic as adults
Try to avoid making an unrealistic world view part of anti-discriminatory practice. Children have a strong sense of natural justice and they will object if, for instance, your bullying policy in the setting suggests that some kinds of insults, perhaps racist ones, are more significant than personal taunts such as 'You're adopted, your real mother must have hated you!' Trouble between the users of your setting will sometimes follow the lines that suit naïve adult sensibilities, but children from social and ethnic groups that experience discrimination will sometimes be inconsiderate and rejecting in their turn.

PLAYWORK WITH BOYS AND GIRLS

Part of children's individuality is that they are male or female. Good practice in anti-sexism is not achieved by claiming that there are no differences between boys and girls. Clearly, differences do exist, but most of these are accentuated by adult beliefs about how men and women, and so also boys and girls should

behave. ('Gender' is the term used to describe the socially determined expectations of the two sexes.) British culture has been, and in many ways still is, shaped by gender stereotypes about the potential and limitations of males and females. Children and young people will be influenced by these attitudes. (See page 37 on this issue in children's development.)

Your aim in playwork will be to ensure that neither boys nor girls shut themselves away from learning particular skills or joining in certain activities solely for reasons of their sex. Users of play settings may believe that they will be incompetent at an activity because of their sex, or perhaps friends and family tell them firmly that an activity is inappropriate for a girl or a boy. Good practice can never be to force children into activities that counter gender stereotypes. Playworkers need to consider how the play setting as a whole could encourage boys and girls to extend their interests and skills.

Example

You would neither discourage Josh from playing football nor Maekesha from joining a cooking activity on the grounds that these were traditionally gender-typed activities. Good practice would be to ensure that the play setting worked in such a way that Maekesha could join a football game, and learn footballing skills, without being teased or rejected by either sex. The same would hold for Josh and cooking, or any other, more traditionally female activities in which he showed an interest.

GOOD PRACTICE

It is certain that you will have at least some working assumptions that will affect your approach as a playworker. It is impossible to plan ahead without some assumptions about what is likely to interest users of your setting and approximately how many children might wish to join in given activities. Playworkers' assumptions need to be reviewed and particularly so when there is any element of grouping by sex – intended or not.

PLAYWORK IN A MULTI-CULTURAL SOCIETY

It is important that playworkers show respect for, and give time to understand the ways of cultures represented by the children, and within British society as a whole. No playworkers should tolerate racist words or actions from users within the play setting, or from their parents. A stance against racism has to be even-handed and playworkers have to be ready to challenge black users just as much as white if they are rude or dismissive of groups to which they feel they do not belong. (See also page 160 on this issue.)

Sensitivity to different cultures does not mean that playworkers are expected to accept any way of treating children solely on the grounds that it is a traditional approach for a given group, or religion. Look, for instance at page 33 for a discussion of two points on which good practice in playwork is a direct challenge to tradition.

Other chapters in this book show the practical ways in which you can show respect and support all the children's learning beyond one culture. The acknowledgement of childhood in a multi-cultural society raises some basics of good practice in playwork which are addressed now.

Choices with reasons
Playwork practice could not possibly encompass the details of all social, cultural and religious traditions. Choices will always have to be made. So, any play setting has to communicate honestly, through the behaviour of the playworkers and any written material, what kind of approach is taken in the setting.

You need to be honest if what parents are asking, or what children expect you to do, is not easy to deliver. Some potential problems may be resolved, but requests cannot be granted if they go directly against centre policy. For example, some play settings may find that parents' wishes are for a play programme that is different for boys and girls, or that parents may wish to determine their children's play companions on the basis of race, sex or religious belief. Whatever the apparent reason behind such requests, playworkers cannot agree to follow such a line.

GOOD PRACTICE

You need to understand the reasons for policy and the details of practice in your setting. Then you can explain courteously to parents, and children when they ask you, what you do and why you do it that way.

Don't assume – ask
You cannot know everything. Even very experienced playworkers will continue to learn about cultures with which they are less familiar. Sometimes you will not understand what is being asked, or perhaps you will not realise the importance of what a parent, or child, is saying to you. For example, for cultural, sometimes religious, reasons, families may require that their children, usually their daughters, keep their head covered and do not remove clothing to the extent that would be required in a swimming trip. This is not optional.

GOOD PRACTICE

Be ready to check your assumptions, and breadth of knowledge, about cultural or social groups, or the implications of religious beliefs. Responsible playworkers do not dismiss a request or a suggestion out of hand because it seems odd, or unnecessary to them.

Activity   3.1
With colleagues discuss the sensitive issues raised in the Good Practice above.

Variety within a group
When you are learning about family patterns from a range of cultures – perhaps of minority ethnic groups to which you do not belong – or the major world

religious faiths, it is very important to remember that there is usually as much diversity within particular cultures or faiths as there is between them.

For instance, all the major world faiths have different sects, some of whom disagree vehemently with each other. For any given set of culturally-based beliefs, for instance about diet, dress or religious observance, there will be some families who follow the practical requirements more strictly than others. The only way that you can follow the advice just given of 'Don't assume – ask' is to take opportunities to talk with parents and children.

CHILDREN WITH DISABILITIES

The main themes of good practice in playwork are the same regardless of the pattern of abilities and disabilities of the children and young people who attend the setting. Positive relationships cannot be developed between playworkers and users if children are seen largely in terms of their disabilities, and certainly not if adults' feelings are dominated by pity or personal discomfort.

However, responsible playworkers would not pretend that a serious heart defect or total hearing loss are irrelevant for a child's options in play, since this is untrue. Whether in integrated or specialist play settings, playworkers will need to offer a full range of play, shared activities and enjoyable communication. Playwork teams may need to adjust how the activities are offered and the kind of equipment needed as appropriate to individual users. Careful risk assessment should ensure that disabled children are not over-protected and therefore restricted in their play.

PROGRESS CHECK

1   Describe three broad ways in which anti-discriminatory practice can work in play settings.
2   Why is it important that children are not directed away from play activities that are more traditional for their sex?
3   Explain why it can be misleading to generalise from your experience of one family to expectations of other families sharing the same culture or religion.

Developing relationships with children and young people

EARLY CONTACTS

Your first contacts with children or parents will vary depending on your play setting. In schemes with a register of users you will have a more formal start to the relationship, perhaps involving visits and the completion of an information sheet about the child or young person. If you are working in an adventure playground, a drop-in club or running a mobile playbus, children or young people will simply turn up.

A good welcome is fairly low key!

Open-access settings

The beginning of the relationship in an open-access play setting will be informal, but playworkers can still take a consistent approach of acknowledging the arrival of 'new' children or young people by taking the first opportunity to talk briefly with them. Users can be made welcome and, if appropriate, introduced to other users.

Activity 3.2

If you work in an open-access setting, note down the ways in which you deal with early contacts with children and young people.

If you have no experience of an open access setting, then arrange to visit your nearest play facility that works in this way. Discuss with the playworkers and take notes on the way in which they welcome new users.

Write up your notes into a concise report. Add photos or sketches, if possible.

GOOD PRACTICE

If your setting runs for more than two hours a day and you have any children under eight years of age, then your play facility needs to be registered and inspected by Ofsted. If not, the facility may still choose to voluntarily register – see page 22 for details.

Settings with regular attenders

You are much more likely to have a definite pattern of first meetings and discussion if you are working in an after-school club with a register of attending children and an explicit understanding that you take responsibility for the children between agreed hours.

Good practice would be that, before a child attends for the first session, there would be a meeting between an individual playworker, the child and his or her parent(s). This meeting would include a tour of the club itself. There are two sides to this first meeting:

1   Key information that playworkers need to give to parent(s) and child.
2   Questions that child and parent(s) want to ask about the play setting.

On the basis of this meeting it should be possible for parent(s) and child to make an informed decision about whether to accept a place in the club.

To think about   3.3

First meetings with parents and prospective users should cover the most important points about the running of a play setting, but not be so full of information that parents cannot recall the details.

■ How do you make sure in your play setting that first meetings cover the essentials? For example, do you have a list to jog your memory?

■ Even a short list of practicalities can be a lot for parents to remember. Do you have something written that they can take away?

■ What kind of general questions do you find are most common? From parents? From children?

■ In your experience do parents have queries about the form you ask them to complete for their child? What sort of queries are common? (You will find more about good practice in record keeping in Chapter 5.)

■ Discuss your thoughts, and any new ideas, with the team.

Short playschemes

School holiday playschemes can be a halfway stage between the practice of an open-access facility and that of a regular after school club. Good practice will include attention to two issues:

1   Effective contact with parents and children prior to the start of the playscheme so that they have an accurate view of what the scheme is offering.
2   Collection of basic information about children for reasons of safety and planning the play programme.

You may address these two issues by written communication, through an open meeting for potential users, or both methods.

What are the essential items of information to know about children, even during a half-term playscheme? How do you ensure that you gain this information? What are the risks if you do not?

LEARNING CHILDREN'S NAMES

Using names

It is not good practice to refer regularly to users of the play setting as if they were an undifferentiated group. It is fine to call out 'Can everyone come over here please!' when users are scattered over the yard or in a large hall, but you should make an active effort to get names into your memory and address children by their own name most of the time. It is neither good practice, nor at all courteous to users, if playworkers depend most of the time on phrases like 'you lot!'. Admittedly, in a large playscheme that only lasts for the week of half term, learning names may be tough, but do try.

Children's names should be used in the way that they ask. Evalene may definitely want to be known as Eva, but Kevin may hate being called Kev. Occasionally, a child may use a nickname and playworkers should follow what he or she wants – perhaps Frances has always been known as Fizzy and she prefers it.

Some names will be more familiar to you than others and, in an ethnically diverse neighbourhood, you may meet children whose name is completely new to you. You can ask children to repeat their name and then you make sure that you are pronouncing it correctly. Practise if you need and, if you are having difficulty with a name, consider making yourself a discreet note on how to say it.

GOOD PRACTICE

No child's name should be shortened or changed just because playworkers think it is too long or find the name difficult to pronounce. Rarely, you may find that a name is genuinely hard for you, because it uses sounds or sound combinations that do not appear in your own language. If you find your difficulty persists, then ask the child for a suggested variation that you can manage. In the same way offer children another version of your name, if they are having genuine difficulty.

KEY POINT

Children's names will never be 'difficult'; it is you who are finding a first or surname hard to pronounce. Neither are names 'odd'; it is that you have never encountered this name before. Playworkers should bear this point in mind for themselves but you may also need to intervene, with care, if children take the line of 'that's a funny name'.

Personal and surnames

At first meeting you will be finding out a child's personal name. For one of a number of possible reasons, some children and young people attending your play setting will not share the surname of the parent(s) whom you meet. So it is important to check rather than assume.

It is appropriate to refer to 'personal' or 'first' names, since the description of these as 'Christian' names is a consequence of the long-term influence of the Christian religion on British society and is not, therefore, universally applicable.

The Western European naming system is that the personal name comes first, followed by any further personal names, and the surname comes last. Not all cultures follow this pattern – neither the order, nor in having a family surname. The best guideline for you to follow is, 'If in doubt, ask'.

In most play settings children and young people will call playworkers by their first name. Children can be informal with adults and still look to you for guidance and follow what you say. Children will feel respect, or liking, for you on the basis of your behaviour; it does not depend on whether they use your first name or your surname.

THE ROLE OF THE PLAYWORKER

As a playworker you are in a different position from a child's parent who has a long-term and continuing responsibility for a son or daughter. You are responsible for children and young people while they are with you, although this responsibility will take different forms depending on whether your play setting has a register of regular attenders or is open access.

Neither are you attempting to step into the role of children's teachers who have a responsibility for their education in the context of schooling. Playworkers can support and extend children's learning, but in a different context from school, and with some opportunities that are not available to teachers.

KEY POINT

As a playworker you are not a child any more, but you can bring the qualities of enthusiasm and excitement that will make activities with children come alive. You can be a good friend to users of your play setting, so long as you recall that you are an adult friend. This point will hold even if you are still in your late teens or very early twenties, and are not that many years removed from the eldest users of your play setting.

THE END OF A RELATIONSHIP

Some relationships in play settings will last for years. But, at some point, users of the setting will move on, as will the playworkers. In open access schemes users may simply stop coming and it will dawn on playworkers that what were familiar faces of children or young people have been absent for weeks. In schemes with regular attenders there may be more warning that a child or young person will stop attending.

Different play settings will vary but part of a friendly relationship with users will be to acknowledge when it is coming to an end, or will be interrupted.

- When children are about to leave or pass the maximum age for the play setting, then playworkers should acknowledge this change in some way. It may be an organised leave taking, like a party, or simply making sure that the last day or session for a user is recognised through conversation and a proper goodbye.
- Playworkers should warn users if they are going to leave the job and say their goodbyes. It is not good practice to give children the experience that familiar adults simply go away without a word.
- The end of a half term or school holiday play scheme may be marked with a party and with goodbyes that include, 'Hope we see you next time.'

PROGRESS CHECK

1 Describe briefly the role of the playworker in any play setting. Are there responsibilities for children that definitely lie outside your role?
2 Describe three ways in which you could build up a personal relationship with users of your play setting.
3 Under what circumstances might you not call a child by her or his given name?

Communication in playwork

You will have many different opportunities to communicate with the users of your play setting. Many of these will arise naturally as you spend time with children and young people focused on shared activities. Some play facilities will have scheme or club meetings which offer a scheduled time to exchange views and put forward suggestions.

KEY POINT

In most instances you will be alert for opportunities to talk with and listen to the users of your play setting. With the exception of planned consultation with children and young people, conversation is not an activity to be timetabled into the day or session.

CONVERSATIONS WITH CHILDREN AND YOUNG PEOPLE

The focus of communication

You may have conversations with children about a wide range of general topics as well as exchanges focused on a given activity. There will be opportunities within the playwork setting to support children and young people as they extend their skills of communication and become more confident in speaking out. For example:

- Talking about what interests the children. These could be plans for the playground, television, films or videos, books, school, local issues – anything that holds their attention.
- Specific requests for the opinion of a child or young person. The opinions might be about the play setting – 'The afternoon snacks are getting boring, what else do you think we could do?' Or about something outside the setting – 'My nephew has been on at me to take him to see that film. He's only six, do you think he'd like it?'
- Inviting children to be part of planning or working out how to progress an activity. You might draw them in with 'I wonder what's possible here – what do you think?', or 'How are we going to go about this – any ideas?'

Children and playworkers who have developed a relationship will also have shared memories. It might be the picnic and hike across the heath, made especially memorable because one of the playworkers slid off the stepping stones into the stream. Or it might be reliving the sense of achievement when the impressive structure was finished in the adventure playground. Children and young people often enjoy reminiscing, so long as the content is driven by their interests and the memories are not a source of upset or embarrassment to them.

SHARING SOMETHING OF YOURSELF

A positive relationship of individuals is two-way. So, it can help to build a friendly relationship with users of your setting if you share something about your own interests, your personal likes and dislikes. Depending on the activity in which you are involved, the conversation that develops might focus on your own likes and dislikes or your memories of school or childhood.

Children and young people are often genuinely interested in playworkers' personal lives, away from the play setting. They will ask you about your family,

your partner and your own children, if you have any. They may well press you with questions without considering whether they are being intrusive. The younger children, especially, will not think about your possible wish for privacy. It will be up to you to call a halt, in a way courteous to the children, if you do not want to answer further inquiries. You might say, 'That's enough questions for me. I'd be interested to hear about you and... .' If children do not take the hint, you might need to be more specific, although still polite to them. Perhaps you could say, in a pleasant manner, 'I don't want to talk about that. It's personal to me.' You can even stop a more dubious line of questioning in an assertive way, which does not depend on putting children down or accusing them of outright rudeness.

CASE STUDY 3.5

During the previous weekend, Adrian (14 years) ran into Elroy at the cinema. Adrian picks up on this when they next meet at the adventure playground.
Adrian: Was that your girlfriend then, Elroy? The one with you?
Elroy: Yes, it was. That's Kimberley.
Adrian (grins and goes on): Are you knocking her off, then?
Elroy: That's private, Adrian.
Adrian: That means you are then! That proves it!
Elroy: All it proves is that I choose not to talk about my private life with you, mate. *(Said firmly but with a friendly grin, since Elroy knows Adrian well.)*

Question
Have you or your colleagues needed to divert a child or young person away from what feels like an inappropriate conversation with you? How have you managed this?
   Share ideas with some of your colleagues.

GOOD PRACTICE

In forming a friendly relationship with children you might share memories that are personal to you, mention experiences of relevance or interest, and express your opinions occasionally. You would not tell children intimate facts about yourself, your family or anyone else.

USING QUESTIONS

Generally, open-ended questions will tend to encourage more communication from children than closed questions, which tend to invite a one word reply.

Example

Sam is telling Dawn about what he watched on television over the weekend. Dawn might just ask questions such as 'Do you like Beth (a character) ... ?' or 'Are nature programmes your favourite?'. Sam could then reply 'Yes' or 'No'. On the other hand, open-ended questions from Dawn can invite opinions, descriptions and explanations from Sam. He has a range of choices in his reply to questions such as, 'What's Beth up to now?' or 'I meant to watch that programme on wolves. What was it like?'

The words 'How?' and 'What?' can be positive beginnings when you are inviting children to explore the opinion they have just expressed. When adults ask, 'Why?', or even 'Why do you say that?', some children feel put on the spot to justify their view. Depending on their previous experience, they may also assume that the adult is disagreeing. However, open-ended questions can support a child or young person in explaining the thoughts that have gone towards the opinion.

Example

Matt is expressing a firm opinion. Whether Angus agrees with him or not, he can encourage Matt to explore his view with, 'I'm not sure I follow you, Matt. Can you tell me how you decided that ... ?' or 'That's a different way of looking at it, Matt. What makes you say that?'

Of course, good communication will never just depend on using a particular form of words. Meaning also comes from how something is said and from the messages of body language (see page 43).

Routine events, such as a club's school pick-up, can be an enjoyable opportunity to talk

Through conversation you can build children's confidence as well as their ability to communicate. You will do this as you show an interest in hearing their views and ideas. You will also learn from children and young people themselves – they often have a fresh outlook on a topic and impressive knowledge in their area of special interest.

IF YOU DO NOT SHARE A LANGUAGE

Some play settings are situated in an area with families who do not all share the same first language. When families are long-term residents, it is most likely that the children will be bilingual. However, if some families have recently arrived, perhaps with refugee status, then the children may be fluent in a language of which playworkers have no knowledge.

It is still very possible to make children welcome to your play setting and to encourage them to become involved when there is currently no shared spoken language. Several practical points will help everyone:

- If at all possible, you should learn some key phrases in the child's language – 'Hello' or 'Goodbye' would be a friendly start.
- Continue to talk with a child who is learning your language, but keep what you say in a simple format. This means shorter sentences and using words that are directly grounded in what the child can see, or is watching you doing.
- Support what you say with normal, not exaggerated, gestures of pointing or demonstrating.
- Encourage the other children to talk with the new arrival in a similarly straightforward way, and at normal volume.
- If bilingual children using the play setting share the new arrival's first language, then they may be willing to help you, so long as this does not become an onerous responsibility.

HEARING AND SPEECH IMPAIRMENTS

You may have children attending the play setting who have specific impairments affecting their hearing or speech.

It is very important that playworkers never assume that a child with disabilities will automatically have trouble with communication. Likewise, playworkers should be ready to intervene, with care, if other children appear to be making the assumption that a child in a wheelchair will be deaf or very slow to reply.

First meetings with children and their parents will be valuable in helping playworkers to identify effective ways of communicating with the children.

Examples

- Ben feels self-conscious about his hearing impairment. Although communication is eased for him with a hearing aid he is resistant to using it. He is adept at lip reading but will not remind people to face him. One playworker at Hummingbird Adventure Playground is able to sign and the others want to learn. However, Ben's parents warn them that, at the moment, Ben will only use signing within his family.
- Caitlin, whose development has been severely affected by Down's Syndrome, communicates successfully with a combination of spoken words and signing. Her parents are pleased to teach some of the basic signs to playworkers at the Downham after-school club. They stress that signing does not take the place of spoken words – adults and other children should talk and sign to Caitlin simultaneously.
- Rory's words do not always come out clearly but his sister, Jane, understands the majority of what he says. Their father explains to playworkers at Hummingbird that Jane is happy to help out and Rory does not mind, so long as adults or other children continue to look at him. He gets very angry, understandably, if people act as if he is no longer there.

Activity   **3.6**

Write short reports on children and young people who have difficulties in communication or who become frustrated with the inability of others to understand them. In what way do children make the most of their abilities and how can playworkers and other children help?

If you have very limited experience in this area, then talk with colleagues to build up your understanding. Read some of the resources suggested in Appendix E and consult relevant websites.

PROGRESS CHECK

1 Describe three ways in which you could encourage children and young people to talk with you.
2 Are there topics of conversation that playworkers should avoid with users? How might you close down an inappropriate conversation?
3 Describe three different circumstances in which communication could be genuinely difficult – to the person speaking or listening. What could you do in each case?

LISTENING

Children's ability to communicate will extend with plenty of practice in talking with people who are interested in what they have to say. The essence of a good conversation is a fairly equal turn-taking on talking and listening. Children will tend to copy adults they respect, which will include playworkers. So you can guide children and young people by how you behave, as well as how you sometimes intervene carefully on the children's behaviour.

Listening to children

Children do not learn to listen by being reprimanded with, 'Listen to me when I'm speaking!' They may learn to be silent, but that is not always the same as listening. Children are far more likely to listen to others through experience of adults who pay careful attention to them, and who listen to what the children have to say, at least as often as they ask children to listen in their turn.

You will show that you are listening through what you say in reply, but also in your own non-verbal behaviour. It is important that you:

- Look at children when they are speaking, rather than glancing away or appearing more absorbed in what you are doing. If it would be dangerous to take your eyes away, then say to the child, 'I must keep watching this, but I am listening to you.'
- Avoid interrupting them. If it is necessary, you apologise and get back to the child with, 'I'm sorry, you were telling me about … '
- Add your side of the conversation built upon what the child has told you or expressed an opinion about.
- Show children that not only do you listen, but that you value what they say enough to recall what you have been told earlier. For example:
  – 'Catherine, you told me how you walked the nature trail with your Dad. Do you remember what the path was like? Would Sam get his wheelchair along it?'
  – 'Go on, Dai, tell them that joke you told me yesterday.'
  – 'I remember you were interested in sharks, Josh.'
- Take any worries seriously that children express to you. Playworkers in hospital can be in a good position to help children who are anxious about their health or upcoming treatment. In any setting, playworkers should not ignore signs of possible abuse of a child or young person – see Chapter 7 for good practice in this area.

Activity   3.7

The above points about listening to children may seem very obvious, but as basic guidelines for good communication, they are regularly broken.

Keep alert over a period of a week and notice how often adults, even well-meaning ones, show through their behaviour that they do not really value what children say.

Try to take your examples from different settings and then identify two ways in which you could improve your active listening in the playwork setting.

Discuss or present your findings in a team meeting.

Listening and knowledge of individuals

Communication with children or young people should never lead them to feel uneasy or intimidated. Playworkers need to be alert that what is enjoyable teasing to one child may be uncomfortable to another. One child may relish a challenge, yet another might feel anxious about the same encouragement of, 'Go for it! I'm sure you can make it.' The positive relationship that you develop with the users of your play setting will help you to be sensitive to individual differences. That, for instance, Sam likes and needs the verbal 'push' but, if Kevin says he does not want to try something, then he is serious about not being ready yet.

Helping children to listen

It is discourteous of adults continually to demand that children pay attention to what the adults say – especially if adults do not listen in their turn. However, there will be times when you wish, reasonably, that a child listen to you, or to another child who is currently talking.

As you develop a positive relationship with the users of your play setting, you will find that they are more and more likely to listen to you in general conversation, because you listen to them. Sometimes you will need to give some explanation or instruction to a group, or an individual child. You might wish them to listen to your words, or that they watch you carefully, or both. Depending on the occasion you might do any of the following:

Sometimes children need your full attention

- Make sure you have their attention before you start. You might use a child's name or gently touch an arm before saying, 'Kathy, stop a moment. I can see why you're not managing to cut that wood. Let me show you how to hold the saw.'
- An excited group might need a call, a hand clap or some version of 'Hey, everyone! This is important. Are you listening?' You would then follow up with the message – 'We meet here, by the dinosaur, at 3 o'clock. If you haven't got a watch, then ask one of the museum attendants. Same thing if you can't work out how to get back here.'
- If you wish to be sure that children have listened and are likely to remember, then ask them to summarise what you have said in their own words. In the museum example, it might be a simple, 'So, where are we meeting ... and what time?' If you are helping a child to learn the rules of snooker, you might say, 'Liam, you tell it back to me now. When all the reds are potted, what's the order that you have to pot the other colours?'

Conversations in your play setting will be more enjoyable for children if the more vociferous ones do not drown out the quieter children. The turn taking of listening as well as talking will develop if you intervene with discretion, as well as modelling considerate social behaviour yourself. Your intervention can be positive, rather than the negative, 'Don't interrupt!' For example you might intervene with:

- 'Sachin, hold on a minute. Let Grace finish her bit' ... 'Right, Sachin, it's your turn now.'
- 'Marsha, you started to say something a moment ago.'
- 'Grace, I'm not sure that Catriona was arguing with what you just said. I think she was making a different point. Would you say it again, please, Catriona?'

LISTENING AND UNDERSTANDING

Playworkers and children will not understand each other fully all the time – neither do adults in their communications. There will be different kinds of not understanding, some of which are misunderstandings.

Sometimes you may judge that the children do not understand what you have said. You have several options, depending on the nature of the communication.

- Sometimes you suspect a child or young person was not listening to you in the first place. You might say, perhaps with a friendly smile, 'You weren't listening to my words of wisdom, were you?' ... 'No? Shall I say it again?'
- On some occasions it may help to repeat an explanation, but with different, or simpler words. Sometimes you may need to give one step at a time to children.
- Sometimes a child who appeared to be attending carefully still looks blank or confused. Then you might ask, 'You don't look sure, Naomi. Where did I lose you?'
- It can be helpful to get children to talk you through what they have

understood up to the point where the confusion sets in. Then you do not waste energy re-explaining what they have followed.

- Children sometimes understand every word you have said but they do not grasp the idea that you are putting across. In some cases you may be depending on a level of understanding that the child has not yet reached. (See page 46.)
- It may be more the case that you have failed to go into detail over some aspect that seems obvious to you, but is not known to the children. For instance, in tapestry or binca work the needle is taken up through one hole and directly down through another, and not over the edge of the canvas.

Sometimes it will be you that does not understand what a child is saying. The simplest, and often most effective, approach is to admit you did not understand. For example: 'Fizzy, I didn't follow what you said. Would you take me through that again, please?'

Adults often take roundabout routes by saying 'Pardon?' which can just get a literal repeat of the child's words. This will not help you when you heard the words the first time; your problem is that you didn't understand. Sometimes adults guess or start asking questions, but again the answers may still not help you, since the child does not know that you are confused.

To think about   3.8

Children are learning the social skills of communication. Adults are not necessarily adept or courteous in every single communication. So, watch out that you do not insist on unrealistic standards for the users of your play setting.

INVOLVEMENT THROUGH CONSULTATION

Spoken exchanges, with listening as well as talking, will be an important route for involving children and young people in the play setting. They will appreciate being consulted for their opinions, evaluations and suggestions – either through individual conversations or centre meetings.

Some children may hold back to check that you are serious in this aim – perhaps previous experience tells them that adults say, 'Tell me what you'd like', but do not then take much notice. Consultation with the users of your setting will support a positive relationship with them so long as they can see results from this process. The most important aspects will be that:

- Commitments made to the users are honoured. Promises should not be made if there is any doubt over whether they can be kept. It is much better to say, 'I'll get back to you on that,' and of course to honour this commitment, than to say blithely, 'I'm sure that'll be fine,' when you cannot be at all sure.
- Any changes in plans for the play setting are explained to the users, with apologies if necessary for problems that you had not foreseen.

- The opinions expressed by users are shown respect through listening and consideration. If suggestions prove to be impractical, then explanations should be given.
- In any kind of consultation, all users are treated fairly and with equivalent attention to their views.

PROGRESS CHECK

1 Describe three ways in which playworkers can show that they are listening to a child or young person.
2 How might you help children and young people to listen to each other?
3 Describe three ways in which you might consult with users.

Learning and playwork settings

There are many possibilities for children to learn within the different playwork settings. For example, they may learn specific skills – using their hands in a range of arts and crafts, or gaining in physical confidence in games or moving over large structures. Through the relationships established in the setting, children may also learn more of the skills of communication, of dealing with disagreements and of developing friendships. They also can have many opportunities to extend their skills of self-reliance – see for example page 96.

Just as importantly, children and young people may take on a positive approach to learning – in any sphere. With the support of playworkers, they may become more confident in their ability to learn and to work their way through a task that seems very difficult at the beginning.

HOW DO CHILDREN LEARN?

Children and young people will learn in playwork settings because of a similar set of positive circumstances that are important in other settings, such as their school or their own home.

A blend of variety and familiarity
Users of your play setting will want and need a mixture of activities. Some will be completely new, or different versions of previous activities that they have enjoyed. Children get bored and cease to learn if what is on offer is too repetitious. However, they also need the opportunity to practise in order to improve their skills and, for that, they need the same or very similar activities. It may be another chance to hone their draughts skills, or the same structure to climb today with more confidence and less trepidation than yesterday.

Enough challenge – without anxiety
Children learn from activities of all kinds when the level of difficulty or novelty is enough to challenge, but not so great that the children become worried about their ability. Individual children vary in the level of challenge they relish. Some

are by nature more cautious than others and some children have had their confidence knocked by experiences of failure, or by how adults have treated them over mistakes. Even naturally more resilient children can become anxious if key adults in their lives – home, school or play settings – have spent much more time on highlighting mistakes and failures than on praising successes and encouraging efforts.

KEY POINT

Most learning involves some level of risk. Children need to learn how to cope with the possibility that something will be hard or not go as well as they wished. (See pages 101–2 for more on the different kinds of risk in play.)

SUPPORTIVE ADULTS

Children can help each other to learn and can be supportive. If playworkers have established a positive atmosphere, then children and young people may be pleased for each other when they gain a difficult skill or produce a good piece of work. However, adults are often better placed to help when children get into difficulties. So playworkers, rather than other children, are more likely to be able to stand back enough to see what is getting in the way.

For example:

■ Sometimes, children underestimate how important sheer practice can be. They see another child who is skilled and think, 'I wish I was good at rounders like Andy'. They are not recognising how Andy has spent a lot of time playing and getting to the level of skill he now shows. Even children who have a particular flair have to focus their talent through practice.

- On other occasions, children will benefit from being coached in the best techniques for what they are trying to do. There may be more than one way to hold a racquet or a table tennis bat, but Grace's current style, and the fact that she is not looking at the ball, are making it very hard for her to hit it back accurately.
- Some children set such high standards for achievement that they classify most of their efforts as failures. An involved playworker may be able to draw their attention to how far they have got along the way and encourage the children to be pleased about what they have managed, rather than gloomy about what they have not.
- Trying something new always involves the possible risk of mistakes. Playworkers can support children and young people in a genuine learning from mistakes. You can acknowledge, with children, that something went wrong, but encourage them firmly with, 'What can we learn from this for next time?', 'How did it go wrong?' and sometimes, 'You know, I didn't foresee that either. How did we miss it?'

LEARNING AND PRACTICE

Children often are unaware, or underestimate, how much impressive skills are built up through practice. Playworkers can usefully explain this to them and that most learning goes through a stage of conscious incompetence when children, or adults, are only too aware of what they do not yet know or cannot do. This can be a very uncomfortable stage for anyone. If children lack confidence, or they have no support, they may simply give up.

With the confidence to keep practising, and with support – probably from adults, but other children may offer support as well – children will persevere through to the stage of conscious competence. At this point, a skill has been well learned, but it does not feel automatic, or a natural part of an individual's set of

Sometimes children just want to watch a while

skills. Children, or adults, in this stage of a skill have to keep their mind firmly on what they are doing. For example:

■ Perhaps Liam, in the example from page 76, has to talk himself, just under his breath, through the order in which he pots the colours in snooker, before he gets to that comfortable stage where he 'just knows'.

■ Kathy (also from page 76) will, for a while, have to line up her saw as the playworker showed her, until she has practised to the point where her hands and body move, without deliberate thought, into the right position over the saw and the wood.

With practice and the confidence that you can trust your body, or your mind, then children and adults move into the stage of using the skill or the knowledge without having to concentrate on every aspect. When children have reached that stage of confidence and competence then the lunge for the table tennis ball or the dive into the pool looks automatic, achieved without obvious effort.

To think about 3.9

Recall a skill that you had to gain in recent years. It might be learning to drive or getting used to a new software package on a computer.

Try to get back in touch with your feelings as you learned this skill. Then think about how this experience might guide you in supporting the children.

Activity 3.10

Focus on a child, or young person, in your current play setting who is experiencing difficulties in the skills needed for an activity.

Gather some information on what appears to be the main source(s) of the problem. You could observe or take an opportunity to talk with him or her. But, as well, think about children whom you know who are not having such difficulties. What might be going on for this child that appears to make learning harder?

1 Does this child simply need more practice? Competence can take time.
2 Is there any way to help this child through smaller steps towards an end goal?
3 Look further under the heading of 'Supportive adults' to consider what type of approach might help here (see page 79).
4 Write up your findings into a short report, with line drawings or other visuals, if possible.

PROGRESS CHECK

1 Describe three ways in which playworkers can help children and young people through the stage of conscious incompetence.
2 What factors may get in the way of children's learning?
3 Explain why it may not be helpful to let children avoid all possible kinds of risk.

KEY TERMS

You need to know what these words and phrases mean. Go back through the chapter to make sure that you understand.

Anti-discriminatory practice
Gender
Sexism, anti-sexism
Racism, anti-racism
Stereotypes
Minority ethnic groups
Open-access settings
Role of the playworker
Open-ended questions

Disabilities
Listening
Sign language, signing
Encouragement
Praise
Consultation
Conscious competence and
   incompetence
Reflective practitioner

4 *PLANNING FOR PLAY*

A programme for play

Good quality, enjoyable and safe play for children and young people requires some level of planning. Users of a play setting will soon become frustrated if the setting is bare and any activity that is suggested is followed by a delay while the playworkers sort everything out. But planning for play does not mean that every activity is organised down to the very last detail; good planning allows for flexibility.

Nor does planning contravene the underpinning ethos of playwork – that children should be allowed to choose freely what they want to do in a spontaneous manner. On the contrary, careful and sensitive planning aids such choice. The correct emphasis needs to be struck, where the users are given access to choose from a range of play opportunities and not directed into an activity-led programme. The playworker also needs to recognise the potential of the environment itself to engage the child's interest. This requires an understanding that whatever options are open to the users in the form of materials and equipment they may still find more play value in a puddle, just digging the earth or making a monster from a pile of chairs and a curtain. Peaceful activity should also not be overlooked. The child's or young person's need to read, chat, listen to music or just sit and observe must be accommodated in any programme planning.

WHAT IS MEANT BY A PROGRAMME?

Any play setting will benefit from planning a programme of play. There are several inter-related features to this kind of planning:
- Looking ahead to what kind of activities could be provided on a particular day or over the period of a holiday scheme.
- Organising the necessary play materials and making checks on stocks.
- Working out the pattern of work for the playworkers, so that children and young people will be adequately supervised and the whole team can be involved in the activities.

An aim of playwork is to help children and young people to enjoy themselves

- Taking account of the environment in which this play setting operates.
- Taking account of the individuality of users and of their interests, abilities and preferences.
- Responding with flexibility to the events of the day or session.
- Making sure that children will have plenty of scope for free play as well as the planned activities on offer.
- Taking time to review how well the programme, and the built-in options, are working for all of the users of the play setting.

Some playworkers express concern that planning for play will inevitably mean destroying the spontaneity for children and young people. This will not be a consequence unless playworkers misunderstand their role, and insist that users follow a rigid pattern in use of the activities. Some playworkers are now using the term 'play curriculum', with much the same meaning as the description of 'programme' as above. Once again, the term does not imply a rigid set of requirements, nor an insistence on specific end products and targets.

KEY POINT

A play programme is a plan with flexible possibilities and not a rigid schedule which everyone has to follow.

A FOCUS ON THE USERS

Planning for play should be user centred. This means that playworkers always have the individual children and young people to the forefront of their minds in the planning and the running of any play setting.

A good play programme will leave space for children's choices and for their own ideas. However, the playworker may still have to make some final choices or even veto some wilder flights of imagination. Children often like to dig holes, but they cannot be allowed to do this in the playground of a school play centre.

Given a completely free choice, some children might wish to spend the whole session rushing around in games that are rich in fantasy, but also high on noise level and collisions with other people. This group might be sharing the same indoor play space with other children who want to sit quietly for a time and read a book.

GOOD PRACTICE

A focus on the users – sometimes called a child-centred approach – does not mean that children and young people's wishes should be followed automatically. The demands of some users may impose on others, or expose children to an unacceptable level of risk. Playworkers have the responsibility to hold all the users in mind, not just the more vociferous or active ones.

CASE STUDY   4.1

Hummingbird Adventure Playground has the motto of 'Children choose here'. The playworkers have been adamant that children should be left to decide the games they play and their own companions. This has worked fairly well up until recently. Now, half a dozen children have formed an exclusive group and staked a claim to the rope swing and platform as their own territory. Playworkers realise that children not in the group are being warned off the swing with tough words and physical force.

Questions
1   What are the key issues here? What are the conflicts?
2   How might playworkers challenge the territorial group over their behaviour?
3   In what ways might the playworkers need to consider the ground rules of the playground?
    (Chapter 6 will also help you with these questions.)
4   Write up your ideas and discuss them with one or two colleagues.

A RANGE OF ACTIVITIES

Different play settings will have different sets of opportunities and possible restrictions, but all should be aiming for a range of activities to be on offer to children and young people. The varied types of activity could be chosen from:
- Choices in physical games and the chance to use physical skills, such as climbing and building.
- Some choices in craft and creative activities.
- Helping out in the routine of the play setting.
- Shared activities such as board games or cards.
- Time for conversation with other users and with the playworkers.
- Enjoyment of books and story time.

- Selected use of television or DVDs.
- The scope for imaginative play.
- Plenty of opportunities for free play and the encouragement to do this.
- Trips out – either local or more special trips, further afield.
- Activities chosen to help children. For instance, playworkers in hospital have sets of play equipment specifically collected to help children come to terms with injections or the after-care stage of a serious operation.
- Selected use of CDs.
- Selected use of computers.
- Selected use of console games.

Some play activities will have an end product that the children have created, perhaps with the help and involvement of the playworkers. They may have completed a structure or overhauled an existing one. Or some of the users may have enjoyed making something during a craft or cooking session. In other activities the only result is a sense of pleasure and satisfaction at having enjoyed a really good time.

Different play settings will have perhaps more opportunities for different kinds of play. However, good playworkers can make the most of the play environment in which they work. For instance, playworkers in hospital have been able sometimes to give children opportunities for the messier activities such as water play and to bring in animals like rabbits to be the ward pets.

PREPARATION

Part of planning will be a decision about how much to prepare in advance and how much to leave until it is clear what children and young people would most like to do today. It is important that playworkers review play programmes in order to identify whether the current balance is more or less right.

Activity   **4.2**

Activity   **4.2**

In your play setting keep a record over the period of a week of:

■ the play activities that you planned in advance
■ the activities or games that emerged from children's initiatives.

Look back over your notes of what exactly happened in the play programme of a day or a session.

1 What can you learn?
2 Were there days when you did not have enough ready?
3 With hindsight, were there other days when you had over-structured the programme?
4 Discuss your main findings with colleagues or present to a team meeting.

PROGRESS CHECK

1 What is meant by a play programme?
2 Give two reasons why any programme should be flexible to the users of a play setting.
3 What would be the disadvantages of a narrow range of play activities?

PLANNING FOR CHILDREN

Playworkers have to do their best to get to know the individual children and young people who use their play setting. Admittedly, this may not be easy, especially in a short scheme or one with few regular attenders.

In any play setting, the users will differ in:

■ Their interests and abilities.
■ Their individual temperaments – some will always be keener on the quieter activities and some on the physically active choices.
■ Their age, although actual years will only be a rough guide to playworkers.
■ Whether they are boys or girls, and whether the children believe this difference should be reflected in a different choice of activities or play companions.
■ Cultural background, although some play settings may benefit from considerably more diversity than others. It will depend on the neighbourhood and usage of the setting.

The age range

Compared with other types of facilities for children and young people, many playworkers are planning a programme for a wide age range. Children attending a scheme may range from 5 to 12 years, but the span could be as wide as from children of 5 years right up to young people of 15 years, who are on the brink of young adulthood.

Occasionally you can plan an activity that will engage the interest of the entire age range. However, this is most likely to be a special event, for instance, a sporting tournament, a fete or a camping trip. It is more likely that you will need flexible plans that consider the different ages. Within a programme it is

very possible that an activity, particularly at the end of session, might engage the interest of all the children or young people. A game of run outs or charades might be an enjoyable way to bring all the ages together, so that they feel like a more coherent group.

Young users of play settings will be discouraged by too high a level of challenge, but can feel patronised by too low a level. They may need closer supervision than older users, especially perhaps with tools, but the focus should always be on what they can do, rather than what they cannot. In deciding about activities you will then also have to bear in mind the organisation of playworkers' time for careful supervision.

Activity 4.3

Discuss with your fellow playworkers which activities in recent weeks you found were:

- best suited to the under 8s in your setting
- most successful with the over 12s in your setting.

Consider how you might approach the situation, when a child who is young in age is ready and able to be part of an activity more designed for the older ones.

Similarly, how do you ease the entry of an older child into an activity that has been viewed as more suitable for the younger end?

Ethnic and cultural diversity

Part of the planning and reviewing of a play programme is close attention to how far the programme is genuinely multi-cultural. You will need to ask yourself:

- From what ethnic groups do the children come who use the project?
- Does this reflect the make up of the area in which the project is located?

- What can we do to encourage more children from the different ethnic groups?
- What can we introduce that could give all the children a broader awareness of different cultural traditions?

If some of the users of a play setting are of Asian origin, then playworkers can, of course, find out what interests the children from their own cultural traditions. However, a majority of Asian users would not be a good reason to avoid introducing activities that stem from Chinese or African culture. In fact, many play activities in common use do originate from a range of different countries – for instance, fighter kites from Japan or mask and mime from Italy. Sometimes it may be more a case of introducing children to the information about the cultural origins of an activity that they already enjoy.

Boys and girls
Playworkers need to remain alert to any patterns in how the play programme is used by the girls and boys. Playworkers also need to be aware of their own behaviour with users.

To think about   4.4
Perhaps your playwork team has worked hard to remove the more obvious signals towards boys' or girls' activities, but try to look at your setting with an outsider's eye for whether there are any remaining subtle signals to boys and girls by:
- The words used to introduce children to an activity.
- Surprise, even unspoken, that a child wants to join a particular group.
- Whether the activity is run by a male or female playworker.
- What the playworker says about his or her abilities for this activity.
- Whether remarks from children or young people about boys' or girls' activities are allowed to pass without comment.
- Present your ideas in a positive way within a team meeting.

Perhaps in a play setting the boys have laid claim to the football area, snooker or the carpentry table. You may then need to include special time in a programme to ensure that the girls get access to the equipment, and also to boost their confidence for the future. In the same way, some boys-only groups may be needed so that playworkers, perhaps the male playworkers, can undertake play activities to redress the balance in the other direction. Boys may be unwilling to try out what they view as 'girls' stuff', unless a male they admire encourages them through example. Boys who would like to extend their skills and interests may benefit from a boost to their confidence before the mixed-sex group. Girls can also be scathing in words and rejecting in their behaviour of a boy who is trying to cross the gender line that previous experience has encouraged the females to draw.

INCLUSION

Disabled adults and children have a right to be included in society and to participate within it. We call this the right to "inclusion." To support children with additional needs and their families, play settings must work in line with the current legislation, regulations and codes of practice that apply in their home country. It's important for settings and individual staff to work in ways that promote inclusion within the setting.

THE DISABILITY DISCRIMINATION ACT 1995

The Disability Discrimination Act 1995 (DDA 1995) was devised to support the rights of disabled people to take a full and active part in society. It gives them equality of access, or in other words, the same opportunities to participate in society as non-disabled people. This important piece of legislation gives disabled people (adults and children) rights regarding the way in which they receive services, facilities or goods. This includes education, care and play services.

The DDA 1995 was introduced in three stages:

■ In 1996 it became illegal for service providers to discriminate against disabled people by treating them less favourably than non-disabled people.

■ In 1999 service providers became required by law to make reasonable adjustments for disabled people, such as providing extra assistance.

■ In 2004 service providers became required by law to make reasonable adjustments to their premises. This means that it mustn't be unreasonably difficult for disabled people to access the provision because of physical barriers, such as narrow doorways or steps. If a premise's physical features cause a barrier for a disabled person, that feature may be removed or altered. Or a service may provide a reasonable way of avoiding the feature or may make their service available in a different way, i.e. an out-of-school club may replace steps into the front of their building with a ramp. Or they may open a fire door around the side to let a wheelchair user in.

A disabled person is defined in the DDA 1995 as someone who has a physical or mental impairment that adversely affects their ability to carry out normal day-to-day activities. This will be long-term – it will have lasted for 12 months or be likely to last for more than 12 months. This includes some chronic illnesses, such as ME, which affect some people's ability to carry out normal day-to-day activities.

EVERY CHILD MATTERS

Every Child Matters: Change for Children aims to improve outcomes for all children and young people, including disabled children. As many disabled children's needs are complex and cross traditional service boundaries, they are one of the groups who stand to gain the most from this programme of change.

Every Child Matters is supported by a number of policies and strategies that should work together to improve outcomes for disabled children, young people and their families. Every Disabled Child Matters is a campaign to get rights and justice for every disabled child. It is jointly led by four organisations that work with disabled children and their families – Contact a Family, Council for Disabled Children, Mencap and the Special Educational Consortium. The organisation "will challenge politicians and policy-makers to make good on the Government's commitment that every child matters." Visit www.edcm.org.uk for further details.

KEY POINTS

All play settings should promote inclusion. It is good practice for staff to undertake disability equality training. (For details of "Everyone Can Play," a short course on inclusion specifically for playworkers, visit www.playwork.co.uk/index.asp?page=ecp)

Staff should work in partnership with disabled children and their families to assess and review how individual needs can best be met within the setting. Adaptations or extra staff support may be needed.

Some disabled children and young people have complex needs. Their families may feel that these will be best met in a specialist play setting which has been purposely designed and staffed - some specialist adventure playgrounds are fully accessible for instance, and some special schools have out-of-school clubs. Non-disabled siblings often attend alongside their disabled brother or sister.

ADAPTATIONS

As you'll see when you carry out the activity on page 92, a wide range of special equipment and resources are available to support disabled children. Children may also bring their own specialist aids with them to the setting. But often it takes just a very simple adaptation to make games or activities accessible, as shown in this case study.

CASE STUDY 4.5

Adapting for Kierra

Playworker Will works at a holiday club. Ten-year-old Kierra, a wheelchair user, has recently started attending the club. The staff have planned some parachute games and Will needs to ensure that Kierra can participate. He thinks that she could join in effectively if the other children played kneeling down instead of standing up. He asks Kierra what she thinks of this idea. Kierra says her teacher plays parachute games in the same way at school, and that this adaptation works for her.

Questions

Why did Will consult Kierra when deciding how to adapt the activity?

Activity   4.6

Have a look at an educational or care catalogue or website (such as www.essen-tialaids.com, www.independentliving.co.uk/disabled-children.html, www.dlf.org.uk/public/suppliers/play.html and www.nesarnold.co.uk). Make a list of specialist aids, equipment and play resources that may help children aged 5–12 years with the following impairments:

■ A physical impairment of the hands, leading to difficulty with fine movements including feeding and fine motor play.

■ A visual impairment, leading to difficulty locating and tracking moving objects such as balls.

An example of planning ahead

The following case study takes one example through in detail to illustrate planning a play programme.

CASE STUDY   4.7

Willow Tree adventure playground has a permanent staff of playworkers. They are open every afternoon in school time and run regular half-term and holiday playschemes on a drop-in basis. They need to plan the details for the next half-term scheme.

The playground has:

■ A building with two play spaces, one medium and one small, and a small kitchen.

■ Outside there is a free play area with two adventure swings and a climbing structure and a hard surface area for ball games.

■ The playground is not financially well off, but they have built up over the years a reasonable selection of basic tools and equipment. Their running costs allow them to buy consumable essentials such as paints, paper, modelling clay and balsa wood.

■ The playworkers have access to a scrap store and can hire equipment such as jewellery and candle making kits from the local play association.

In their planning session the playworkers have to allow that on past experience:

■ They will have an average of 45 children on site, but it could be as many as 70.

■ The age range of the users will be 5–15 years.

■ The group of children will probably include white European, Asian, Afro-Caribbean and Chinese children.

■ So far, when children have been bilingual they have been fully confident in English, which is the first language of all the playworkers, none of whom can speak more than a few words of welcome in other languages.

■ The children vary in their physical abilities and skills in communication. One child in regular attendance is a wheelchair user, and one has an artificial hand. Both are alert, confident children, but sensitive to comments from other users.

The playworkers lay out the following plan shown on the opposite page:

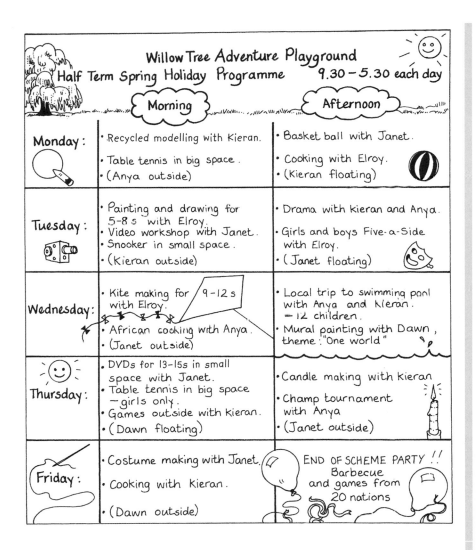

Willow Tree Adventure Playground

Half Term Spring Holiday Programme   9.30 – 5.30 each day

	Morning	Afternoon
Monday:	• Recycled modelling with Kieran. • Table tennis in big space. • (Anya outside)	• Basket ball with Janet. • Cooking with Elroy. • (Kieran floating)
Tuesday:	• Painting and drawing for 5-8 s with Elroy. • Video workshop with Janet. • Snooker in small space. • (Kieran outside)	• Drama with Kieran and Anya. • Girls and boys Five-a-Side with Elroy. • (Janet floating)
Wednesday:	• Kite making for 9-12 s with Elroy. • African cooking with Anya. • (Janet outside)	• Local trip to swimming pool with Anya and Kieran. – 12 children. • Mural painting with Dawn, theme: "One world"
Thursday:	• DVDs for 13-15s in small space with Janet. • Table tennis in big space – girls only. • Games outside with Kieran. • (Dawn floating)	• Candle making with Kieran • Champ tournament with Anya • (Janet outside)
Friday:	• Costume making with Janet. • Cooking with Kieran. • (Dawn outside)	END OF SCHEME PARTY !! Barbecue and games from 20 nations

QUESTIONS ABOUT THE PLAY PROGRAMME:

■ Is there a reasonable breadth of activities?

■ Take one activity, perhaps 'Drama with Kieran and Anya', and jot down some details of how this might develop. What sort of drama? How might they set up possibilities with the children?

■ Does the programme look as if they will be making the best use of each member of the playwork team? What is important to make the role of floater work?

■ What play materials and equipment will they need for the week? Are there activities that might need additional planning or permissions? What will have to be bought or ordered?

- What may have to be checked? The state of outdoor equipment – but what else?
- In what way is the range of activities taking account of the likely range of users?
- What happens if an activity does not last for a full morning or an afternoon session? What kind of contingency plans may be necessary if the weather is bad?

CASE STUDY 4.8

Wooden Towers Adventure Playground welcomes disabled children with profound and complex needs. The overriding aim of the playwork team – Denise, Sejeeven and Ed – is to offer a full play programme (similar to the list on pages 85–6). They then adjust the play activities and equipment depending on the children who are attending. The team is currently getting to know Sajida, Winston and Gemma who have joined the group in the last month.

- Sajida is 10 years old. She was knocked down by a lorry a year ago. Serious head injuries left Sajida with difficulties in her speech and movement. Her parents say that, compared to how she was prior to the accident, Sajida is now very withdrawn, has sudden temper tantrums and her sleep is disturbed most nights.
- Winston is 8 years old. He has cystic fibrosis and follows a strict routine of antibiotics, vitamins, inhalations and physiotherapy. Winston's parents wanted him to attend Wooden Towers because they felt confident that the playworkers would keep to his routine and be alert to possible infections. Winston is relatively healthy and he is beginning to rebel against taking his pills.
- Gemma's mother was exposed to rubella (German Measles) during pregnancy and her daughter was born with a weak heart and partial loss of vision and hearing. Gemma is now 6 years old and attends local primary school. Her parents are pleased about her progress but concerned that the teachers are keeping Gemma in a very sheltered small group and she is missing out on play opportunities.

Questions
1. In what ways might the team need to personalise their programme for these children?
2. What other kinds of information would you need to know in order to make more detailed plans for Sajida, Winston and Gemma?
3. Write up your ideas in a short report.

PLANNING FOR SPECIAL ACTIVITIES

Taking children on trips and outings is, for many projects, an integral part of the play programme.

Activity   4.9

The next time there is a possible trip from your play setting, look at how you can involve the children at different stages of the planning.

- In choosing the places to visit, start with the children. Can you get a group together to discuss possibilities?
- What do the children know about the possible venues? Has anyone been already? Do they know someone who will help get permission for a particular visit?
- Within the capabilities of the children, what kind of fact finding could they do on their own? What kind of fact finding could they do with the support of the playworkers?
- Share your ideas through a short presentation to a team meeting.

Trips and outings, even local ones, require careful planning. The age of the children will be particularly relevant as will your knowledge of them as individuals. Can they cope with a long train journey? How many of a group get horribly sick in a coach? The age and dependability of the children will also affect what will be a safe adult–child ratio for the trip. In the example of Willow Tree adventure playground (see page 93) the team has planned a swimming trip, but with more ambitious ventures there would be more to check out and plan. (See page 222 for more on this part of a play programme.)

GOOD PRACTICE

Any special trips will require parents' written permission. (See page 124 for more on this issue.)

PROGRESS CHECK

1 Give three examples of the kind of unchecked assumption about children that can arise in playwork.
2 List at least four issues, other than activities, that have to considered in planning a play programme.
3 Explain why all children need a full play programme, regardless of their individual needs.

Play and social skills

LEARNING SELF-RELIANCE

Play settings offer good opportunities for encouraging children to become more self-reliant because of the possibility of involving children in the daily running of the setting. Playworkers remain ultimately responsible for many issues, not least of which is health and safety. However, it is worth looking carefully at any aspect of your play setting that has no input from the users and asking yourself why this is the case.

After-school clubs with a register of attenders are taking on the responsibility for children's care that otherwise would be taken by parents, or by the children themselves in their own home. Users can be encouraged to take responsibility, and show they can be trusted with part of the club's running. A club that is too highly organised by playworkers can discourage children from learning self-care skills, since the playworkers do it all.

There are many options for encouraging children in self-reliance.

Information, ideas and making decisions

Playworkers should have plenty of ideas themselves and not depend utterly on the children for 'What shall we do?' Yet many of the activities of a play setting offer chances to involve children in:

- 'Where could we go for our whole day out?'
- 'How can we find out?'
- 'That looks like a problem – what could we do about it?'
- 'These three options look promising – how shall we decide?'

- Any play setting needs the boundaries set by a clear set of rules and these are far more likely to work if the users are involved in establishing and reviewing the key rules and how they are working in practice. (More on this in Chapter 6.)

CARE OF EQUIPMENT

Taking care of and tidying up equipment should not be the sole responsibility of playworkers. However, any playwork team will have to decide how best to involve the setting users, in the knowledge of these actual children and young people:
- Are they more prepared to clear up some kinds of equipment than others?
- What incentives may help?
- In what ways can playworkers show that they trust children? In what aspects of the setting can they risk trusting the children?
- Is there a time to stop replacing equipment that users break?

SAFETY ISSUES

The safety of the play setting has to remain a prime concern of playworkers but in what ways could the users be involved?
- Routine safety checks, alongside a playworker.
- Group discussions with users about how to deal with unknown visitors to the setting.
- Encouraging children to coach younger or less experienced children in a safe approach to skills.
- Acknowledging any child's safe behaviour or avoidance of possible accidents.
- Letting children observe, or safely help in, minor first aid in the setting.

DAILY RUNNING

Food and drink will be a part of some play settings. Usually, children and young people can be involved in preparing snacks or sorting out drinks and in the clearing up afterwards. Playworkers can be pleasantly surprised that what seems a fairly tedious routine task to them can be attractive to setting users, since helping out offers the undivided attention and company of a playworker. It will be appropriate to invite children and young people to get involved and help out in a range of daily activities that are necessary for the smooth running of the play setting.

Children with disabilities need just as much encouragement towards self-reliance. Playworkers will need to attend to the children themselves, as well as liaise closely with parents, to make sure that disabilities are not assumed wrongly to prevent some forms of self-reliance. Children with physical disabilities may have a full understanding of the tasks of self-reliance but be frustrated by the physical movements or need special equipment. Children with severe learning disabilities may need to be shown how to complete tasks by fine steps until they

follow an entire sequence. Playworkers will need to give patient attention when children are encouraged to make possible choices within the daily routine – the process can take time.

Activity   4.10
Look back at the case study on page 94 of the Wooden Towers Adventure Playground. Note down the individual issues in learning self-reliance as they could affect Sajida, Winston and Gemma.

Conversation and the play programme

The striking advantage of a play setting over school is that your communication with children and young people can be free-ranging. A well organised play setting will have a planned play programme. But, even if you decide to call this programme a 'play curriculum', you do not have to ensure that children are gaining skills to a given standard that will be assessed. Although you may often be talking about what you are doing together, your conversations do not all have to be directed on the play activity. If children or young people wish to discuss in detail the merits of the film they watched at the weekend, you can follow the conversation enjoyably wherever they wish to take it.

KEY POINT

In your review of a day, or session, in your play setting you would consider your total involvement with the children or young people. A planned craft activity or the completion of the new playground structure should not be seen as more important than conversations with play setting users, when they wish to use their time in that way.

Grafton Road holiday playscheme

Anthea had prepared materials for a painting project which would help children to explore the effects of different textures in paint mixes. The painting activity was part of a longer-term objective to introduce the scheme users to a range of economical arts and crafts that they might wish to pursue as leisure interests.

Six children, varying in age from 7 to 11 years, settled at the table and started on their paintings. They chatted as they worked and eventually the conversation became the dominant activity.

Sachin had started with a dramatic account of how some of the eldest boys in his primary school had been caught smoking. The other children around the table joined in, expressing strong views about whether it was or wasn't a good idea to start smoking.

Anthea listened carefully to the views being put forward and made sure that nobody got talked down. She joined in at one point to explain, briefly, how boys and girls can feel pushed into doing something because their friends are doing it. Grace picked up on this theme and started to tell the group how her school class had discussed ways of dealing with dares.

The conversation rolled easily from one child to another and suddenly it was time to clear up. Marsha said doubtfully to Anthea, 'We haven't really done anything, have we?' Anthea replied, 'I think we've done a lot, Marsha; it just wasn't what we started out to do. I really enjoy listening to what you all think. And we can come back to the painting tomorrow, if you'd like.'

Questions

1   Have there been occasions recently in your play setting when one child, or group of users, have been keen to talk?
2   What kind of topics interest the children or young people in your play setting?
3   Anthea made the decision that the conversation absorbing the children should become the activity, rather than telling the children to concentrate on their paintings. Are there any occasions when a playworker should direct children back to the activity at hand?
4   Discuss the issues with a colleague and compare your ideas.

PROGRESS CHECK

1   Give at least four examples of how playworkers can encourage children and young people in greater self-reliance.
2   In what ways can playworkers' conversation with children be an important part of the play programme?

The involvement of playworkers

PLAYWORKERS AND PLAY

In any play setting, the playworkers will be looking for a balance between:
- joining in the play or standing back
- initiating an activity or following the children's lead.

Playworkers as a resource to children

A good playworker is interested in and acknowledges the ideas and suggestions that users of the setting can bring. Playworkers are also present because they will be a valuable resource and support to children and young people in areas about which the playworker is more knowledgeable or experienced.

An active and involved adult does not have to be intrusive in an unhelpful way to children and young people. There are a number of ways of being a very useful resource to the users of your setting. You can be:
- An experienced adult who offers help and support to children as they learn skills.
- A friendly companion in activities, games or conversation.
- An impartial referee during games or in disputes between children.
- A rich source of ideas and suggestions.
- A gatekeeper of the boundaries and a protector of the users of your setting.
- A good model of how to behave – which does not mean perfect.

Activity   **4.12**

Note down examples from recent weeks in which you have been a resource to the users of your play setting in line with each of the six suggestions above. For instance, perhaps you have supported a group of young people as they learned how to plan and build a new structure in your adventure playground. Or you might have successfully intervened on an escalating row over the rules of draughts and calmed the children down sufficiently that they completed their game.

Write up your experiences in a short report.

HELPING CHILDREN'S INVOLVEMENT IN PLAY

Challenge and assessing risk

Adults caring for very young children have to protect them from risks that the children can neither cope with, nor foresee. Younger children may therefore be prevented from joining in some activities, but this is not a strategy that will work with older children and young people.

Children often do not realise how much adults worry about them

KEY POINT

Information about child development (see for instance Chapter 2) can give some guidance about ages and likely skills. However, this is when children are ready to learn and be helped to learn, not an age at which a skill simply appears ready formed.

GOOD PRACTICE

Whenever the opportunity is there, playworkers should inform parents about the full play programme of the setting and how potential risks are handled.

The majority of interesting and challenging activities involve some level of risk. For children and young people, 'extremely safe' tends to equate with 'extremely boring'. Learning anything new will also bring some level of risk – emotional, psychological or physical – and children can cope with adult support along with their own personal resources.

Physical activities can bring the risk of minor or major physical injury. No play setting can guarantee 100% safety. Even a very carefully supervised play environment can have excited children crashing into each other or tripping over their own feet. (Chapter 8 addresses good practice in health and safety.) Children and young people will learn about physical risks and how to keep safe enough by:

- Warnings from playworkers – specifically targeted and not so frequent that users dismiss the playworker as a total fusser.
- Copying playworkers' safe behaviour – both the actions and an outlook that includes looking ahead. For instance, 'What are we going to have to really watch out for as we're building this structure?'

- Specific help from playworkers as children and young people learn skills.
- Practical everyday tips, such as, 'It is safe to feed the ducks on a trip to the local park, but keep well clear of the swans and the geese.'
- Calm and sympathetic handling of accidents, rather than, 'I told you so!'

Creative art and craft projects can bring risks to children and young people. Sometimes these can be physical, for instance through a poorly controlled tool. But this learning also involves emotional risk and a child's self-confidence can be shaken. An important project for children may go wrong or the reality may be far removed from their plans. Yet, if playworkers protect children to such an extent that nothing ever goes wrong, then children cannot learn that, with support and sympathy from adults, perhaps they can put right a mistake or learn to live with it.

Becoming skilled in domestic activities, such as cooking or even pouring out drinks for everyone, will not go perfectly every time. Juice will be mispoured, egg shells will be mistakenly dropped into the cake mix. Social relations with other users and with playworkers also include potential risks. So part of children's learning in this sphere is the reality that friends will not always be completely friendly and groups do not always accept a good idea.

GOOD PRACTICE

Playworkers cannot, and should not, try to create a play setting in which all possible risks have been removed. The setting and the activities should be safe and the playworkers alert to dangers. Beyond this caution, children should be supported as they discover that dealing with a manageable level of risk can be a challenge to be enjoyed, and not a threat.

BUILDING CONFIDENCE

Some children have very low self-confidence and are all too ready to blame themselves when a project does not go perfectly, or to belittle what they have achieved with 'It's not as good as Ben's' or 'That doesn't count – anyone can do that.'

CASE STUDY   4.13

Maureen and the other playworkers in St Dunstan's play centre have become concerned at how Eva is so quick to run herself down. Having heard Eva's father mocking his daughter's efforts, Haki suggests that Eva has probably experienced a continuous chipping away at her self-confidence. The playworkers do not set themselves the impossible task of making everything right, but they agree to take every opportunity to counteract Eva's very negative view of herself.
- Haki sees Eva staring at the materials that the group has for the jewellery project. Eva looks miserably at Haki and says, 'I'm stupid. I can't do this.' Haki

replies, 'Well, we could decide that I'm stupid. Perhaps I didn't explain it very clearly. Let's try again.'

■ Joseph is close by when Eva moves to tear up her painting, saying, 'I'll never be as good as Matt!'. He stops her with, 'Hold on a moment, Eva. I know Matt's paintings are really good, but that doesn't mean yours are bad. I would like to have them both up on the wall this afternoon.'

■ When she summons up the courage to speak out, Eva has shown that she has an impressive store of general knowledge. Maureen manages to persuade her to join the children's team for the play centre's fund raising quiz night.

Questions

1 Do you have children like Eva in your play setting?

2 In what ways are you looking to build their confidence?

3 If you have a friendly relationship with a child's parents, you may be able to broach the subject of their son or daughter's low confidence. Have you managed a positive conversation in this way?

4 Discuss the issues and ideas with one or two colleagues.

WHEN USERS SEEM NOT TO WANT TO GET INVOLVED

Some children and young people may prefer to watch than to get involved – at least some of the time. It is not the playworker's role to push children into activities that they do not wish to do. Yet, sometimes you will realise that your intervention could support a child in doing what they would like.

Activity 4.14

Read through the following examples of events in Hummingbird adventure playground. Consider what you could do if you were a playworker in this setting. Compare ideas in discussion with a colleague.

■ Jane is the smallest regular user at the adventure playground. She has been standing on the platform for 15 minutes, waiting for a chance to swing on the rope. Six larger children continue to dominate the rope and Jane finally gives up and climbs off the platform.

■ Freddy has shown an interest in the needlework project. He looks on but turns down an invitation to pull up a chair around the table. Sandra has taken responsibility for this project and the six children around the table are all girls today.

■ Ben turns down the invitation to join the football game that is about to start. 'No thanks! I have enough of that at school – everybody calling you a "wally" and Mr James going on about why did we lose.'

Children will sort some issues out for themselves

BRINGING SESSIONS TO A CLOSE

Some play activities have a natural ending, brought about by the children or
young people themselves. On other occasions, part of the playworkers' responsibility will be to bring an activity or a whole session to a close, and ideally in such
a way that children do not feel rushed.

Playworkers may have to:

■ Plan an activity so that it will be realistic, given time constraints and the number of children or young people involved.

■ Keep an eye on the time, so that the activity can be completed and there is
time for clearing up – ideally involving the children and young people.

■ Give warnings that an activity will be coming to a close, or that the whole setting will be shut up soon.

GOOD PRACTICE

Some activities may have a natural ending but some will need to be brought to a
close in a way that, ideally, does not rush the children and does leave them feeling
a sense of completion.

To think about 4.15
Look at the play programme on page 93. Take three of the planned activities and jot down the ways in which you would bring them to a satisfactory close.
Present this to a team meeting as part of a theme of 'Good beginnings and endings in play'.

Reviewing the play activities

Playwork can often unfold at a fast pace. There may be limited time for quiet reflection or discussion during a day or a session. Yet the experience of the play session is important. Playworkers can remain alert and observe what is going on within the play setting.

WAYS OF REVIEWING

A review of the play programme as a whole will include the valuable sources of:
- Playworkers' observations and their opinions about how particular activities have unfolded.
- The views of children and young people who use the play setting – either gathered through informal conversations, or in a group meeting of users.
- A deliberate attempt to observe and evaluate a particular activity or aspect of the programme.
- Informal conversation between playworkers.
- Group meetings in which the playwork team gets together to review the programme at a time when the children and young people are not present.
- Keeping notes for the setting of what you did and how it went.

- Opening a file on useful resources and the local community, and keeping this up to date. See, for example, page 262.
- Parents and other adults may be a useful source of feedback, as may your local Play Officer.

To think about   4.16
In which of the different ways do you review and evaluate your play programme in your own setting? Are there some possibilities which you are overlooking?

THE FOCUS OF A REVIEW

The work in any play setting can develop more effectively if playworkers have a focus to their review, at least some of the time.

On some occasions you will have a general discussion, or simply listen to what children, young people and colleagues wish to raise. On other occasions it will be useful to take a particular approach. For instance, you might want to review any of the following:

- The range of activities within your play programme. Are you overlooking some types of activity? (Look back at page 85.)
- How well has an activity, or a week's programme, gone? What can you learn for next time?
- The level of involvement of individual children. Do some appear to be more closely involved than others? Does this matter?
- Are you making any unchecked assumptions about who might like to be involved?
- Is there a pattern of involvement according to age of users, their sex or ethnic group – and does this matter?

CASE STUDY   4.17

St Dunstan's play centre has a commitment to promoting equal opportunities on gender. They decide to pay special attention to this side of the activities for a fortnight and then discuss their observations in a team meeting. The conversation unfolded like this:

Angus: It's the little things that creep up on me. They were all helping me to carry the rounders kit out to the yard and I heard myself telling Eva not to strain herself with the heavy bag. Now why do I tell her that, but assume that Matt will be fine?

Maureen: And especially Matt. I've watched him; he's going to give himself a hernia the way he picks up heavy boxes. I think that we all act like we should warn the girls more about risks, especially on the more physical activities. And the boys are the careless ones!

Joseph: I don't think you can say that for certain, Maureen. We get more boys' names in the accident book, but maybe we let them take more risk.

Maureen: Fair enough. On the other side, I'm going to admit something. I've kept track of myself in how I praise the kids. I found out that I was much more likely to tell one of the girls that she'd done a good job or that she'd handled a situation well. I can only think that I was assuming the boys would think praise was soft. The last week I've made a serious effort to praise the boys, and not just for physical things.

Angus: I saw Josh's face when you admired that enormous collage of his. He didn't say anything, but this grin just spread all over his face. Joseph, you were keeping a log of who did what activity.

Joseph: Yes, I've got a lot of information. But, I'll start with football – we were worried about what might be going on there. I've definitely noticed that the girls who enjoy football are much more likely to join a game if Aaron isn't playing. He's the one who gives them a really hard time and then the other boys follow his lead.

Angus: I'd thought it was Josh who gave the girls a rough deal. He's always shouting at them.

Joseph: Yes, but he falls to the ground and yells 'foul!' whenever a girl tackles him successfully. Naomi and Maekesha worked this out; they just tell him where to get off. It's Aaron who says the really offensive stuff, and I reckon he barges into them deliberately. Maekesha didn't complain, but she had a huge bruise after yesterday's game.

Maureen: We should decide how we tackle Aaron then. Who's going to talk to him?

Angus: I think it will have to be me or Joseph. Aaron's got a foul mouth and he should realise how insulted the girls feel. It's not only in the football games. But, I think he'll dismiss you just because you are a woman. What do you think?

Maureen: That's okay. I'd like to believe he'll respect me in the end. And you know, he's not half as rude to me when there's no audience to impress. But we have to deal with Aaron as he is at the moment. So, how's it going with the group that wanted to watch your 'Baby it's you!' videos?

Angus: Pretty good. We had a group of six girls and two boys for the first one. And then we had a really lively discussion about whether men were any good with babies. I told them that I was the one who stayed home with my daughter when she was a baby. Then Eva announced that I was different and so I didn't count; most men were still hopeless. Interesting, eh?

(And so on...)

Questions

1 What were the main issues that emerged through the discussion at St Dunstan's play centre?

2 In your own play setting, how have you addressed the individuality of boys and girls in playwork practice? In your own assumptions, or those of the children themselves? In patterns of behaviour? In choices in the play programme?

3 Some situations will need to be tackled precisely because a boy has behaved towards a girl in an unacceptable way – or a girl to a boy. What situations have you recently faced and how were they resolved?

4 Make a short presentation on this topic to a team meeting. Illustrate it with line drawings or cartoons.

PROGRESS CHECK

1 How should playworkers approach the element of risk in play activities?

2 Give three reasons why playworkers might work to involve children who did not seem enthusiastic at the outset of an activity.

3 Give two reasons why it is important to bring activities to a close.

4 Suggest four ways of reviewing a play programme

KEY TERMS

You need to know what these words and phrases mean. Go back through the chapter to make sure that you understand.

Play programme or curriculum

User centred

Free play

Planning

Self-reliance

Risk in play and learning

Review of programmes

---

5 THE DAILY RUNNING OF PLAY FACILITIES

This chapter covers:
- Opening up and closing down procedures
- Administration and record keeping
- The design and maintenance of the user-centred environment
- Materials and equipment
- Finance and budgeting

A successful play project depends as much on the quality of its administration and organisational procedures as it does on the quality of relationships between workers and users. A strong organisational framework will support those relationships and help them to flourish and prosper.

These basic points will apply whether you are working in an all-year play centre or playground or on a six-week holiday scheme. There will be different procedures for different settings and we will look at some of these through examples and case studies. The basics of good practice, however, are the same.

Opening up and closing down procedures

OPENING UP

After arriving at the project you will be involved in a number of pre-session routines that will enable you to be prepared for when you open up to the children and young people. These will include:
- picking up any messages via mail, e-mail, answer phone or other building users
- undertaking any 'start of day' administration tasks
- checking to make sure that all the play spaces are safe
- preparing the materials and equipment for the session
- speaking to colleagues
- if appropriate, preparing for registration.

It is important that all workers know their own job tasks and areas of responsibility before they arrive so that time can be used effectively. A rota prepared at a staff meeting is the way most play projects facilitate this.

In some circumstances, a residential holiday scheme or large multi-use play centre for instance, it will be necessary to have a hand-over meeting. The outgoing worker or staff team can pass on keys and information to the incoming

Checking equipment before opening up will avoid disappointments later

worker or team, thereby ensuring continuity. This becomes particularly important when:

- there has been an emergency or special incident
- new children have joined the project
- the out-going team have been told of something that will be occurring after they have left.

This sort of information, of course, should also be recorded in writing but a verbal exchange at hand over is both direct and helps convey the atmosphere of the session.

CASE STUDY 5.1

St Dunstan's Play Centre is a school-based play centre operating between 3.30 and 6pm Monday to Thursday during the school term. Maureen is the Worker in Charge and Joseph, Angus and Haki are her assistants. Angus is also a teacher at the school.

At 3pm Maureen and Joseph arrive at the school to prepare for the evening session. Maureen first of all visits the head teacher's office to confirm her arrival, collect any messages and receive any information relating to the play centre. Meanwhile Joseph opens up the play centre room – they have one room in the school which is solely for play centre use – and starts getting out the materials and equipment needed for the first activities. They have planned games in the main hall, a craft activity in the play centre room and free play in the playground.

Maureen soon joins him and together they set up the craft activity which Haki will be running when she joins them later. Joseph also has a quick walkabout of the playground to make sure that all is as it should be. Once they are satisfied that everything is in place for the first three activities of the evening they prepare two tables in the main hall to administer registration, one for infants and one for juniors. At 3.30 Haki and Angus join Joseph to register the children in, and Maureen welcomes and talks to the children as they wait.

Questions

1   Play centre workers, particularly in schools, are often limited in preparation time. How do you ensure that you are ready for when the children arrive?
2   In shared-use space liaison with other users is essential. How much time do you allow and which people do you speak to?
3   The safety of the play space is essential. What daily checks do you run?
4   Discuss issues raised with a few colleagues.

KEY POINT

Although all workers should assure themselves that the play spaces are safe for play the setting will affect how thorough these daily checks should be. A school or community centre which has already been in use during the day will be less likely to suffer potential misuse than an open space visited by a mobile project, or an adventure playground where trespass might have occurred during closure. (These checks will be dealt with more fully in Chapter 8.)

CLOSING DOWN

Playworkers will similarly need to run through a routine set of procedures after the children have left. These will include:

■   ensuring that all the children have either left the project or been collected
■   collecting up and storing all materials and equipment
■   generally cleaning and tidying the play areas as necessary
■   making any entries into the log book or diary
■   turning off lights, switching on alarm and answer machine if appropriate
■   checking out with other users of the premises if appropriate
■   ensuring that all lockable doors and cupboards, etc. have been made secure.

KEY POINT

If a child has not been collected at the end of the session you will need to put into action the procedures operating at your play project. These should include:

■ allowing a reasonable time for the parent or carer to collect them
■ contacting the parent/carer once that time has elapsed
■ contacting any other known contact person if the parent/carer can't be reached
■ contacting the next appropriate person with responsibility in such situations, e.g. social services area officer
■ leaving any messages for the parent/carer at the project or, if possible, at the parent/carer's home, before leaving the child in care of, for example, the social worker.

You should not take a child or young person to your home and it is important that parents and carers are informed of the procedures when children aren't collected on time.

CASE STUDY   5.2

Hummingbird Adventure Playground is a voluntary managed project with a brick-built play building and a large open space with timber play structures. On dry evenings there is invariably a lot of activity outside with children building camps and tending to the playground garden. After the children have left, Yousiff and Michelle, the two full-time workers, run through a similar routine each evening before closing up for the night. Together they will use the ladder to take down the rope swings and then walk round the site to ensure that all the tools and equipment have been brought inside. At the same time they will pop their heads into camps and under play structures to make sure there are no children hiding. If there has been an outside fire or barbecue they will check that all flames have been doused.

Inside the building any remaining materials and equipment from the session activities will be cleared away and stored including food items into fridge and cupboards. Before finally leaving they will make sure that all the electrical equipment is switched off except the answer phone and security alarm which should be switched on, and that all doors and windows are locked.

Questions
1   Different procedures will apply to different play settings. What are the key tasks where you work?
2   Would these key tasks be transferable to another setting?
3   What new tasks might you have to carry out in another setting?
4   Exchange ideas with colleagues.

To think about   5.3
With your colleagues, run through your opening up and closing down procedures.
- Are they comprehensive enough?
- Are the task areas and responsibilities clearly allocated?
- Are you giving enough time for them?
If you are still preparing for play when the children arrive, and closing down before they have left then the answer to the last question is probably no. List what you need to do each day and rotate the tasks.

GOOD PRACTICE

Opening up and closing down procedures are routine and may seem boring, but sharing the tasks and taking turns as appropriate alleviates the tedium. These procedures are important tasks and need to be taken seriously.

Administration and record keeping

Since the Children Act 1989 came into force in October 1991 (see Chapter 1), one of the key areas of administration and record keeping in play settings which have any children under eight years is the registration of children in and out of the facility and the keeping of records of children using the project.

KEY POINT

The word registration tends to be used in three different ways to mean:
1 Checking children in and out of a project by marking a daily register of names.
2 Recording children as members of a project.
3 That your play facility is registered with Ofsted.

The majority of play projects work with children in a broader age range than the under eights, typically 5–12 or 5–15 years of age.

Settings registered with Ofsted must keep the following records and hold them for two years:
- the name, home address and date of birth of each child who is looked after on the premises
- the name, home address and telephone number of a parent/guardian/carer of each child who is looked after on the premises
- a daily record of the names of the children looked after on the premises and their hours of attendance
- accidents which involve the children being cared for occurring on the premises where childcare is provided
- any medicine administered to any child who is cared for on the premises, including the date and circumstances and who administered it, including medicine which the child is permitted to self-administer, together with a record of a parent/guardian/carer's consent
- the name, home address and telephone number of every person living or working on the premises on which childcare is provided (or the part of the premises where the childcare is held, in the case of premises such as community/leisure centres, where only parts of the premises are used for childcare).

Settings will also hold the following information:
- child's ethnic origin and gender
- family doctor's name, address and telephone number
- names of persons authorised to collect the child
- details of any needs relating to diet, medication, allergies or behaviour
- first language of child and parent.

GOOD PRACTICE

Having a full factual record of all your children has several benefits. It will help you to:
- monitor how well your project is serving the community in terms of the ages and location of the children
- monitor how well your project's equal opportunity policy is working in terms of tracking the gender and ethnic origin of your children
- deal more effectively with illness and emergencies
- maintain an overview of your project
- write reports and funding proposals within the bounds of confidentiality.

REGISTRATION FORM

All children who attend must be registered with the playscheme. Children remain at the playscheme until collected by a named adult.

Child's name (full) _____
Name to be called _____
Address _____
Date of birth _____ School attended _____
Name of parent/guardian _____
Address _____
Tel. nos: Daytime _____ Evening _____
(please give both parents' numbers if appropriate)
Does your child have any known medical problems? _____
Does your child have any known allergies or major dislikes, e.g. certain food or materials? _____

Name and address of person collecting the child from club if different from above (child will only be allowed to leave with the named person).
Name _____ Tel no: _____
Address _____

Details of second contact other than collector who may be able to collect the child in an emergency.
Name _____ Tel no: _____
Address _____

Details of child's doctor
Name _____ Tel no: _____
Address _____
When would you like your child to start the club? _____
Any other information? _____

Some of the routine activities of the club may involve short trips including visiting parks or local libraries. For your child to take part in these activities you must give your permission.

I agree to my child taking part in the activity described above YES[ ] NO[ ]

I consent to any emergency medical treatment necessary during the running of the club. I authorise the play/care staff to sign any written form of consent required by the hospital authorities if the delay in getting my signature is considered by the doctor to endanger my child's health and safety. YES[ ] NO[ ]

I have read, understood and agree to abide by the Regulations.

SIGNED: Date:

For personal information to be given freely the giver must feel secure that confidentiality will be respected. Whilst it is unlikely that a parent or carer would object to the use of information in an abstract way, e.g. 11 children are nine years old, 25 are girls, 10 come from the north of the city and 12 are of Asian origin, they should always be informed. On no account should personal details be used that might, in any way, identify the child or child's family without discussing it first with the parent and, if appropriate, the child, and obtaining written permission.

GATHERING THE INFORMATION

In many after-school clubs and play centres there is no drop-in facility and every child has to be registered as a member. Membership operates through an admissions procedure which requires every parent or carer wishing to admit their child to fill in an admissions or registration form. An example is shown on page 115.

In applying the form there are some key good practice points to be remembered.

- Have the forms translated into the main languages of your users. Although the child may be fluent in English their parent or carer may not.
- Wherever possible meet with the parent or carer to help fill in the form. This will not only enable the form to be filled in accurately, but will reinforce the information verbally. If this isn't possible make sure that the form is accompanied by an information sheet on the project, again in a relevant language if appropriate.
- The children and their families are entitled to confidentiality and all personal information should be kept in a safe and secure place at the project, e.g. a safe or lockable cupboard.
- A back-up of all records should be lodged with an appropriate designated person, e.g. the chairperson of the management committee or the local authority play manager, and the parent or carer informed.

Whatever records you keep at your project it is essential that you devise a reliable system for their storage and retrieval. Here are some reminders:

- Ensure you have a separate space for administration paperwork, an ordinary metal filing cabinet is still the best choice.
- If information is confidential keep it in a locked drawer, safe or metal box.
- Devise a simple filing system with names and numbers that will enable you to locate information quickly, and keep it regularly 'weeded' of out-of-date information.
- The above applies equally well to information stored on computer; give all your documents names or codes, make sure they are written on the hard copies and keep a list of all your files.
- With very crucial information make back-up copies or, when using a computer, back-up disks and lodge them with your employer.

SPECIAL ARRANGEMENTS

If you are entering into a specific arrangement with the child's parent or carer, a particular collection time or an occasion when an older child can leave the project on their own for instance, put this in writing and have it signed by both parties. Keep a copy on site and give a copy to the parent.

DEALING WITH INFORMAL ENQUIRIES

Often a parent or carer will approach you in an informal way, perhaps even walking down the street, to ask about their child using the project. It is essential that you know the process and the availability and conditions of the facility. Your project may already be fully subscribed, but you have a waiting list that they can put their name on. There may be a fee structure to using the project and there will always be certain conditions regarding ages of the children. All this essential information needs to be passed on to the enquirer and their request dealt with quickly by the appropriate person.

GOOD PRACTICE

An enquiry is often the first point of contact between you and the child's family and will be the first building block in the relationship. Filling out forms is difficult at the best of times. Your patience and understanding will enable the process to be accomplished efficiently and the adult to immediately feel welcomed to the project. Many of us are naturally wary of giving out personal information. Carefully explain the need for keeping records and that confidentiality will be respected.

Activity   5.4
With other playworkers, discuss any issues about questions asked or reluctance from a family.

When parents or carers enquire about their child joining your club or play centre they will not only want to know about the admissions procedure but also about how the club operates and what codes of conduct or rules of behaviour it maintains. See example on page 118.

GOOD PRACTICE

Always offer to talk through any aspects of the material that is given out. You will need to be sensitive to the needs of parents or carers who may lack confidence in reading or writing.

Once a child has been accepted into the club a letter welcoming the new child and parent will be sent, or given, out. The letter also serves as a check and reminder about any previous information that the parent or carer should have had, and the need to report to the club any changes to names, addresses and telephone numbers, etc. that might occur in the future.

RULES AND REGULATIONS

1. **Registration:** Only children for whom Registration Forms have been filled in may attend.

2. **Opening times:** The club will run from_____
   Monday to Friday during term-time (except bank holidays) unless parents are otherwise notified.

3. **Payment of fees:** For those children who attend the Club on a full-time basis, fees will be £_____ per week, payable on a Monday when they are collected. Parents are reminded that they are paying for the space at the Club, so if your child cannot attend one week you will still be required to pay for that week.

For those children who attend on a part-time basis, fees will be £_____ per day, payable on the day when they are collected.

4. **Collecting your child:** Children need to be collected from the Club by _____. If you collect your child after this time, you will be charged a penalty of £_____ due to the Club incurring extra staff and caretaking costs. Frequent late collections will result in your child's space being withdrawn.

Please give us written details of who will be collecting your child other than yourself, as we will not allow your child to leave the club with someone who is unknown to us. Any regular collection arrangements you may have should be recorded on your child's registration form.

5. **Absences:** Please inform the Club supervisor if your child is going to be absent.

6. **Behaviour:** If any child's behaviour is still unsettled after a period of time, and all attempts made to accommodate them have failed, we may have to advise the parent to remove them from the Club. Our concern is for the happiness and well-being of the child. He/she may be re-admitted at a later date.

If any child disrupts the Club, e.g. bullying, being rude, racist, or badly behaved, and does not respond to reasonable attempts of correction, we reserve the right to withdraw their space.

7. **Notice:** If you wish to remove your child from the club, please give us two weeks' notice.

If you require further information on the Rules and Regulations, please ask the Club supervisor to explain before you sign the Registration Form. We hope you and your child enjoy the facilities we offer you.

THE DAILY REGISTER

Some play settings run a daily register to check children both in and out of the facility. These usually come under the overall term of playcare but may also be referred to as registered or closed-door facilities.

KEY POINT

In a registered or closed-door facility children are checked into the project and can leave only if:

a   they are collected and signed out by a parent or carer, or
b   they have permission from their parent or carer to notify a playworker and leave unaccompanied.

In an open-access, open-door or drop-in facility children can enter and leave the project freely.

Checking in
The register is usually taken like a school register, though perhaps less formally. Essentially the children's attendance is ticked off in a book. This happens at the beginning of the session when the children first enter the play project and is usually facilitated by one or more playworkers marking off names at a table. To make it more efficient in clubs or centres with large numbers, the age groups may be split.

Checking out
As the children are collected by a parent or other nominated person, a playworker will sign them off in the book. At the end of the session the senior worker will check that all the children have been signed out.

OPEN-ACCESS PROVISION

Open-access provision exempt from registration

It is good practice for open-access or drop-in facilities that are exempt from compulsory registration on the Childcare Register to apply to join the voluntary part of the register, and to adopt the same approach to administration and record keeping as those facilities registered on the compulsory part of the register. See page 22 for further details.

KEY POINT

Although, by their nature, open-access projects do not require formal agreements about dropping off and collection, many have adopted an informal approach through a negotiated understanding between the parent, the user and the playworker. For example, a child may drop in to a project after school on their own and remain there with the exception of going to the local shop under supervision until the parent arrives to collect them. The child, the playworker and the parent would agree these parameters together with the clear understanding that the playworker's responsibility, apart from normal on-site duties, is to organise a supervised visit to the local shop during the session. The child's responsibility is to remain at the project until collection and the parent's to collect on time. For children who can operate this degree of personal responsibility it is a workable solution for busy parents who have a good relationship with their local open-access project.

Activity   5.5

Take the registration form on page 115 and compare it with what you currently use to record information on users at your project:

1   Is there anything you would adopt from the example, or adapt to suit your project?
2   What could remain as it is?
3   What needs amending to suit your circumstances?
4   What would you omit?

Very occasional users

Although at open-access unregistered projects children are free to come and go as they please there is always a core of regular users. However, these facilities will also be used by children who come infrequently and perhaps only on one or two occasions. This can be particularly common in the school holidays and especially in the summer. In these circumstances it can be difficult to keep records that are as detailed as those maintained for regular users. However some basic factual information is useful to monitor the number and geographical location of children using the project and necessary for use in an emergency. Wherever possible the name, age, address and telephone number of a new child using the project should be sought.

CASE STUDY 5.6

At Hummingbird Adventure Playground, Michelle, the senior worker, has devised a rota which ensures that a worker is always responsible for checking the basic information required from new children who have casually dropped into the project. With colleagues she has also established some key points about when and how to carry out the process. For example:

- **Give the new child time to settle in**
  Enquiring after factual details, however scant, isn't the way to welcome children to a project. Get a relationship going on simple friendly terms first.
- **Do not push for information if the child is reluctant**
  There are several issues here. The child may have strict instructions not to give out such information. They may be vague about the details. They may be generally hostile to anyone they see in a position of authority. They may just feel uncomfortable.
- **Explain why the information is important and, if necessary, follow it up with a form**
  If a child is reluctant, provide them with a simple form to take home and return, filled in, the next time they visit the project.

If the child becomes a regular user, the registration form can be issued. Compare this pattern with the process in your own setting. Write a short report on the differences and your suggestions.

PROGRESS CHECK

1 The term registration has several applications in respect of play projects. Do you know all of them?
2 What are the good practice points of record keeping in respect of:
   a making the process accessible to parents and carers?
   b keeping records safe and secure?
   c maintaining confidentiality?

THE LOG BOOK OR DAILY DIARY

A log book or daily diary is essential in every play setting and is used to record:

- who uses the project
- what the children do and any special incidents that may have taken place
- special visitors to the facility.

Keeping a daily record not only enables the project to collect research material that will be useful for report writing and planning later on but also contributes to a safe and smooth-running play environment through the recording of special occurrences. Here is an example page from the daily diary of a school play centre:

```
2009                                                              APRIL
                                                        Tuesday    14
                                               Week 16 · 109–257
STAFF IN   Mrs Jones    Mrs Brown    Mr Black    Mr Johnson
NO OF CHILDREN          30 Boys      21 Girls    Total 51
           14 INK       SRN 27       ETH 30      SN 1
WEATHER       RAIN - STORM
ACTIVITIES
    Hall - Registration Mrs Jones  Mrs Brown  Mr Black  Mr Johnson
    P.C. Room - Snack time         Mr Black
    Drawing, Mr Johnson
    Medical Room - Mrs Jones + Animals      Lego Play People
    Hall - Games       Mr Black
    Library - Mrs Brown            Quiet Games
*INCIDENTS Bob was rude to Mr Johnson and one of the girls.
Mr Johnson spoke to him but was not too happy with his attitude.
I will speak to him on Wednesday 15th.*
PHONE CALLS IN: Ms Smith to say Katie and Susan could go home
alone.
PHONE CALLS IN: Michelle from Hummingbird Playground checking if
football match was still on for Wed. 15th weather permitting.
Spoke to all children* about sharing cotton wool that had been
given to one child for a bump on the head and he had passed it on
to another who was wiping it all around his face; also mentioned
about blood — not to touch each other's or soiled cotton wool as
you can catch germs and be very sick.
```

CONSENT FORMS

Whenever a trip or outing is being planned a consent form must be filled in and signed by the parent or carer of each child. It is essential that the following information is stated on the form:

- the destination of the trip
- how the children will be travelling
- what activities they will be involved in
- what they will need to take with them (packed lunch, rain proofs, good walking shoes, etc.)
- the time of leaving and time of return
- what arrangements, if any, are to be made for collecting the children
- the telephone number of the play project to contact in an emergency.

The form should also give space for the parent or guardian to inform the playworkers of:

- any special needs of the child such as limited physical mobility or travel sickness
- whom the playworkers should contact in an emergency.

Page 124 shows a sample consent form for trips not requiring an overnight stay. See also Chapter 4.

RECORDING ACCIDENTS

Even the most efficiently run projects will have the occasional accident from time to time and for some a serious injury may, unfortunately, also occur. Sometimes minor injuries will be too insignificant to record. However, accidents that require some sort of treatment will need to be recorded. That treatment might be bandaging a cut or it could be sitting the child down in a quiet place to recover from a minor collision. If the accident is more serious then the incident will also need to be logged with the appropriate authorities – the local authority and/or the Health and Safety Executive. See Chapter 8.

GOOD PRACTICE

If you are an assistant worker and uncertain whether an accident should be written down, then ask your supervisor or team leader for guidance.

Your individual project will have its own methods and procedures and you may be required to use a standard sheet or fill in an accident book. Whatever method is used the information should include:

- the name, age and address of the injured person
- the date and time of the incident
- the details of the incident
- the nature of the injury
- the treatment given and/or action taken

OUTING CONSENT FORM

Dear Parent or Carer

Your child/children have expressed an interest in joining us on an outing. We need your written permission so that they can attend. Full details of each child will be carried by the Playworker in charge of the outing as well as being left with the staff remaining at the Playground. Please complete the form below and return it, with any fees, to the Playground as soon as possible.

If you have any questions about this outing please see or call the staff at the Playground. Telephone no: _____

DESTINATION _____

ON _____ TRAVELLING BY _____

LEAVING AT   PLEASE ARRIVE 20 MINUTES BEFORE DEPARTURE

RETURNING APPROX _____

PLEASE BRING   A packed lunch   ☐ Warm clothes   ☐

                        A waterproof coat ☐ Swimwear and towel ☐

                        Trainers   ☐ Spending money   ☐

THE COST OF THE TRIP WILL BE   _____

PLEASE RETURN THIS FORM AS SOON AS POSSIBLE
TO ENSURE YOUR PLACE.

✂ ✂ ✂ ✂ ✂ ✂ ✂ ✂ ✂ ✂ CUT HERE ✂ ✂ ✂ ✂ ✂ ✂ ✂ ✂ ✂ ✂ ✂ ✂

CHILD/CHILDREN'S NAME(S)   _____

TO ATTEND THE OUTING TO _____ ON _____

NAME OF PARENT/CARER (BLOCK CAPITALS)   _____

ADDRESS _____

_____

HOME TEL. NO. _____ DAYTIME TEL. NO. _____

NAME AND TELEPHONE NUMBER OF ALTERNATIVE EMERGENCY

CONTACT PERSON _____

PLEASE TELL US IF YOUR CHILD/CHILDREN HAVE ANY MEDICAL OR

SPECIAL NEEDS _____

_____

_____

_____

_____

SIGNATURE OF PARENT/CARER

_____

OFFICE USE: MONEY RECEIVED _____   DATE _____

- if the person was treated elsewhere
- who was informed.

Here is an example accident form filled in to record an injury to a child's arm and further information on accidents and emergencies can be found in Chapter 8.

ACCIDENT REPORT FORM   Form number: 3

Date of accident: 02/05/09   Time of accident: 3.45

Weather conditions: DRY AND BRIGHT

Injured person

Name MAXINE KELLY   Date of birth 06.01.00

Address 14A BRADSHAW ESTATE
         BRIGHTON TERRACE, BRIGHTON

If the injured child was visiting the playground with a school or other organised group, please give details below:

Name of school or group N/A

Address

Details of accident

What happened? MAXINE WAS PLAYING WITH JENNY WITH A BAT AND BALL WHEN SHE SLIPPED, FELL AND TWISTED HER ARM

What was the child wearing? SHORTS AND T SHIRT

Who was it witnessed by? JENNY AND MYSELF

Who was supervising the area/activity at the time?
    ME - DAVE SHANTON

Nature of injury

TWISTED ARM - IT WAS SORE BUT NOT CUT, BRUISED OR OUT OF SHAPE

What treatment was given? I TOOK HER INTO THE HUT AND LET HER SIT DOWN. I COMFORTED HER BUT SHE DIDN'T NEED A SLING

Does the child have any allergies or medical conditions, or receive any medication? NO

If so, was this taken into account when giving treatment?
    /

Hospitalisation

Was the child taken to hospital?   NO

If so, which one?   /   What time?   /

Was the child's information sheet sent with the child?
    /

Other information

Who else was informed about the accident, and when?
    I INFORMED HER MOTHER WHEN SHE CAME IN AT 6PM

SIGNED D. Shanton   Playworker in charge

SIGNED Lucy Langton   DATE: 02/05/09

STAFF AND VOLUNTEER RECORDS

All projects will need to keep some basic information on the staff who work there. Full names, contact addresses and telephone numbers will enable workers to be contacted by telephone or letter if necessary during days off, leave or other periods of absence. If you are in a senior position it may be your responsibility to induct and supervise a member of staff, which will mean keeping a file where you can store such things as the worker's job description, the induction process, and any notes on the worker's progress. With the latter it is important that the information is shared with the worker and that he or she has access to the file. In the statutory sector the more detailed and, perhaps, confidential information on workers such as job applications, references, interview records, sickness notes, etc. will be kept at the town hall or recreation office. With voluntary managed projects this information may be stored at the chairperson or secretary's home. If it is necessary to keep such records at the project they should be stored in a safe and secure place.

VOLUNTEERS

Many projects rely on the contribution of volunteer workers to assist in the daily running of play facilities, particularly with regard to planning and running activities with the children. Volunteers may be:
■ parents or carers
■ students
■ local residents
■ workers from related occupational areas.

They may be involved with a project in different ways. For instance:
■ helping with the general running of the project
■ helping to plan and run an activity session
■ accompanying playworkers and children on an off-site trip
■ planning and running a special project
■ joining the management committee or users' group.

In the case of volunteer workers it is good practice to create a file storing information on the volunteers who help on your project. This should include basic information such as:
■ the name of the volunteer
■ their home address
■ a contact telephone number
■ their status in respect of the project, e.g. parent, carer, local resident, ex-user.
■ how they would like to help, e.g. running arts and crafts activities, building play structures, supervising outings.

Volunteer help can be invaluable on trips

It is now essential that all staff and volunteers go through a vetting procedure on previous criminal convictions to clear them for work with children. It is the responsibility of employers to ensure that the relevant paperwork is completed and sent away. The Criminal Records Bureau (CRB) will carry out checks, and issue a Disclosure to those permitted to work with children.

To think about   5.7

With your colleagues, discuss how well your project makes use of volunteers. Are there ways that you could:

■ recruit more volunteers?

■ make better use of those already involved?

Are there any agencies locally who might provide students for a special project? There are also some businesses who, similarly, second employees to help charitable organisations.

In this section the focus has been on the keeping of records. Further information on good practice regarding staff and volunteers can be found in Chapter 9.

PROGRESS CHECK

1   What are the key areas of record keeping apart from information on your users?
2   In what circumstances might you wish to look up previous records?

The design and maintenance of the user-centred environment

One of the principal values of playwork is that the child or young person should be at the centre of the process, and, whenever possible, empowered to make their own choices about the nature of the play experience (see Chapter 1). In particular, children use their surroundings in their play. There will be the secret places, the places that are good to climb, the areas that serve as 'safe' places in games, the rooms and sheds and objects that to us may be functional but to them are the settings and artefacts of their imagination. Supervised play projects have, in some areas, become the only places where children have a real opportunity to influence their environment. It is, therefore, crucial for the playworker to:

■ understand how children operate within the play space
■ plan for real choice and ownership to take place
■ ensure that all children and young people have equal access
■ ensure that the play space is safe and stimulating.

THE INDOOR PLAY ENVIRONMENT

Image
When the children and young people enter the play space they should feel as if they belong and, equally important, experience a sense of excited anticipation. This can be conveyed by, for example:

■ children's art work displayed on the walls
■ children's crafts shown on shelves and tables
■ photographs, drawings and paintings that the children like can be displayed.

As children enter the play setting it is good to convey a busy atmosphere and give an indication of the sorts of things that the children can participate in if they wish to. Paper and paints, scrap materials, board games and other items that can be used without direct supervision can be in place and ready for use.

You may wish also to have the name of the playground or club displayed on the wall with opening times and the names of all the playworkers. If the children themselves have designed this and included a club logo it will contribute to the feeling of ownership by them.

An important issue when considering the image of your play environment is how well it reflects the ethnic and cultural diversity of your users. Make sure that you do not reflect only the majority culture in your displays and, equally important, guard against images which are, or could be, a cliché or patronising. Pictures, posters and arts and crafts materials need to reflect a range of ethnic groups.

Accessibility

If, as an adult, you went to your local library and found that all the books were for under eights, all the shelves of books ended at your chest height and all the chairs and tables were no more than eighteen inches off the ground you would feel very disorientated. In fact children experience the world in this way most of the time only, of course, in reverse. For them most things in the built environment are too large and adult centred to be comfortable. In the play environment, however, things should be different.

When you are involved in the design and purchase of furniture and equipment, make sure that they are accessible to children and remember that children do not all come in the same size and shape. You will need to consider the age range of your users and plan accordingly. It is only recently that playworkers have been able to be fully involved with the design process and we are now able to see play buildings with not only toilets and wash basins at child heights but also working surfaces and equipment in kitchens and craft rooms.

KEY POINT

Although your project may not be used by children and young people with disabilities on a regular basis, you never know when such a user may visit or become registered with you. To ensure access for all children and to meet the requirements of the Disability Discrimination Act, it is essential that your project has ramps and other facilities such as special toilets to accommodate users with disabilities. It may not be your responsibility, but you can bring it to the attention of your line manager or management committee if your building, and access to it, assumes no users (or their parents) will have any disabilities. Of course, finances may be an issue but all projects should strive for these minimum requirements.

Resources of space

In considering the use of your indoor environment take an overview of all the play spaces at your disposal. You may well have the use of a number of different indoor play spaces, including:

- a main play space for flexible activity
- a craft room
- a darkroom
- a kitchen
- a gym
- a computer room
- a quiet room
- a club or games room (with table tennis or snooker table for instance)
- a music room.

Should you be fortunate in having many of these facilities you will probably not be concerned about limitations of space. You will, however, be presented with a different set of demands in terms of staffing. Buildings with multiple spaces can be difficult to supervise and specialist activity rooms such as music rooms and darkrooms will require workers with the appropriate skills. There will need to be a fairly structured programme to ensure safe and effective management of all the rooms when in use. (See Chapter 4.)

Of course, the above is an exceptionally good range of facilities. In most play projects the task for the playworker is often to offer as varied a choice of activities as possible within a limited choice of space. So you will be making decisions all the time about what goes on where.

Children and young people should be consulted about the use of your available space but you may not be able to please everyone. You will be making decisions with regard to safety and the use of the space by others. You will also need to consider the underpinning values of the project. Without adequate facilities, it just may not be possible to accommodate football on site for a few enthusiasts without severely disrupting the activities for most of the other users. Whilst recognising that television and video can be a positive experience, your project may have taken the view that children can have access to this provision in other settings and wishes to provide alternative activities.

Activity 5.10

With your colleagues discuss what range of indoor play spaces you have at your disposal and how you use them.

In your discussion consider the following factors:

- Within the confines of safety and the care of the space with regard to other users, does your use of the indoor environment reflect the needs and wishes of the children?
- How much choice do the children have in what they do?
- Is there room for flexibility and spontaneous activities?
- Do you need to make special provision for older and younger groups? For example 5–8 year olds could use the main play space from 3.45–5.00pm, 9–11 year olds from 5.00–6.00pm.
- Have you utilised all the spaces to their full advantage?
- Is there room for improvement on the storage and display of the children's art and craft work?
- How much can you adapt and change the spaces?

KEY POINT

It is very important to be honest with children and young people and avoid giving them false expectations. Talking to children with a 'We'll do whatever you want' attitude is as unproductive as a 'We know what's best for you' stance. Even 5–6 year olds can understand, if you are clear, about options within a framework and choices with boundaries.

THE OUTDOOR PLAY ENVIRONMENT

On visiting the outdoor space children should be able to identify and relate to what they see in the same way as they do with indoor spaces. There is, however, an even wider differentiation between play settings in respect of outdoor environments.

In the adventure playground setting, the playworker can enable the children to stamp their identity onto the space through murals, timber constructions (which can be brightly painted), animal enclosures, gardens, camps, dens and, under supervision, open fires.

CASE STUDY 5.11

When Elroy started his new job as the senior worker at the Willow Tree Adventure Playground he decided that the playground needed a complete re-think in terms of its outdoor environment. Janet and Kieran, the assistant workers, agreed that the playground had got a bit run down and uninteresting.

There were only two features on the site designated for play, a hard surface area in front of the playground building which was used for ball games, and the timber play structures which, apart from one rope swing, were all large platforms, many of them unconnected and only accessible by a vertical ladder nailed to the side. Although there was a mature willow tree with some flowering shrubs in one corner they were not used in any way. There was an old concrete sand pit on one side, which was now used only for storing old timber – a bit of an eyesore and potentially dangerous.

After discussions in staff meetings and with their local voluntary management committee to estimate how much time and money would be available for such a project, Elroy, Janet and Kieran decided to put into operation a strategy that would make the playground both more stimulating and more visually attractive. Their strategy employed the following steps:

1   They listed all the features that they, as a team, thought would enhance the playground.
2   They spoke to the children to get their ideas about what the playground could feature. By showing them their own list of ideas, but stressing that these weren't the only possibilities, they encouraged them, in a realistic way, to make a contribution. This included drawing, and designing play ideas on a map of the site, for those children who were interested.
3   They incorporated the children's ideas with their own and came up with a draft plan of the 'new' site, a schedule of work and a budget estimate.
4   The draft plan was discussed with the management committee and a final version eventually agreed.

After much discussion and deliberation Elroy, Janet and Kieran's final plan included the following:

■   The concrete sandpit was to be replaced and any suspect play structures dismantled.
■   The hard surface games area was re-sited away from the building and equipped to facilitate a practice area for basketball, badminton and football.
■   Two large playground signs, designed and painted by the children, were to be erected by the main and side entrances.
■   The hard surface area outside the building was to become a seating and picnic area where children and adults could sit and socialise.
■   A special area, fenced off and equipped with scrap materials, was designated for the children's own constructions.
■   The corner area with the shrubs and willow tree to be further planted and landscaped and designated as a wild life and garden area.
■   A major part of the site was designated for timber play structures which would include large and small swings, climbing platforms, walkways and bridges and wherever possible these would be accessible by ramps to facilitate use by children with mobility difficulties.
■   In various parts of the site children would be encouraged to design and construct sculptures from timber and durable scrap materials.

In other play settings the scope to utilise the environment is invariably much more limited. Consequently the playworkers need to apply their imagination in different ways.

CASE STUDY 5.12

At the St Dunstan's After-school Play Centre, they have the use of the school playground during the session. It is a hard surface area with a wet-weather shed. The playworkers are not allowed to have a permanent play centre sign on display outside and they cannot construct anything unless it can be dismantled on the same evening. They respond positively to this situation in the following ways:

- A 'sandwich board' sign painted by the children is erected in the playground each session.
- They take out trestle tables and draw and paint in the wet-weather shed.
- There is a selection of bikes and go-karts for the children to ride on.
- There are a number of light wheelbarrows and plastic and rubber blocks that children can transport and play with.
- Weather permitting, table tennis and pool tables are used outside.
- Large junk modelling sessions are run, using cardboard to make such things as animals, houses, cars, etc.
- The playworkers regularly play with and organise games for the children.

Questions

1 What are the restrictions on the use of your outdoor space?
2 How do you organise a broad range of activities for users?
3 Organise your observations and ideas to make a short presentation to your team.

Activity 5.13

Take some time to visit other projects in your area to see how they look and what features they have. Talk to the playworkers and find out what the issues were for them in designing and adapting their project. Talk to the children also and, in particular, watch how they use the play space. Where do they congregate? What are their secret places? How do they make use of the play features in their play? Is it different from the original concept?

Watching how children interact with the play environment will reinforce the importance of consulting with them before implementing changes to the play space.

Write up your observations with a range of illustrations.

Materials and equipment

Materials and equipment must, of course, be safe. They must also be accessible to the child and ideally offer flexible use. What you choose will depend on your play setting, the ages and interests of your users and the extent of your storage space. A basic play store for a project that is catering right across the 5–15 age range should have examples of most of these kinds of equipment:

- arts and crafts, e.g. scissors, pens, brushes, craft knives
- games, e.g. bats, balls, parachute, skipping ropes, shuttlecock, pool table
- small games, e.g. ludo, chess, cards, dominoes
- outdoor tools, e.g. spades, forks, wheelbarrows
- carpentry, e.g. saws, hammers, set squares, work bench
- drama, e.g. old clothes for costumes, face paints, mirrors.

Materials may include: paint, paper, glue, clay, nails, wood, ropes, nets, and an assortment of junk materials.

Of course you may, depending on the age of your users, the scope of your project and the availability of your budget, be able to provide more sophisticated items such as:

- a pottery wheel
- a kiln
- jewellery making kit
- camping equipment
- mountain bikes
- canoes
- musical instruments
- computers.

GOOD PRACTICE

When obtaining materials and equipment, make full use of all the available sources. The local scrap project will be as rich a source of materials as the borough play store or the high street craft shop – and a lot less expensive. Your neighbourhood shops and businesses can also be useful, e.g. the supermarket for cardboard boxes, the garden centre for bamboo canes, the timber yard for wood off-cuts, the clothes manufacturer for fabric.

Activity   5.14

Monitor how many times over the next fortnight children show interest in an activity which you do not have the resources to provide for. Did the activities require specialist materials and equipment, e.g. a video camera? Could you have had the materials and/or equipment in your store? If so, why not stock up.

Check out your suppliers. Are you making full use of all the possibilities? Are there untapped sources of materials in your neighbourhood?

Organise your information into a simple numerical presentation and present it, with other ideas, to your team.

MAINTAINING THE SUPPLY OF MATERIALS AND EQUIPMENT

Every project will need a system whereby:

■ materials and equipment are regularly monitored
■ suppliers are kept listed
■ correct procedures are in place to order and receive goods, whether purchased or on loan or hire.

If you are a senior worker this will be your overall responsibility, but as a team member you will also need to understand how the system operates.

As a team you will need to:

1 Regularly review your core supply of materials and equipment to ensure that sessions can run smoothly and that you are prepared to meet most of the spontaneous requirements of the children.

2 Plan special sessions well in advance and take stock of any materials and equipment that may not be part of your core supply and order accordingly.

3 Keep an updated list of supplies on file with names, addresses, telephone numbers and prices if appropriate. Part of the list could be those organisations or businesses in your locality who will donate or lend to the project.

4 With your list of suppliers keep any paperwork that you need to either order materials and equipment, or which tells you the particular procedures needed for purchase, loan or hire.

5 Implement a system that ensures goods can be received and checked. This may involve enlisting help from other people if yours is a part-time project and the supplier can't guarantee delivery when you are on the project.

PROGRESS CHECK

1 In a shared-use setting what measures should you take to ensure that the children have choice in their play activities?

2 Name three features which might enhance an outdoor environment for younger children.

3 How might you ensure a regular supply of junk materials such as cardboard, paper, and old clothes?

Finance and budgeting

The role you will play on your project in respect of finance will depend on the nature of the facility and your own position within the team. Generally speaking playworkers on voluntary managed projects have more responsibility in this area than those on projects run by local authorities. Senior workers will have more responsibility than assistants although, as is often the case in playwork where workers are operating in small staff teams, many of the tasks will be shared out. Staff salaries, however, are usually the sole responsibility of the management committee treasurer or the local funder – usually the local authority or play association. Leaving aside the payroll aspect of finance there are five main task areas:

- planning expenditure (budgeting)
- recording income and expenditure (accounting)
- petty cash
- purchasing goods and services
- fund raising.

PLANNING EXPENDITURE (BUDGETING)

CASE STUDY 5.15

The Hummingbird Adventure Playground receives an annual grant from the education department of the local council. Most of this is to meet the playground's most important item of expenditure, the playworkers' salaries, and the remainder is spent on running costs. Each year Michelle, the senior worker, leads the team in finding additional money through fund-raising activities. This extra money is often very important to the service the playground provides.

The playground is managed by a voluntary committee of local people with a treasurer Doreen who, with the chairperson Larry, oversees the financial management. Each year Michelle, Doreen and Larry get together to review expenditure and plan for the future. At these annual meetings they will look at all the different areas of spending. For example:

- heating
- lighting
- telephone
- stationery
- site and building repairs
- materials for play activities
- play equipment
- trips and outings
- staff training.

They also prepare a forward plan for the coming year. The plan will include their annual grant and what they hope to achieve through fund-raising. Once the financial forward plan has been completed this will be shared with the other playworkers and the full management committee. Opposite is an example of a financial forward plan.

Questions

1 What are the methods of reviewing and planning budgets in your play setting?
2 If you are a senior worker, how do you involve the other members of the staff team?
3 Discuss the key issues with your team, including a presentation of basic budgetary limits in numerical terms.

PLAYGROUND FINANCIAL FORWARD PLAN 09/10 April—March

Income:

Borough: Annual Grant	£46800.00
Play Association: Equipment Grant	200.00
Fundraising (1) Based on last year:	
Easter fete	350.00
Children in Need Grant	1000.00
Occasional donations	150.00
Fundraising (2) Anticipated income:	
Joshua Clement Fund — to buy table tennis table	500.00
Sainsbury — to fund outings for children with special needs	750.00
Fees:	250.00
	£50000.00

Expenditure:

Salaries:

Senior worker including NI	£17000.00
Assistant worker ×2 including NI	24000.00
	£41000.00

Running costs:

Training	200
Rent	250
Water rates	300
Insurance	750
Light/heat	450
Maintenance	300
Cleaning	150
Furniture and equipment	500
Outings and events	300
Play materials	500
Refreshments	200
Telephone	400
Admin.	400
Misc.	250
	£4950.00

Special projects:

Table tennis table	500.00
Outings for children with special needs	750.00
Easter and Summer holiday schemes	1500.00
Drama project	500.00
Residential trip	800.00
	£4050.00
Total:	**£50,000.00**

RECORDING INCOME AND EXPENDITURE (ACCOUNTING)

A simple accounting book will normally be enough for most play settings to record income and expenditure through the petty cash system, and any small amounts of money coming in through voluntary donations or fees for trips and outings. It is important to establish a clear understanding as to who keeps the book up to date so that there is no danger of items being forgotten or lost.

PETTY CASH

Many play projects operate a petty cash system for expenditure on such items as:

- refreshments
- small items of materials and equipment
- travelling expenses
- minor repairs.

	PETTY CASH BOOK		PAGE 6	
Date	ITEM	RECEIPT	INCOME	EXP.
9.5.09	CARRIED OVER		£23.00	
	TOP UP OF FLOAT		£27.00	
			£50.00	
11.5.09	FOOD AND DRINKS FOR CANTEEN			7.99
12.5.09	FELT TIPS			3.99
17.5.09	TEA, COFFEE, MILK			5.29
21.5.09	TENNIS BALLS			5.20
24.5.09	FOOD FOR CANTEEN			6.70
25.5.09	BUS FARES TO PARK			3.15
25.5.09	COLD DRINKS			6.06
29.5.09	TELEPHONE BOOK FOR OFFICE			7.12
				£45.50
	CARRIED OVER		£4.50	
1.6.09	TOP UP OF FLOAT		£45.50	
			£50.00	
2.6.09	CRAFT KNIFE			4.60

The senior worker will be allocated a float and spending will be accounted for by collecting a receipt and entering the transaction in the playground accounting book. As the float gets low the receipts will be 'traded' in for money to replenish the float to its original amount. The money is kept in a secure place such as a locked metal box in the playground office, and all the workers should be familiar with, and able to operate, the system.

PURCHASING GOODS AND SERVICES

Although you may not be actually handling the money itself, it is usually the playworker who decides or recommends what needs to be bought or repaired. This may involve you in obtaining an invoice that you can forward to your management member or council finance department. Most play projects make their own distinction between what is a 'major', and what is a 'minor' item of purchase. 'Major' items will need the authority of the line manager or management committee whereas 'minor' items can be ordered direct. For instance an electric drill costing £120.00 could be 'minor', and a bar football table costing £450.00 could be 'major'.

KEY POINT

Some play settings do not handle 'real' money in their purchasing of materials and equipment. They have no petty cash system and all purchases are made through the finance officer of the education department who settles accounts with council suppliers or pays cheques to local shops and businesses.

FUND RAISING

All play projects can make use of extra funds. In the voluntary sector major items of expenditure have been secured through the fund-raising efforts of the playworkers and managers – a new building for example. There are many sources of extra funding from the local jumble sale to the European Social Fund and which type you employ will depend on the nature of your project and the purpose of the extra money. In preparing medium to large fund-raising applications here are a few useful indicators:

- Read the application form thoroughly so that you do not waste time filling in unnecessary information.
- Make sure that what you are raising the money for meets the objectives of the organisation or charity donating the funds.
- Sell yourself well, pointing out all the unique points about yourself and your project.
- Do your sums thoroughly – some organisations now require business plans with applications.
- Be clear about the aims and objectives of your fund-raising project.
- Make sure you build in an evaluation process.

Do you feel you have a clear understanding of the financial systems in operation at your project?

What improvements do you think could be made to the system?

KEY TERMS

You need to know what these words and phrases mean. Go back through the chapter to make sure you understand.

Record keeping	Consent form
Admissions procedure	Accident book
Confidentiality	Staff and volunteer records
Log book or daily diary	Vetting procedure

6 RESPONDING POSITIVELY TO CHILDREN'S BEHAVIOUR

> **This chapter covers:**
> - **The focus on behaviour**
> - **Boundaries and realistic expectations**
> - **Patterns of encouragement**
> - **Dealing with unwanted behaviour**

The focus on behaviour

Children and young people are still developing towards adulthood. They are relatively open to learning different ways of dealing with people and everyday situations. They need three basics from playworkers:

1   A clear understanding of what you want from them in the play setting.
2   A positive boost to their motivation to cooperate with you, especially when they find it hard to behave in the way that you wish.
3   A consistently good example set by your behaviour, but not impossible perfection.

KEY POINT

A central part of playwork practice in any setting will always be how individual playworkers behave towards the users of the setting. Policies and guidelines are an important part of playwork, yet they have no meaning unless the words come alive through actions.

AN AUTHORITATIVE APPROACH

Some playworkers are concerned that positive management of children's behaviour is somehow tantamount to a cynical manipulation. This is not the case; the two approaches are very different. Manipulative adults are inconsistent with children, because the only real consistency is with the adult's hidden agenda. Adults whose aims to manipulate are insincere, tend not to respect children as individuals and they often do not keep to their own rules. An approach of positive management of children's behaviour has completely different qualities from an intent to manipulate.

Honesty and openness
There is no pretence – either that playworkers are perfect or that 'anything goes'. Some kinds of behaviour will be unacceptable in a play setting, no matter

who is involved. Feelings are dealt with in an honest fashion and discussed between playworkers and users. The ground rules of a setting are established and reviewed in consultation with users. Yet, playworkers are open in stating, and explaining, any non-negotiable issues – for instance, no racist behaviour or no drugs on site.

KEY POINT

Attempts to guide and direct children's behaviour only become manipulative if playworkers are dishonest and fail to value children and young people.

Authoritative – not authoritarian

Playworkers who act in an authoritative way will give explanations and listen to the users' perspective. They will work towards a friendly relationship with users, but will not pretend they are 'just one of the kids', because this is untrue. Authoritative playworkers will be capable of firmness, but will not be dismissive of users' concerns or experience. They will be ready to step in when a situation is getting out of hand or to offer choices without making the decision-making process feel a burden to the children or young people.

In contrast, an authoritarian approach urges children to do what they are told, without any discussion, simply because of the position of the person giving the instructions. Authority might be claimed because, 'I'm the one in charge', or 'I'm older than you' or 'I know a lot more than you'.

KEY POINT

Playworkers have a role to fulfil. Children and young people are often very relieved when adults act in line with their responsibilities. A dithering or overly permissive adult is often as much trouble to them as an uncompromising authoritarian.

Children will often support each other

Feelings and behaviour

A focus on behaviour does not mean that playworkers deny the importance of feelings. Good communication skills will help you to support children in expressing their feelings. (See, for instance pages 51 and 73.) Sometimes you will be working to help them do this in a way that is less hurtful to others or disruptive of other users' enjoyment.

Feelings are important and they influence everyone's behaviour – playworkers too. But, this effect can be rather unpredictable. For instance, one child who is distressed may turn in on himself and another may lash out with her fists. Strong feelings may be an important reason to explore in dealing with unacceptable behaviour, but they do not excuse ill-treatment of others.

PROGRESS CHECK

1 If children are to learn different ways of behaving, what basics do they need from playworkers?
2 Describe three differences between an authoritarian and an authoritative approach to children and young people.

Boundaries and realistic expectations

Most people prefer to know where they are. They like to have boundaries that are clear and practical rules that are implemented fairly and have to be followed by everyone. Children and young people are no different from adults in this respect. Any play setting will need to have a set of ground rules that emerge from realistic expectations of everyone involved.

GROUND RULES FOR A SETTING

The exact details may differ but the process of reaching the rules should be very similar in different settings:

- Ground rules work much better if children and young people are involved in developing the rules in the first place and then in reviewing them from time to time.
- Rules should be stated simply and briefly and phrased positively whenever possible – as a 'Do' rather than a 'Don't'.
- The set of rules should not be very long – certainly no more than ten. Several concerns may reduce down to a basic such as 'Respect other people in the centre'.
- The ground rules should apply to everyone – users, playworkers, parents and any visitors.
- The setting's rules should be written down and easily available to new users, playworkers and to parents.

The ground rules of a play setting cannot cover absolutely everything about all the activities and events. For instance, you may have a ground rule about 'Watch out for the safety of other users', but a more specific notice is posted up within the playground that says 'One person at a time on the pole'. On the other hand, playworkers should not try to resolve all issues by establishing further rules. Some disagreements or irritations have to be talked through between workers and users of the setting.

Useful ground rules are never a list of Don'ts

GOOD PRACTICE

Even a clear set of sensible rules does not run a play setting for you. Playworkers need to acknowledge and thank children who follow rules and bring home the consequences to children who do not. (See pages 148–157.) You also need to review the ground rules, with the children, from time to time.

REALISTIC EXPECTATIONS

Age of the users
One consideration will be the age of individual users. For example, 6 year olds cannot be expected to have a grasp of the possible dangers that 14 year olds can have gained through experience. On the other hand, 14 year olds may be a lot less willing to back down from a physical challenge and they may therefore put themselves at risk for the sake of self image. (More on children's development in Chapter 2.)

Whatever the age of the users, it is no use expecting close to perfect behaviour. Nor is it at all wise to push children into the position where they have no chance to save face, to apologise or to wipe the slate clean and start again.

Different expectations

Users of any play setting have to become familiar with the expectations of the playworkers, which are unlikely to be identical to those of children's teachers or their family.

KEY POINT

Differences do not automatically mean difficulties for children. Even the youngest children in a play setting will have some experience of dealing with different sets of adult expectations.

It can be best to discuss any direct contradictions between the settings known to users of the play setting. Playworkers can show respect for the rules of other adults in the children's lives, while still being clear about 'how we do it here'.

For example:

- In Downham after-school club, Zoë explains to Liam: 'I know that your teachers don't let you go in the store cupboard at school, but here we've decided that we can trust you all to get what you need.'
- In St Dunstan's Play Centre, Joseph is talking with Aaron: 'Aaron, it's your Mum and Dad's business how they run things at home, but here everybody is expected to take their turn with the washing up. We don't think it's "girls' stuff"; it's everybody's stuff.'

To think about   6.1

Adults often do not do what they are asked in their work or personal life, nor do they always do it with good grace. They do not always think ahead with care, nor do they consider the feelings of other people. In summary, supposedly mature grown-ups can be a right pain in the neck, so it is unreasonable to expect something completely different from the younger end of the species.

Discuss this sensitive area in an open way with your team.

Children with disabilities

Specific disabilities will have an impact on a child's development. Playworkers need to establish accurate expectations of children in the light of their capabilities. It is very important that expectations for children's behaviour do not underestimate a child or young person. For instance, it would be very poor practice to take a pitying approach of 'Poor little Caitlin, she's got Downs. We shouldn't expect too much of her.'

Playworkers need a good enough understanding of a child's disability that they can develop realistic expectations. You will be able to achieve this through:

- Good communication with a child's parents, who will be able to give you a rounded sense of what their child can manage so far and the kind of boundaries that they draw at home.

For example: Caitlin's parents could show playworkers the relevant signs to support simple messages such as 'No, Caitlin, stop that now' or 'Well done, Caitlin.'

■ Talking issues through with the children themselves, when possible. Playworkers can empathise with the frustrations associated with a disability, yet still expect children or young people to take the level of responsibility for their own behaviour that is within their direct control.

For example: Ben has a hearing disability but chooses not to wear his hearing aid. He then uses the fact that he couldn't hear to excuse himself for being over an hour late rejoining the group at the end of the day trip. He denies any responsibility for causing everyone to wait for him.

■ Talking together as a playwork team, to pool observations and experience of all the play setting users, including those with disabilities.

For example: Sam complains to Kieran that other children make rude remarks to him because he is in a wheelchair. Kieran talks with three children named by Sam and then raises the issue in a team meeting. It seems that one girl is offensive to Sam on the grounds of his disability. The other two children are adamant that they only shouted at Sam because he ran his wheelchair into their legs. Other playworkers have observed that Sam sometimes uses his chair rather like a battering ram.

CHILDREN'S EXPECTATIONS OF PLAYWORKERS

Children who are consulted are usually realistic. They know only too well that adults are neither perfect, nor capable of pulling off miracles. Children may use different words, but they tend to ask that playworkers should be:

■ Fair – in that they treat all the users equally, with no favourites.
■ Consistent and reasonably predictable – playworkers do not change formal or informal rules depending on their mood.
■ Encouraging – at least as much 'Well done' as 'Stop that!'
■ Willing to listen and not liable to jump to conclusions.
■ Considerate of feelings – and definitely not likely to make children look foolish.

Children also ask that playworkers should:

■ Keep their promises and avoid empty threats.
■ Obey their own rules.

PROGRESS CHECK

1 Describe four practical ways to ensure that ground rules for a play setting are likely to work.
2 Outline three general points you need to bear in mind for holding realistic expectations of any child or young person.

Patterns of encouragement

Discussion about the behaviour of children and young people all too often follows the negative pattern of focusing almost entirely on behaviour that adults do not want, and on the individuals who are seen as troublesome. Responding positively to children's behaviour includes not only looking carefully at behaviour adults wish to discourage (more on this from page 150 onwards), but also directing more attention and energy towards encouraging the behaviour that is wanted.

GOOD PRACTICE

Any playwork team needs to ask themselves the key question, 'In what ways are we actively encouraging the behaviour that we want from children and young people?'

To think about 6.2

In your work or personal life, you would find it very disheartening if every wrong move were criticised and yet you hardly ever received compliments for your efforts. Life might also be confusing, since you would be trying to deduce what people really wanted from a long list of what they did not want.

WAYS OF ENCOURAGING

Playworkers have a range of possibilities to draw from in order to encourage children and young people.

Thanking children

This is a simple and effective way of acknowledging what children have done or the effort they have made. The thanks may be in words. For example:

- 'You were very patient in waiting for me, Winston, I appreciate that.'
- 'It's a good thing you came with me to the scrap store, Kevin. I'd have missed all those cardboard tubes on my own.'
- 'Thanks for reminding me, Eva. The trip letters had gone straight out of my mind.'

Or you may thank some children or young people more by a gesture – a smile, a nod or a friendly pat on the arm.

KEY POINT

You may know inside that you are pleased with a child, or grateful for a young person's help, but there is no way that they can know, unless you communicate this feeling.

Acknowledging effort and achievement

There will be many occasions when you can encourage a child on the basis of what they have done. These do not have to be striking achievements, nor do they all have to be for something tangible. Children deserve acknowledgement for the small, everyday actions, as well as for their craft activities or physical skills. For example:

■ 'Adrian, that was some fantastic shot. I never thought the ball would go in.'
■ 'Grace, I noticed how you held your temper when Kelsey was giving you a hard time.'
■ 'Good idea, Sam. Let's go for it!'
■ 'Katie, you did the right thing to call me over to deal with that strange bloke. I wouldn't have wanted you to try to handle it on your own.'
■ 'Well done, Fizzy, you remembered how it works.'
■ 'Winston, thanks for taking your pills. I know you're fed up with it but it's really important if you're going to keep well.'

To think about   6.3

It is not always appropriate to compliment a child in front of others. Sometimes it will be better to have a few quiet words with her away from everyone else. You will make this decision from a judgement about the situation. Your knowledge of the child or young person will also be a factor – some will be embarrassed by public praise. Read over the examples given above and think which comments might best be made to users when the playworker is alone with them.

Discuss your ideas with a colleague.

Most people who work with children and young people can safely double their level of encouraging comments without going over the top. The atmosphere of the play setting becomes that much more positive. This only works, of course, if:

■ Encouragement is genuinely meant. Children and young people soon spot compliments used just as a technique and will dismiss the adult along with the insincere compliment.

■ The words of encouragement are varied and appropriate to the situation. The same phrase repeated again and again will no longer sound genuine.

Activity 6.4

Over a period of 3–4 days note down at the end of each day or session all the examples you can remember of encouraging comments that you made to any user of the play setting. Are there any patterns in your list?

■ Do you rarely, if ever, compliment some individuals? Be honest with yourself!

■ Are you commenting on some events more than others? For instance, are you more likely to compliment a child on his drawing than on his calmness in tackling an argument.

■ Do you have a clearer memory of telling children off than of complimenting anyone? If so, what is going on?

Describe two ways in which you could adjust your behaviour as a playworker to make your play setting a more encouraging place.

Discuss some of your ideas with fellow playworkers.

SHOWING TRUST

Anyone – adult or child – has to earn the trust of others. Fortunately, a play setting gives many opportunities for trusting users in small matters, before taking any risks over more important responsibilities in the setting. Trusting children works very well as encouragement if:

■ The task is manageable for the child.

■ Playworkers acknowledge that they have trusted or relied on the child.

■ If any children show that they cannot be trusted, the consequences are dealt with simply and without lots of recriminations.

Children or young people in your play setting might be asked to check up on the stores of drink in the cupboard, to take responsibility for one part of the clearing up or to help a playworker to remember to do something. Children can then be thanked for effectively sharing the responsibilities of running the play setting. For example:

■ 'Rory and Jane – thanks for finding the lost piece of the jigsaw. I was sure I could depend on your sharp eyes.'

■ 'Debbie, I want to thank you for your special help in settling Caitlin in. It made a real difference to her that you were so patient.'

If children fall down in their responsibilities, then it can be important to acknowledge this; but, as far as possible, this should be without lengthy complaints and with a view to checking out what went wrong and how soon can they be trusted in the future.

REWARDS AND INCENTIVES

There can be a place for tangible rewards or prizes within a play setting – so long as they do not get out of hand. Incentives are simply rewards promised for the future on an 'if...then' basis. Neither rewards nor incentives should ever take the place of the encouraging approach described so far. There should never be any sense of 'paying' children to behave well. It is more that play settings, like any other setting for adults and children, can benefit from the occasional special event and some activities may genuinely not be possible unless something else happens first. For example:

- 'I think we all deserve a treat after that hard work. We'll open the tin of shortbread that Sam's mum brought today.'
- 'That was the speediest clearing up job that I've ever seen. Brilliant! So we have got time to finish the video.'
- 'I promised you we could get a table tennis table once you showed me you could take better care of the equipment. Well, you've convinced me. Good for you! I'll order the table tomorrow.'

PROGRESS CHECK

1 Describe at least four different ways in which playworkers can encourage users.
2 Why will insincere encouragement fail to work?
3 Give two reasons why you think that adults may hold back from praising children and young people.

Dealing with unwanted behaviour

A strong focus on encouragement will promote a more positive atmosphere in your play setting. It can build a strong basis from which to deal with troublesome behaviour but will not make all the users of the play setting behave perfectly. When playworkers are responding to the unwanted sides to users' behaviour, they need a clear, shared view of:

- The kinds of behaviour that the team wishes to discourage.
- The range of strategies that everyone will use, and those which are not available.

DISCUSSION WITHIN THE TEAM

You will not have much opportunity to consider and review within a busy day or session. So it is crucial that any playwork team makes time to discuss the general issues of 'how well are we handling the kids' behaviour?'. Individual playworkers will also need the opportunity to talk about an incident with hindsight so that they can learn for the future. This discussion might be within supervision or an informal conversation with a colleague.

Discussion about individual children or young people can be more productive if playworkers discuss the following:

- What, exactly, is this child or this group doing? Don't depend on labels as a shorthand. All playworkers will not mean the same by 'aggressive' or 'rude'.
- What are the reasons why this behaviour matters? What are the consequences of what this child, or group, does?
- What might be the best approach(es) from individual playworkers, from everyone?
- What is this child or young person doing well? Are the team taking up any opportunities for encouragement?

OPTIONS IN DEALING WITH UNWANTED BEHAVIOUR

Clear direction and telling

Often, you will not have time to deliberate over how you are going to tackle a child's troublesome behaviour. You will need simply to tell them that a certain kind of behaviour is not on. This will not always be some huge confrontation with a child. Often, your intervention may be a firm, yet friendly; 'Come off it, Kevin. I saw you jump the queue. Haven't you realised yet; I've got eyes in the back of my head.'

Sometimes playworkers can remind users of a ground rule of the play setting – all the more reason for involving users in the development of the rules.

Children stop listening if adults go on and on

For example: Mike may only need to say a simple, 'Remember the Clearing Up rule, Josie.' And if Josie goes to start tidying, then she deserves a 'Thanks'. Or else, Mike may need to be more persuasive – 'We came to that rule because everyone was so fed up with the mess. You too, Josie, I seem to recall.' Mike will not lose face by offering a compromise of, 'Come on, Josie. I'll give you a hand.'

Careful ignoring

Some children thoroughly enjoy winding playworkers up and it is these situations that are often better ignored – at the time. It is far too easy, once you have become irritated by a child or convinced that he is a troublemaker, to start to tell him off for very little things, perhaps things that you would let pass with a child you liked more. It is worth discussing this sort of situation with a colleague since a playworker who is a favourite target may be able to behave in a way that reduces the wind-ups.

Sometimes you may see an incident brewing up and there is time, although not much, to decide, 'Should I get actively involved in this?' Sometimes children will sort out situations themselves and they will feel stronger for having managed to resolve them.

KEY POINT

You should never set about ignoring a child; you are choosing not to rise to certain kinds of behaviour. You are ignoring the behaviour, not the individual child.

Redirecting users

It is sometimes possible to defuse a situation by offering alternatives. A squabbling and shouting group may be broken up by a playworker who offers another activity or places some clear direction on the current one. Children who appear to be misbehaving largely because they are bored may be redirected into more absorbing and possibly physical games. A firm, 'Pack it in, Gaven' can be followed with 'Bet I can do the obstacle course faster than you now. I've been practising!'

Using consequences

It is reasonable that children or young people should experience the consequences of their own behaviour.

The objective underlying active encouragement of children is that they can experience and enjoy the positive consequences of their behaviour. For instance, making an effort in a group project is greeted with thanks and compliments. Taking care to carry out their responsibilities in the settings brings trust from the playworkers and chances to do more grown-up tasks.

There are also consequences to troublesome behaviour and these can be used in responding positively to children and young people. Using consequences only works if:

- The consequence is a natural or logical follow-on to the behaviour. Unexpected or inconsistent punishments from playworkers do not work as consequences of the child's behaviour. Punishments tend to look, and are, consequences of playworkers' frustration or anger.
- Children and young people are given warning – either as individuals on an 'if-then' basis or because this is an established group rule.
- Imposing consequences is done calmly by playworkers, with a clear and simple explanation and within a time scale whenever that is relevant. Nagging is avoided.

CASE STUDY 6.5

In Hummingbird adventure playground, three children have been using wood for the new structures as weapons. Michelle, who is in charge of the woodworking group, gave them two clear warnings, which included, 'If I can't trust you to behave safely, then you'll have to leave this group'. The children persisted and so Michelle said, 'That's it. You leave for today.' She offered them a choice of other activities and said, 'I'll let you try again tomorrow.'

When the children come to the woodworking group the next day, Michelle greeted them and then recapped on the rules of safe woodwork with the entire group. There was no harking back to what happened the day before.

Questions
1   For what kinds of behaviour can you use consequences in your play setting?
2   How do playworkers behave in order to use consequences positively in your setting?
3   Present your ideas to a team meeting.

Later discussion with children
Depending on your relationship with users, it can sometimes be productive to have a conversation with children or young people after an incident. When relations have become fraught it may help to have another playworker or user present – so long as the other parties remain objective and don't crank up any sense of taking sides.

KEY POINT

Discussions will not work if the conversation is a one-way lecture at the user. It will only be helpful if there is a sense of joint problem solving.

CASE STUDY 6.6

In Downham after-school club, Mike is talking in a quiet corner with Debbie:
'I understand now that you had a hard day at school, Debbie, but I want you to understand how hurt I felt when you cussed me out in the street. I'll admit I felt worse because of those people watching us. I'd like us to talk about it – now, if that's okay with you.'

Mike is being honest about his own feelings and is not pushing all the blame onto Debbie. There is more chance, although never a certainty, that Mike and Debbie may have a conversation that resolves the issue.

Questions

1 How do you think the exchange might have gone if Mike had taken the line of, 'You were so rude to me in the street, Debbie!' or 'Don't you think you were out of line on the walk home?'

2 Think over a similar exchange that you have had with a user. What went well and what did not develop so positively?

Sometimes you may need to mediate in disputes

KEY POINT

The problem-solving approach affirms the child or young person. It is part of an authoritative approach that communicates, 'I am not prepared to let this go', but it also says, 'I like you and I want us to come through this. I value you enough to want us to talk about it.'

Banning

Some users may not respond to any of the positive approaches to get them to change their behaviour. Playworkers have to consider all the users of a setting and it is unjust that unacceptable behaviour from a few users should be contained only because others tolerate being ill treated or playing in a wrecked setting.

KEY POINT

Users and playworkers have a right to physical safety and to freedom from persistent and offensive verbal attacks. Users who insist on their wish to threaten or insult other users or playworkers may forfeit their right to come to the play setting.

Persistent problems with users should be discussed in the playwork team and preferably with a user's parents, although that may not be practical in an open access facility. Neither a total ban, nor a ban from specific areas of the play setting should be imposed in the heat of a confrontation.

GOOD PRACTICE

In most instances, playworkers should not unilaterally decide to restrict individual users or to ban them from the play setting. It is reasonable for an individual playworker to tell a child or young person to pull out from an activity and calm down before returning. It would not be reasonable for that playworker to tell the user he or she was banned from the activity until further notice.

The possibility of a ban should be:
■ Discussed within the playwork team.
■ Communicated to the user in such a way that he or she has the choice of behaving in such as way as to avoid the ban.
■ Discussed with the child's parent, or other carer, if possible.
■ Set for a fixed period, and not be left open-ended.

Activity   6.7
It is very possible that the line management beyond your play setting will want to be consulted about the intention to ban a child for more than a given amount of time.
Find out the information on this point.

'Catching them out' doing well
Playworkers need to watch out for expecting too high a standard from any of the children, but especially when there is a risk that annoying behaviour from a child in one situation may generalise to another. Children will be very disheartened by any sense of 'I'm still cross with you about that business with the water. So it doesn't matter how helpful you are now. It won't count!'

GOOD PRACTICE

Incidents have to be dealt with and then let go. It is only fair that children and young people can start again with a clean slate. There will be consequences that children have to accept as following from their behaviour, but being nagged into the distant future should not be one of them.

CASE STUDY 6.8

In St Dunstan's play centre, Aaron is rude and aggressive towards the girls who play football. And he has a long way to go before he treats Maureen with the same respect he gives to the male playworkers. His unacceptable behaviour needs to be tackled and changed, over time. This change will not be speeded up, and will probably be slowed down, if the playworkers let their dissatisfaction with some of Aaron's more sexist behaviour spill over into the way that they generally treat him.

For instance, Aaron has worked with great dedication on the mural and fully deserves the compliment from Angus of, 'That is so good, Aaron. The figures just leap off the wall.' Later he helps Maureen to clear up all the pots and brushes. Aaron grumbles about having to help, but since he does it he still deserves the acknowledgement of, 'Thanks, Aaron. And I appreciate you getting everything back on the high shelf. I'd have had to get the steps out if you hadn't been here.'

The playwork team have discussed their approach to Aaron and agreed that they must avoid any remarks that turn potential encouragement into criticism. So Angus was not about to moan, 'Pity you can't always be so cooperative' and Maureen did not complain, 'You wouldn't have grumbled if it had been Angus or Joseph who asked you to clear up.'

Questions

In your setting, think of a few children or young people whose behaviour is troublesome to you.

1 You may be clear on what it is they do that you would like them to stop, but what are they currently doing that you could be pleased about? Consider this even if there seem to be only a few examples!

2 When was the last time you complimented them on anything – on what they had made or on behaviour such as helping out?

3 Discuss with your colleagues the approach that you are taking to the instances of reasonable behaviour from children whom you see as a difficulty.

4 You could make a short presentation to the team on the key issues as you see them.

UNACCEPTABLE TACTICS FROM PLAYWORKERS

This chapter has described many aspects to an authoritative approach to responding to children's behaviour. This is far removed from an authoritarian and punitive approach. A number of tactics in dealing with children are seriously unproductive and can form no part of good practice in playwork. These are:

■ Physical punishment of children through hitting, slapping, shoving or shaking. This is an abuse of adult strength and gives a clear message to children

Some things you will let go

that physical attack is an acceptable way to deal with problems or strong feelings. Threatening to hit children is equally unacceptable.

■ Ridiculing or humiliating children through words or gestures. Even if children have been very rude to playworkers, there is no excuse for a deliberate attempt to hurt or offend in return.

GOOD PRACTICE

Playworkers have a right themselves to physical safety and may have to use adult strength to protect themselves or users, or to pull children apart for their own safety. Playwork teams need to discuss very carefully the kind of incident which could require self defence. Any actual incidents in the play settings should be reviewed in detail and written up as a report.

PROGRESS CHECK

1 Why is it important that playworkers do not depend on labels when discussing users' behaviour?
2 Describe three ways in which playworkers might discourage unwanted behaviour.
3 Name two tactics that playworkers should never use.

UNACCEPTABLE BEHAVIOUR

All children and young people have their off days. Playworkers who have a good relationship with users can often bring them round, without serious trouble. Some kinds of behaviour are seriously unacceptable in a play setting and a playwork team needs to be clear over how incidents will be handled.

Aggression and fighting
Undoubtedly some children indulge in a great deal of play fighting and general rough and tumble. Very physical girls tend to be persuaded out of play fighting by social pressures, so it will mainly be the boys who show this behaviour in your play setting. Playworkers will need some guidelines to follow in order for the team to act consistently over play fighting. It might be that there is no scuffling

whatever inside, but that a certain level of rough and tumble is tolerated out-doors, so long as no one is hurt. Play fighting might be judged to have turned into unacceptable aggression when individual children are involved who do not want to join in. For instance, the group will not let a child go, or a chasing game has become a hunt-and-hurt game. See also the section on bullying in Chapter 7, page 182.

KEY POINT

Playworkers will need to step in and split up fighting groups whilst recognising that this physical energy will need an outlet that is more acceptable.

Prejudice and discriminatory behaviour

Attitudes are basically individuals' own business, but they become the concern of playworkers when those attitudes emerge through behaviour. Good practice in any play setting will be to ensure that no users, playworkers, parents or other visitors behave offensively or in a discriminatory way to anyone else for reasons of their group membership. This includes:

■ Ethnic or social background.
■ Culture, language or religion.
■ Sex and sexual orientation.
■ Any form of disability.

The kind of behaviours that could concern playworkers and should not be ignored are:

■ Physical assaults following a pattern.
■ Persistent refusal to cooperate or to let particular children join in.
■ Derogatory name calling and offensive remarks or ridicule.
■ Offensive graffiti, whether on walls, bags, badges or clothing.
■ Bringing in to the play setting offensive leaflets, comics or magazines.

Playworkers' reactions will need to depend on the behaviour, and the extent to which children or young people persist. At different times and in different situations you might sensibly take a slightly different line, but this would never include letting any of the above behaviour pass without comment or action, as if they did not matter. Playwork teams need to discuss how they will all approach such situations. Individual playworkers may not agree on exactly what to say, but handling the kind of examples that follow cannot be postponed indefinitely.

An appropriate response from playworkers

In work with children and young people, a major objective is to encourage them to relate to others as fellow individuals and not as Caitlin-who-has-Downs or Hamid-who-is-Pakistani. So it is crucial to bear in mind that a group difference is a necessary condition for considering whether any prejudice is playing a part in troubles between users. But, this difference is not a sufficient condition to take as absolute proof that one individual is behaving in a discriminatory way towards another.

Consider the following examples and discuss with colleagues how you might deal with the situation.

- Some children copy a word like 'queer' or a phrase such as 'Paki shop' without any real thought. A playworker might say, 'That's an offensive word, Dai. I don't want you use it in the centre.' Further conversation could follow if the child wishes.

- Some children and young people are bringing attitudes into the centre that are accepted elsewhere. At the Grafton Road holiday playscheme Bill takes Kelsey to one side: 'I know that the rappers call women 'bitch' and 'ho', but the girls find it really offensive, and so do I. Kelsey, I want you to cut it out when you're here.'

- Playworkers need to take a firm line on offensive material. A worker might say, 'I'm taking this National Front stuff away from you. You can have it back when you leave. But, this is a warning, if you bring in anything like this again, then it goes in the bin for good.' (The same approach would apply if users bring in pornography.)

- Sometimes it is appropriate to ask, 'What did you say?' to get them to repeat a remark like 'Deaf idiot!' Playworkers can follow up with, 'Ben is partially deaf but he's not an idiot – any more than you are. Now what happened between you two?'

- Sometimes the ground rules may need to be re-stated. 'I know that your Dad doesn't like Jewish people; you've told me this before. But your Dad doesn't attend this centre; you do. And here every boy and girl is treated with respect. What you said to Naomi was cruel and disrespectful. I would like you to apologise, but it has to be your decision.' The playworker might continue with, 'Kevin, how are we going to handle this? I like having you here, but I'm not having you talk to anyone like that.'

For example, further discussion may reveal that:
- 'It's not that Rory can't speak properly. That's not why we didn't want him in our board game. It's that he hates losing; he's such a pain if he doesn't win.'
- 'Kelsey is going around saying that I'm "racist" because I won't go out with him. But I turned him down because he's a sexist prat.'

It is also important to recognise genuine interest in differences. If your play setting has 5–8 year olds, you will encounter the kind of unselfconscious curiosity that lessens as older children realise that it is not socially acceptable to ask lots of personal questions. Playworkers can guide children sometimes about when and how to ask questions, so as not to be intrusive, but, often, a straight question deserves a straight answer and certainly not any kind of, 'Ssh, that's rude.'

For example: Tom (just 5 years) is the newest arrival at Downham after-school club. The first afternoon he watches Caitlin signing to Zoë and says loudly, 'Look at that silly girl waving her arms about.' Zoë completes her signed and spoken answer to Caitlin and turns to Tom, 'No, Tom, Caitlin's not being silly. She has trouble speaking, so she talks with special signs. We could teach you some signs, if you like. Bet there aren't many people in your school who can sign as well as speak.'

Alcohol and drugs
Play settings may have a non-negotiable rule of no alcohol, no drugs and no smoking within the play setting or on any centre trips. A playwork team has to decide how many warnings will be given and may agree that some of these substances are more serious than others, and may warrant an immediate ban.

GOOD PRACTICE

Playworkers need to have information on how to recognise children and young people who are the worse for alcohol, drugs or solvent abuse. They also need telephone numbers for emergency treatment in the case of drug overdose or alcohol poisoning.

Sexual behaviour
Any play setting with young people has to accept that they will be sexually aware to a greater or lesser extent. Older children may show curiosity or interest. Sexual awareness or behaviour becomes playworkers' business when it impinges inappropriately on the play setting. This may be because:

Some activities may simply not be allowed in your play setting

- Young people are getting physically very affectionate in the play setting. Playworkers need to communicate that 'here is not the place to do your snogging'. The remark can be friendly, but the heavier the petting, the firmer the words will need to be.
- Young people or older children are sexually harassing other users in words or actions. This is a kind of bullying and needs to be tackled as such. The same situation holds if users are being harassed because of their presumed or actual sexual orientation. (See page 182.)
- Children are showing a level of sexual awareness or behaviour that seems very precocious for their age. The children may be watching unsuitable adult videos elsewhere, but there is also the possibility that they may be experiencing sexual abuse. Any suspicion of this nature needs to be discussed with the team leader and local guidelines followed. (See page 187.)
- Users have made sexual advances, physical or verbal, to playworkers. A playwork team will need to decide with some care how such incidents are tackled.

CASE STUDY 6.10

Willow Tree adventure playground backs onto a stretch of open common. The children move freely from the open access playground to the common. Dawn, a volunteer, asks to speak with Elroy, the team leader.

Dawn is confused and distressed after an incident last week with three boys, of about 10 or 11 years old. They had urged her to come and see the wild flowers on the common. When they were out of sight of the playground, the three boys had tripped her up and, as she expresses it, 'tried some really serious groping'.

Dawn is cross at having been 'jumped on' and as she explains to Elroy, 'They were just young boys. It sounds stupid now, but I believed them about the flowers'. Partly because she had hit two of the boys in order to get away, Dawn had felt uncertain about whether to speak up. However, this afternoon, one of the boys had cornered her on a high part of the playground walkway and groped her again, with the comment of, 'You like it really.'

Questions
1 What kind of comments does Elroy need to make in this conversation with Dawn? What will be supportive (and what might be unsupportive)?
2 Are there any practical issues to be discussed with Dawn?
3 In what way does Elroy need to tackle the three boys involved in the incident? What might he say? Should Dawn be present? Should any sanctions be imposed on the boys? If so, what kind?

Incidents that concern playworkers should, ideally, be raised in a team meeting, so that there can be a proper discussion of not only this incident but any broader issues. Playworkers may also need the support of their colleagues.

PROGRESS CHECK

1 Describe at least three kinds of unacceptable behaviour that should never be ignored in a play setting.
2 Describe three possible approaches to dealing with offensive language.
3 Why would it be bad practice to assume that any conflict between users of a different race must be racist in origin?

KEY TERMS

You need to know what these words and phrases mean. Go back through the chapter to make sure that you understand.

Positive management of behaviour	Encouragement
Authoritative	Trust
Authoritarian	Rewards
Unacceptable behaviour	Incentives
Realistic expectations	Consequences
Ground rules	Banning

---

7 HELPING TO KEEP CHILDREN SAFE

> **This chapter covers:**
> - **Understanding child abuse**
> - **Good practice in child protection**
> - **Bullying between children and young people**
> - **Helping children and young people with personal safety**

Understanding child abuse

THE ROLE OF PLAYWORKERS

General reviews of good practice in child protection during the 1990s recognised the importance of people like playworkers who have regular contact with children and young people. As someone who is often seeing children on a daily basis, you may be the first person who notices something of concern. However, you will also develop close relationships with children and young people, sometimes over a long period of their childhood or adolescence. So, you may well be the person whom they trust to tell about an experience of abuse or bullying.

Playworkers may feel uneasy about the sense of responsibility in situations where child protection could be an issue. However, you will become more confident as you gain a clear understanding of what is good practice in this area of work. This understanding includes knowledge of which responsibilities lie within your playworker role and which belong to another professional in the local network. So part of your role is understanding when to consult and pass on your concerns, and to whom in the local child protection system.

Good practice in child protection for playworkers includes an understanding of the:
- signs of possible abuse of children or young people
- procedures to follow if your concerns are aroused through your own observations or disclosure by a child or young person
- elements of good, daily practice, including how to create a play environment through which children learn about keeping themselves safe.

LEARNING ABOUT CHILD PROTECTION

There are several, equally important, strands of how you learn good practice in child protection.

- Reading can help you extend your knowledge about types of child abuse and its impact on the children and young people themselves. Television documentary programmes can also support your knowledge.
- Personal reflection is important as you explore your own assumptions and experiences relevant to this area of practice.
- Discussion within your playwork team is crucial in airing concerns, assumptions and any uncertainties about what should be done in actual situations you all face.
- It is important to make contact with other professionals in your local child protection network and ideally get to know other parts of the system before your setting faces a crisis.
- Training workshops and courses can be valuable in extending your knowledge, as well as providing a forum for discussion of issues and practice dilemmas.

WHAT IS CHILD ABUSE?

Child abuse broadly covers:
- doing something to children or young people that causes them damage, either physically or emotionally, or that seriously disrupts their development, health or well-being
- failing to do something for children or young people, when the consequences are damaging to their development, health or well-being.

Child abuse can fall into one or more of four broad categories: physical abuse, neglect, emotional abuse and sexual abuse, which are discussed below.

Who are the abusers?
Since society at large became more aware of the abuse of children and young people, it has become ever more clear that there are no neat predictions about circumstances when abuse is more or less likely to occur. Child abuse has occurred in all social classes, ethnic, cultural and religious groups. Children have been abused within their own families, but also by individuals trusted by the family to take responsibility for the children. There have been cases of child abuse within day and residential care, education, special schools for disabled children, play and recreation settings. Children are abused by adults of either sex, even within sexual abuse which is sometimes presented as something that only men do to children. There is also now increased awareness that children may be abused by other children or young people.

KEY POINT

There are no certainties within child protection and playworkers must be careful about making assumptions of who is, or is not, likely to abuse children.

There are no shortcuts to recognising abusers

PHYSICAL ABUSE

Physical abuse, with accompanying neglect (see page 168), is the most common form of ill-treatment of children and the most common cause of death in children as a result of cruelty. Physical abuse is defined as the actual or likely physical injury to a child or young person. Younger children may be physically less able to defend themselves, but abusive treatment can extend into the teenage years. Abuse may also continue with children whose disabilities mean it is harder for them to protect themselves or to talk about the abuse to other people.

Children and young people have been physically ill-treated in many different ways. They have been:

- hit, kicked, shoved or shaken hard – the actual blow can injure the child but sometimes greater damage is caused by a resulting fall
- bitten, burned or deliberately scalded, squeezed with violence or half-suffocated
- deliberately poisoned with household substances, alcohol, drugs or inappropriately given prescription medicines
- ill-treated through deliberately frightening or neglectful tactics by adults, such as shutting children in cupboards or cellars
- caught in the crossfire of domestic violence within their home
- deliberately made ill by their carer – this unusual situation is recognised as a form of physical abuse and is called Illness Induction Syndrome or Munchausen Syndrome by Proxy.

It is right that playworkers should avoid rigid expectations of children based on age or supposed developmental stage. However, good general support for children depends on realistic expectations grounded in age in years, sometimes gender and level of ability or disability. Good practice in child protection has to be well grounded in an understanding, explored in team discussion whenever necessary, of what is, or is not, within normal range development and behaviour for this child or young person.

Activity 7.1
Within your team, discuss the sensitive issue outlined in the Good Practice above.

Making sense of signs that concern you

The most likely warning signs of the physical abuse of children or young people are injuries, perplexing illnesses, or a continuing pattern of accidents to a child for which there is no credible explanation, given the age of the child and any disability. The role of a playworker is to be alert for the welfare of children and young people, to talk with children as appropriate (see also page 176) and to share any concerns within your setting with a more senior playworker or local adviser.

KEY POINT

There will be some indications that should arouse your concern, but none are certain evidence of abuse and, for this reason, you will not find short checklists of 'signs and symptoms' for physical abuse or the other categories of abuse in this section. Checklists can mislead playworkers, especially the less experienced, and discourage a crucial observation of individual children's behaviour, age, abilities and current development.

Accidental and non-accidental injury

It is not your responsibility to assess whether an injury is accidental or non-accidental and even thorough medical examinations do not always establish the facts beyond doubt. However, your knowledge of the individual child, of development in general and your observations of the child in your setting will all be valuable in building an accurate picture. It is necessary to bear some key issues in mind:

- Children and young people can hurt themselves during normal, energetic play. However, most accidental injuries are on the parts of the body that stick out, like elbows or knees. Children are less likely to hurt themselves on the insides of limbs, on the cheeks of their face or to get symmetrical injuries like two black eyes.
- Naturally occurring differences of skin colouration can look like bruising on children of African–Caribbean, Mediterranean and Asian origin. These so-

called Mongolian blue spots have a defined edge and are a consistent slate blue in colour, whereas genuine bruising varies in shade and changes over a period of days. Admittedly, it can be harder to see genuine bruising on dark-skinned children and young people.

- It is necessary to consider the visible injury to the child and any explanations of how this injury was caused. With genuine accidents, the responsible adult is likely to have acted quickly to help the child, the description of the incident is reasonably consistent between everyone involved and the child does not appear to be fearful or wary.
- Disabled children and young people may be more vulnerable to accidents but be just as aware of a sequence of unexplained accidents as you would with any child. Some abused children have been overlooked because carers have been too quick to explain away signs in terms of the child's disability.

Some behavioural signs should concern you, and are probably indications of emotional distress but these are not certain signs of abuse.

- Be wary if a child seems keen to hide any injuries, although do not assume that an unwillingness to undress, for instance for swimming, is necessarily evidence of abuse. Some children may have cultural or religious reasons for modesty or be self-conscious about their body for some other reason.
- You need to explore what is happening if a child is very resistant to going home with a particular carer or being with an individual playworker or volunteer.
- You should be concerned if a child or young person harms themselves or threatens to do so; this is not a normal developmental phase.
- Be aware of significant changes in what has been the normal behaviour for this child, including regression (going backwards) in development but there may be different explanations, only one of which is abuse.

GOOD PRACTICE

Signs of distress and possible abuse are not a two-way street and it is crucial that playworkers do not develop a simplistic outlook in child protection. For instance, you will find bed wetting on some checklists for behavioural signs of child abuse. Some older children, who have been abused, do start to wet the bed at night, when they have been reliably dry. However, many children who start to bed wet have not been abused. They are likely to be distressed or worried about something, in addition to the embarrassment that they are wetting the bed.

ABUSE THROUGH NEGLECT

Persistent and severe neglect can include different kinds of failure to care properly for a child and this pattern can be especially dangerous with very young children or children whose disabilities mean they are dependent on their carer for basic food, hygiene and health needs.

- Children may be given inadequate food so that they are malnourished or actually starving. Young or disabled children may be fed in such a careless way that they cannot swallow or keep food down.

Children and young people may show their distress even if they say nothing

■ Children may not be given warm enough clothes for the time of year, so are cold and ill throughout the winter months. They may be in unheated bedrooms with insufficient bedclothes for the temperature.

■ There can be gross neglect of a child's basic physical needs. They and their clothes may be dirty, or they have infections or persistent problems like head lice that would have improved with basic medical attention and home care.

■ Neglectful treatment also covers the carers' failure to provide a minimum level of emotional and intellectual stimulation in order to support children's development and behavioural learning.

Making sense of signs that concern you
Children who are neglected will show the results of their poor care in different ways:

■ Some children are always on the lighter side in weight, but neglected children can be very thin and malnourished children can be tired and lethargic. They may eat surprisingly large amounts when it is available, and may seem desperate to get and perhaps take away food.

■ Children may show the signs of being cold on a regular basis, such as chapped hands, severe chilblains or unnaturally reddened skin in a white child.

■ Children may look dirty and smell unwashed. This can cause serious problems for children because their peers may refuse to play with them.

■ Be concerned for children whose basic medical conditions or infections are left to worsen and their parent or carer seems not to use basic home care nor seek medical treatment.

■ Children who have a considerable number of accidents may be neglected in the sense that their parent or carer fails to take appropriate care and offer supervision suitable for the child, given his or her age and disabilities.

■ Be aware that, although sometimes all the children within a family are neglected, sometimes only one child is targeted for ill-treatment and his or her siblings are reasonably well treated.

You may know that some families whose children attend your setting are experiencing serious stress, financial or otherwise. It is appropriate to offer such support as you can and to avoid unrealistically high expectations of parents. However, your professional responsibility is for the child's safety and well-being. You and your colleagues may need to consult within your local child protection network, because the best that this family can manage is still leaving the child at serious risk.

Activity   7.2
Read the Good Practice above. If this could be a sensitive and relevant issue for your setting, discuss within your team how you might handle the priorities.

EMOTIONAL ABUSE OF CHILDREN AND YOUNG PEOPLE

Emotional abuse is effectively part of all ill-treatment or neglect of children, since adults are undermining children's trust and their human right to see themselves as individuals who deserve security and care. For some children, a pattern of emotional abuse is the only form of abuse in their lives.

KEY POINT

Continuing emotional ill-treatment and rejection of children damages their development and sense of self-worth. Children may be physically unharmed, but so badly affected by the emotional abuse that they have difficulties in making relationships, experience poor health or react by harming themselves.

Children or young people who are emotionally abused may experience some combination of the following cruel treatment:
■ They are regularly told that they are 'stupid', 'hopeless', 'ugly' or 'should never have been born'. Their interests and achievements may be ridiculed in comparison with another favoured child, perhaps a sibling.
■ Adults impose continuous criticism or impossible expectations, given the child's age or experience. Children may be made to feel guilty for circumstances over which they have no control.
■ Children can be emotionally damaged because they are drawn into domestic violence, forced to take sides or to conspire in the family secret.
■ Emotional abuse sometimes emerges through an excessively protective attitude by an adult towards the child or young person, so that the individual is unable to learn to feel and act competently.

Making sense of signs that concern you

No adults are patient all the time, but responsible and caring adults treat children with respect and make the effort to put right their mistakes. Children can be remarkably forgiving of adults' off-days. However, they are worn down by ill-treatment by an adult or young person that is continued, despite the obvious distress of the child who is targeted. Any of the following patterns of behaviour in children should concern you.

- Children who frequently tell you that they think they are worthless, stupid or unattractive. They may communicate through words and their body language.
- Children who frequently blame themselves or seem to expect you to think they are useless or in the wrong.
- Never overlook children who harm themselves, for instance, with fierce hair pulling, picking their skin or head banging. You should also be concerned about children who have compulsive rituals such as very lengthy hand washing.
- Children who have persistent difficulties in making friends and the reason seems to be that they do not expect anyone to like them.

GOOD PRACTICE

Children who have experienced emotional abuse often need considerable amounts of reassurance and encouragement, because they are having to unlearn the negative view of themselves imposed through the abuse. Your support may be a most important experience for an emotionally abused child, especially since a child protection case based only on emotional abuse is very hard to prove.

Activity   **7.3**

Plan and give a presentation to your colleagues outlining the ways in which a playwork team, and specifically your own, could support children and young people who are emotionally abused.

SEXUAL ABUSE OF CHILDREN AND YOUNG PEOPLE

Sexual abuse is defined as the actual or likely sexual exploitation of a child or young person, who is dependent or developmentally immature, either because of age in years or the impact of learning disabilities. The younger or vulnerable individual is unable to give genuine consent to acts that would be acceptable between adults. However, some sexual abuse also involves acts, or levels of force, that would be criminal even if only adults were involved. Available statistics suggest that more girls than boys have experienced sexual abuse, but both sexes are potentially at risk. Some children are abused just once, or for a very short period of time. However, some children or young people experience sexual abuse over many years.

Sexually abusive actions towards children and young people may involve any of the following:

- forced touching of children in an intimate way, sexual fondling and masturbation
- oral or anal sex, or full sexual intercourse
- voyeurism or sexual exhibitionism from adults, or young people, towards younger or more vulnerable children
- coercing children or young people into looking at pornographic photographs or films or taking part in such filming.

The harm of sexual abuse

Children can be physically harmed by some sexual practices, but they are also psychologically damaged by the experience. Adults are responsible for helping children and young people to establish the boundaries for appropriate physical contact and trust of others. Sexual abusers disrupt the very boundaries that they should help to create. They distort children's understanding of relationships because abusers replace proper affection with sexual contact. Children can experience distressing feelings of guilt and emotional confusion, especially since sexual abusers are most often family members, family friends or other people in a position of trust.

Who are the sexual abusers?

The vast majority of sexual abusers are already known to children, or the abuser takes time and trouble to get to know a child. Most identified sexual abusers have been men, but women have been involved and young people sometimes sexually abuse children. Responsible professionals cannot afford to hold neat assumptions about likely abusers.

Paedophiles are people, mostly men, who are only sexually attracted to children below the age of sexual consent. Paedophiles often spend a great deal of time gaining a position of trust with children, through a job or voluntary activity or becoming a friend of the family. This process is called grooming.

GOOD PRACTICE

One way that paedophiles try to gain access to children is by working or volunteering in play and leisure facilities. Careful checks on new workers or volunteers are crucial to protect children. However, an atmosphere encouraging clear communication of any concerns within the playwork team is also essential, since police checks and following up references will only identify paedophiles with a record of previous offences or dubious behaviour.

Activity 7.4

Within a team meeting, review and discuss your own checks and procedures in the setting.

Making sense of signs that concern you

You need to weigh up your observations of children, and what they say, in the context of this individual child and realistic developmental expectations.

- It is not within normal development for children to persist in trying to make physically intimate contact with other children or with adults, especially once the other person has said 'No'.
- Children who are abused may express their experiences through pretend play with dolls or other children, or through sexually explicit drawings.
- Children usually learn that masturbation is a private activity so those who continue to touch themselves in front of others should concern you.
- Be very careful about explaining away sexualised behaviour as part of a child's disability. Such inaccurate clichés have left some disabled children and young people at risk.
- What children say should alert you, if it shows a sexual knowledge or curiosity unlikely for their age.
- Young people who have been abused may indulge in sexually risky behaviour, because they have low self-esteem and only understand sharing affection through sexual activity.
- Significant changes in a child's behaviour, fears, and regressions in their development may be provoked by sexual abuse, but not for certain.
- Some physical symptoms should always lead to a medical check for their origin. Pain or bruising, bleeding, itching or redness in the genital or anal area all need prompt attention and may be abusive in origin. However, untreated thrush or threadworms cause problems and children could hurt themselves in a fall, although this is an unusual site for accidental injury.
- Pregnancy in an under-age girl and evidence of a sexually-transmitted disease in either sex will indicate sexual abuse or risky sexual activity, which would in itself be cause for concern.

GOOD PRACTICE

In the past professionals and parents have sometimes found it hard to believe that anyone would abuse a disabled child. In fact disabled children and young people can be highly vulnerable to all kinds of abuse, including sexual. Be careful that neither you, nor your colleagues, dismiss warning signs. If this kind of behaviour, play or pattern of injury would usually concern you, then ask yourself, 'Why are we not concerned about this child or young person?'

Good practice in child protection

Playworkers need to extend their specific knowledge and understanding of child abuse, but a responsible approach to child protection uses all the other skills of good playwork practice, including:

- respect for children and young people and readiness to listen to them
- alertness to what children are doing and saying in your setting, using your skills of observation and where appropriate good written records

- good communication within your playwork team: that everyone feels able to raise concerns or doubts about children and be heard, rather than being given the message that they are 'making a fuss about nothing'
- established communication with other local professionals, which in terms of child protection means finding out names and telephone numbers before you experience a serious worry or crisis
- good working relationships wherever possible with parents and carers of children, so that you feel more able to raise concerns and the parents feel able to talk with you. Some playwork settings have more regular contact with parents than others.

KEY POINT

Playworkers, like any other practitioners with children and young people, need to take a balanced approach. It is important not to jump to conclusions about a child, nor to be actively looking for problems. However, you need to take your concerns seriously and to avoid any complacency of 'it couldn't happen around here'.

KNOW YOUR PROCEDURES

Any playwork setting should have a clear, written policy and procedures for child protection. Every playworker or volunteer should have read and understood these procedures. Everyone should be clear about the responsibilities of your team and the responsibilities of other professionals in the local child protection system. Local authorities may work slightly differently, but they all share the same legal obligations under the Children Act 1989 for England and Wales and, in other parts of the UK, the Children (Scotland) Act 1995 and the Children (Northern Ireland) Order 1995.

Clear child protection procedures are shared and understood by the whole team. The details may vary slightly from setting to setting but should include procedures for:
- when you have concerns about a child or young person that could indicate child abuse
- when a child makes a disclosure of abuse occurring outside the setting or there is an injury that requires explanation
- when there is a medical or other emergency relating to the safety of children or the team
- when an allegation has been made about another child or young person in the setting, or about a playworker or other adult involved in the setting
- the content of reports that should be written up when there is a child protection issue in the setting. An example of the guidance notes from one local authority is given on page 175.

It *is* your responsibility to:
- be alert to the behaviour, development and well-being of the children and young people in your setting

APPENDIX B

CHILD PROTECTION REPORT

The following information must be included in reports concerning suspected child abuse even if no further action is taken. Such reports are confidential and must be kept in locked files. Reports should be written as soon as possible after an incident but definitely within 24 hours.

· date and place of incident

· Name of child
· Name of parent/carer
· Address
· Telephone number
· Age
· Gender
· Siblings
· School attended

· Name of worker
· Child's level of contact with project

What took place
· Source of information (i.e. indirect or direct disclosure)
· Observed behavioural concerns

Action taken:
· Have parents/carers been contacted?
· When was Line Manager contacted?
· When was Social Services contacted and who was the contact?
· Was anyone else contacted (i.e. Police, Doctor, etc.)?

Summing up:

· It is important to separate fact from opinion

Careful records must be kept of all action taken concerning an incident. For example, time, date and name of Duty Social Worker when reporting suspected child abuse. These records must be kept confidential.

Guidance notes used by a local authority

- explore sensitively any concerns you have, that the children themselves raise directly with you, about themselves or a friend, or that other adults (colleagues, parents or other carers) talk over with you
- pass on to your senior, or decide yourself if you are the senior playleader, whether the matter should be taken further and know whom to contact, including what to do if an allegation of abuse is made about anyone within your team
- know the details of your local child protection system, i.e. the names and contact numbers of relevant professionals to consult and inform.

It is *not* your responsibility to investigate possible child abuse, nor to try to assess whether abuse or non-accidental injury has in fact taken place. That task belongs to the social worker and other members of the local child protection team. Your valuable contribution to the process will be through your observations, communication and support of a child or young person within your setting.

Find out about your local child protection system
You will most probably be expected to contact someone within social services: a named child protection officer, a unit or the duty social worker. The NSPCC has a local branch in some areas and works closely with social services but this organisation, the only national children's charity that legally can investigate child abuse, may not be active in your local area. The local police services will be part of the child protection system, but they would not be your first contact unless you had good reason to be concerned for a child's immediate physical safety or that of your team.

Activity 7.5

Look at the relevant documents that have been drawn up by your local authority and check that you are clear about the principles and procedures in operation for your setting. Make sure that they are understood by all the other members of your team, including any volunteers.

Explore the details, ensure that you are clear about playworkers' responsibilities and summarise these in writing for your team, including any areas of potential confusion or uncertainty.

Talking with the child or young person
In many everyday instances, your first action will be to follow up a concern with children or young people themselves. Often your courteous questions will produce a straightforward explanation from the child which removes your concern; see for instance the case study below.

CASE STUDY   7.6

At the Downham after-school club, Liam turns up one afternoon with a large bump on his head. At registration Mike asks him about it.

Mike: Hiya, Liam! That's a bit of a bump. How did you do that, then?

Liam: Crashed into Betty in the school playground.

Mike: Did you? That must have been some crash! How's Betty?

Liam: She's got a bump too.

Mike: I bet she has. Is it sore?

Liam: No, she's okay, but my bump's much bigger!

Mike: What did your teacher say?

Liam: That I had to sit down for a while. And I should look where I was going. But Betty and me were playing a good game!

Mike: Who was that? Your teacher, I mean?

Liam: Mrs Boyce.

Mike: Okay then. Perhaps you'd better start with a quiet activity today.

Questions

1   What has this exchange told Mike about what happened?
2   Do you think he asked Liam enough questions? Too many?
3   What should be Mike's next step?
4   Share your views on this example with a colleague. Listen to her or his perspective and opinions.

When you are still concerned

In the case study of Mike and Liam, the child's replies and openness will have reassured Mike. He may still have an informal conversation with Liam's teacher, but there is nothing in the exchange to worry Mike that the event is anything other than a normal childhood accident.

You can ask a child who is injured or appears to be in distress what has happened. You may need to broach the topic again or to stress to a child that you are still concerned and this is the reason you are talking privately with her or him. In settings where you have regular contact with parents or carers, you need to ask what has happened, if there is an obvious injury, or to express your concerns about a child's behaviour. When you remain concerned, it is important to support and respond to a child or young person about whom you have worries. However, it is not a playworker's job to investigate, cross-question or interview children formally. Inappropriate questioning may risk further harm to the child or possibly confuse a later child protection investigation.

Playworkers need to be cautious and avoid leaping to conclusions. You are working to separate the ordinary from the extraordinary. You do this by:

■ checking your concerns with the child or young person
■ asking yourself if the incident is a 'one-off' or if it has it happened on a number of occasions and what this might mean
■ allowing for the age of the child or young person and their developmental maturity, including any disabilities

- establishing the child's circumstances and any earlier concerns through your records and discussion with colleagues.

DEALING WITH DISCLOSURES

Sometimes children will tell you directly that someone, outside or inside your setting, is hurting or distressing them. Children sometimes tell or show their concerns in a throw-away or even joking manner. They may want to see how you react, and whether you seem likely to be supportive or to believe them. Other children may ask you a factual or 'What do you think about...' question, and the content makes you wonder. You need to be alert and sensitive to these signals and to any concerns raised in children's play, their relations with each other or the content of their stories or drawings.

GOOD PRACTICE

You should never keep feelings of concern or unease to yourself. No matter how minor it seems, talk your concern over with another staff member. She or he can help you make the important distinctions between fact and opinion, ordinary and extraordinary. A colleague can also sometimes help you locate the observations that underlie what seems to be a 'gut feeling' to you, but is rooted in what children have done or not done, or have said.

When dealing with disclosures the most valuable skills are those of communication, especially listening, that you use in all your work with children. Useful guidelines include:
- Give time and attention for a private conversation as long as the child wants. If you really cannot talk, then make sure that you let them know you have heard and talk with them very soon, certainly the same day.
- Listen to what the child or young person is telling you. There is no need to rush and get someone more senior. This reaction is likely to stop the child, who has, after all, chosen to talk with you.
- Hear the child's words and the way she or he tells you this confidence.
- If children have disabilities then it may be even more important to draw on the full range of communication abilities: yours and those of the child.
- Respond to a slightly worrying question or comment with remarks such as, 'That's an unusual question, what makes you ask that?' or 'I don't think I'd be too happy about.... What's your opinion?'
- Keep your questions open-ended and encouraging. So avoid questions that push a child in a specific direction or assume that you know what he or she is feeling.
- You can also encourage a child by your open and attentive expression and simple questions like 'Yes?' or 'Anything else you want to tell me?'
- Reassure children or young people that you take what they say seriously. If appropriate, reassure or comfort them.
- Explain when you will have to take the matter further. You cannot promise

secrecy, but you can say you will only tell those few people who need to know in order to help the child. Reassure them that they will not be the butt of gossip.

■ Never imply that the child should have told earlier. Children often have difficulty in confiding about abuse. They may be frightened by the abuser or sure that they will be disbelieved. Children also have painfully mixed feelings about an abuser who is within the family.

When disabled children disclose, you need to use your full communication skills

If a child confides possible abuse, you should make full notes on the conversation after it is over, and certainly with no more delay than later in the same day. Your notes should include specific details such as:

■ when and where the child spoke with you
■ what the child said to you – note it down as accurately as you can recall, using the child's own words only when you are sure you recall them correctly
■ any injuries that you observed or that the child showed to you.

Avoid any guesses or speculations about what has happened. You should take the child seriously; it is not your role to work out exactly where the truth lies in the events.

Pass on the details of the conversation and your concern promptly to your senior.

What do children want when they disclose?
Adults have responsibilities in child protection but these will be better fulfilled when you hold onto the likely perspective of the children themselves. When children tell about abuse or being bullied, they want:

■ an end to the abuse or bullying now
■ to feel safe from now on and to able to access help as and when they wish.

They do not want:

- the telling to make matters worse – they may fear that they will not be believed or protected after telling
- to have their life, or that of their family, turned upside down and then to feel guilty about having told.

GOOD PRACTICE

Undoubtedly normal life is disrupted one way or another when a child protection investigation is under way. You can support children or young people by ensuring that they are informed, as appropriate, and do not feel disempowered by the process they believe they started. Your continued willingness to listen can be important but your setting may also offer a vital safe place and relationships where the child can just carry on as normally as possible.

Activity 7.7

Here are a number of scenarios which might occur in play settings. Read them through and for each one ask yourself the following questions:

- If you faced this situation, how concerned would you be? What are the grounds for your concern?
- What would be your first step?
- With whom should you consult?

When you have gathered your own views, discuss some examples with one or two of your colleagues.

1 At Downham after-school club a mother complained to Ian, the club leader, that her son, James, had brought home a sexually explicit drawing. Upon challenging him, her son had explained that another boy, Dennis, had in fact done the drawing and given it to James. Both boys are eight years old. You have been concerned from some throwaway remarks from Dennis that elsewhere he probably watches videos with 15 or 18 rating.

2 During the Grafton Road holiday playscheme one summer Maria, an assistant worker, had taken a group of children swimming. She had been particularly pleased that Tony, a nine-year-old, had come on the trip as he had seemed quiet and fed up recently. When Tony got changed for the pool Maria noticed he had a number of bruises and welts on his back. Some of the bruises were beginning to fade and looked almost healed but some looked new. The welts looked particularly red and sore. The other children noticed and asked Tony how he got them, which he fended off with a non-committal 'I don't know'. Maria intervened to ensure that Tony enjoyed his time at the pool but is now uncertain what to do.

3 Katie is fourteen years old and a regular user of the Hummingbird adventure playground. She has developed a close relationship with Sandra, one of the assistant workers, and enjoys talking to her. Katie's mother remarried when Katie was thirteen and she has never got on very well with her step-dad. Just recently she has been complaining more and more to Sandra, but it is always

non-specific. She says things like: 'He's always unfair', 'My mum always takes his side' and 'My real dad would never do what he does'.

4   At St Dunstan's play centre Maureen, the worker in charge, arrived one day to discover an angry parent waiting for her. The mother asked to see Maureen and alleged that Angus, one of Maureen's assistants, had shouted at and hit her eleven-year-old son during the previous evening's session. The boy had apparently burst into tears on the way home yesterday and his mother says this was the explanation she had managed to get out of him. The mother demanded to know what Maureen was going to do. Maureen finds it very hard to believe that Angus would behave in this way to a child.

5   When the Fun on the Estates mobile playbus visits the Beckton housing estate, John, a boy of fifteen who acts much younger than his age, regularly turns up to play. He likes to play with the younger children but they always shun him because he smells so badly. He is also ridiculed by some of the older users who call him names and push him around in what they claim is 'a bit of a fun'.

6   Fatima is a new user at the Willow Tree adventure playground. Despite the efforts of all the team to make her feel welcome she never participates in any of the group activities. She is always the one on the outside – rarely smiling, biting her nails and looking generally anxious. One evening, Elroy, the senior worker makes a special effort to talk to her and encourage her to join in but she just says that she is not in the mood and wants to be left alone. Later that same evening Fatima has an argument with another child and leaves the playground in tears.

PLAYWORKERS' FEELINGS

If you find yourself dealing with a situation of child abuse, it is important to recognise that your feelings are also involved; the situation is not only about procedures and good communication with the children. You may be distressed or angered when you hear of a child's experience. It is important that your feelings, however valid, do not get in the way of your listening to and supporting the child or young person. However, you also need support and this will most likely come from your colleagues or in a supervision session with your senior.

It is also possible that one playworker within a team, even if this is not you, will have experienced some kind of abuse as a child. The current situation may release unhappy memories and an experience of child protection training can also bring memories to the surface. Personal experience of abuse, or bullying, does not automatically make you either better or worse equipped to support a child now. The main issue, as with any of your own childhood experiences, is that your own perspective and emotional needs do not become entangled with those of this child or young person now.

PROGRESS CHECK

1   Name two signs that would arouse your concerns about:
    i) physical abuse
    ii) neglect
    iii) emotional abuse
    iv) sexual abuse
2   Describe three myths or unhelpful assumptions about likely abusers or abuse.
3   Identify three factors that could make disabled children or young people more vulnerable to abuse.
4   According to the child protection procedures in your setting, what are the steps you should take and who are the people you should inform, if you have reason to believe a child or young person is at risk?

Bullying between children and young people

WHAT IS BULLYING?

Bullying, whether verbal or physical, is a type of aggressive behaviour. It is unprovoked in the usual sense of the word and certainly does not justify the level of response made in return. Bullying is intended to hurt the person on the receiving end, either physically or emotionally.

Bullying between children and young people is not new. Previous generations have always had some experience of bullying, in terms of:

■   direct experience of being bullied
■   trying to help a friend who is on the receiving end
■   remaining a bystander: excited by the drama, too frightened or indifferent to help
■   being a bully or a member of a group that bullies.

There has been a significant change of attitude in recent years, with a greater sense of adult responsibility to take bullying seriously and take effective action in settings run by adults. Playworkers share that obligation to create an atmosphere in which children who are bullied are able to tell and to be helped. The adult responsibility also extends to supporting those children who do the bullying. There are positive parallels in good practice between child protection and dealing with bullying. In fact, some of the actions of bullies between peers would most likely be judged to be abusive between an adult and a child or young person.

KEY POINT

Children's previous experiences will shape how they approach a problematic situation in your play setting. They will have beliefs about how likely it is that they will be able to resolve an unhappy situation and expectations about the possible usefulness of asking adults to help.

Types of bullying

Bullying can include:

- physical attack or the threat of attack unless the child or young person agrees to demands
- intimidation to get money and possessions, or to induce cooperation in activities that the other child initially refuses
- verbal bullying about anything particular to the child or young person or their family – children have been targeted for almost anything that gives the bullies a 'hook' and distresses the child
- harassment with sexual overtones including sometimes coerced sexual activity.

GOOD PRACTICE

Bullying between children does not follow patterns that would meet the expectations of less reflective adults. For instance, girls bully boys as well as each other, children from poor families may be targeted, but some middle-class children have been mercilessly bullied for supposedly being 'posh'. In an ethnically diverse community there will almost certainly be some racist bullying, but black children are also sometimes the bullies. Helpful adults take each situation as it comes and use skills of observation and communication to avoid assumptions about who is the bully and why.

Activity   7.8
In your team, discuss some of the issues outlined in the Good Practice above.

Playwork settings need a clear policy with positive practices to deal with bullying. You may place this within a positive behaviour policy (see also Chapter 6) but you also need links to your child protection procedures. High levels of physical or verbal intimidation between children, and certainly if bullying includes a sexual element, should trigger concern in a playwork team. The child or young person, who is doing the bullying, may have experienced abusive treatment and is playing out strong emotions or paying back the world for the bad experience.

Signs of possible bullying

Playworkers need to be aware of changes in children they know well, without assuming that every change is caused by bullying. For instance:

- Children and young people may tell you directly that they are being bullied in your setting or elsewhere, for instance at school or on the way home.
- Children may have unexplained injuries, torn or dirty clothes, missing possessions or money. They may be very hungry in your after-school club, because someone is stealing their packed lunch or lunch money.
- Children's behaviour may change from how you have known them up to now. For instance, they may have a significant loss of confidence, or appear to be fearful of or subservient towards particular children.

- You may notice compulsive behaviour such as excessive washing or concern about weight, because bullies have called them 'dirty', 'smelly' or 'fatty'.
- Children who are being bullied may have a range of health symptoms, including a general depression. They may express feelings of hopelessness and in extreme cases resort to self-harm.

KEY POINT

Notice that some of the signs of possible bullying are similar to those of possible child abuse. Such observations should always raise your concerns, but it is important not to rush to conclusions about what is happening and who is harming the child.

Activity 7.9

If you are concerned that some children are being bullied in your play setting, you will need to be alert, observe what is happening and record your observations accurately. Be careful to support your concerns and to distinguish fact from opinion.

   If such a situation arises, follow the guidelines in this section and write up your observations.

Why do children and young people bully?

Different reasons can underlie bullying and, of course, reasons are not excuses. However, you will be more helpful if you keep an open mind about what is happening and why.

- Some children and young people bully because they have no idea that they should limit their demands. They may have been indulged by their families.
- Some children are 'victims-turned-bullies'. They had a bad experience when they were younger and now it is payback time.
- Some children or young people have very poor self-image and use bullying, physical or verbal, to boost themselves and feel powerful.
- Some bullies are drawn in as part of a group that intimidates others. The less keen bullies have to leave the group if they refuse to join in and may have a realistic fear that they will then become new targets.

THE ROLE OF PLAYWORKER

All responsible adults, in any group situation, need to create a supportive atmosphere in which children and young people feel reassured that their disclosure about bullying will be taken seriously and that adults will help them resolve the situation. Look again at the section on page 179 on What do children want when they disclose?

Good practice includes the following:

- Listen carefully to what is said by the children or young people on the receiving end.
- Take what they say seriously; it has upset or frightened them, even if it initially seems minor to you. Verbal bullying can make a child desperately unhappy; they do not have to have been hit.
- Have as calm a conversation as possible with the child, young person or group who are accused.
- Model calm problem solving, for example: 'Hamid was telling me something earlier that I find very disturbing. He says that the three of you regularly call him a "Paki bastard". And he says you all kicked him yesterday when he refused to give you money. I want to know your side of all this. Go ahead, I'm listening.'
- Be ready to challenge the bullies. For instance, children who bully will sometimes claim, 'It's just a joke!' You need to communicate very clearly that real jokes are shared by everyone involved. The bullies did not stop when it was very clear that the child they were harassing was distressed or scared. So this was not a piece of fun at all
- Come to as clear a view as you can of what happened. Impose consequences where appropriate: perhaps the opportunity to make an apology and certainly to return or replace anything taken from another child.

KEY POINT

It is very important to avoid adult behaviour that is bullying in its turn. So, no hauling out of the accused, shouting at children and summary justice. Listen to what everyone has to say and be very careful with your own assumptions about who is, or is not, likely to be telling the truth.

Look at what further action needs to be taken.

- Support children on the receiving end in any way appropriate. Affirm that they were right to tell, and work to boost their self-confidence or skills of assertiveness if this might help.
- Consider the possible reasons for the bullies' behaviour and what you could do to redirect them, including supporting them to meet their emotional needs in less harmful ways.
- Less keen bullies within a bullying group may need help to establish other friendships.
- Do you need to talk with bystanders, exploring how they felt unable or unwilling to tell or help?

GOOD PRACTICE

Children have the right to be taken seriously when they confide that someone is ill-treating them. But playworkers should take neither a child's, nor a parent's, accusation as proof without further checking. There are definite parallels in good practice in dealing with bullying and in child protection.

CASE STUDY   7.11

Sian is ten years old. She is currently having trouble with three slightly older girls, who attend her primary school and Downham after-school club. These other girls criticise Sian's clothes and make fun of her hairstyle. The weeks of rude remarks and mocking laughter are beginning to make Sian wonder if there is something laughable about her.

In the after-school club, Zoë notices Sian's hurt expression and catches the end of that day's criticism from the older girls. She asks Sian to help her in getting the snacks ready and takes the opportunity to ask, 'You look sad, Sian. What I heard back there – from Josie and her mates – is that happening a lot?' Zoë sounds genuinely concerned and so Sian explains what has been happening, and her upset that she cannot think what she has done to deserve it.

Zoë listens carefully and helps Sian to think about what she could say to Josie and the other girls. Sian has been held back by the belief that you should not be rude to people. Zoë introduces the idea that perhaps Josie and the others have lost any right to politeness, because of the way that they have behaved. They agree to have a chat with Sian's mother when she comes to pick her up.

Questions

1 What might be the reasons why Sian had not told anyone of her troubles?
2 How might Zoë help Sian from now on?
3 How might Zoë tackle the girls who have been doing the bullying?
4 Discuss some of your views with a colleague.

SEXUAL OVERTONES IN BULLYING

Bullying may have a sexual element through verbal or physical harassment. Or your careful exploration of what has happened might start to reveal sexual activity outside the normal boundaries for this group of young people.

Sometimes children may gang up on an individual

Sometimes children or young people who are being sexually abused start to abuse others while they are themselves still young. The inappropriate or bullying behaviour of a child may be the first warning sign that they are, or have been, sexually abused.

It is often not straightforward to reach a judgement about whether an activity is sexually abusive between older children and young people. As with any delicate issue, you need to discuss the matter with colleagues, especially since your child protection procedures should be followed if you become concerned about possible abuse. You have to weigh up:

- the age of all the involved children and young people and what is within normal range for flirtatious behaviour, rude language, dirty jokes and physical contact for this age group
- relevant factors such as the learning or physical disabilities of individual children involved
- worrying aspects of the situation such as any suggestion of pressure and coercion, or enforced secrecy from one child to another.

PROGRESS CHECK

1 Describe three signs that could alert you to possible bullying in your play setting.
2 Identify three ways in which a playworker could support a child who is being bullied, without placing the child in a more difficult position.
3 Describe one way in which good practice over bullying will link with anti-discriminatory practice and another link to child protection procedures.

Helping children and young people with personal safety

You can take a realistic and positive approach in supporting children and young people to learn about keeping themselves safe, so long as you bear in mind the following:

- Children need to learn to feel competent in many aspects of their daily life. Personal safety is best approached as part of growing up, rather than something children have to face because of a long list of dangers.
- Playworkers can be an important part of helping children learn to keep themselves safe, but remember that other key adults, including parents, should be part of this process. This a shared adult responsibility.
- Children and young people learn about personal safety over the months and years. It is certainly not something that can be covered in one conversation, nor 'done' within a special session at your setting. Be ready to revisit any of the key issues as users wish and as the opportunity arises.

KEY POINT

It is unwise to wait until something happens to unsettle you or the users of your setting. Look at opportunities within the natural pattern of your time with children to support them to keep themselves safe and deal with likely risks.

POSITIVE STRATEGIES

A vital part of your support of children and young people is to build their self-confidence and a conviction of their own self-worth. You will approach this area in many aspects of your playwork and some key themes are described below.

Time and attention within a friendly relationship

- Make a habit of listening to what children want to say to you and take them seriously when they express feelings, worries, confusions, or dislikes about people.
- You would not necessarily agree, especially if children say they find somebody unpleasant or creepy. However, you would ask in an open-ended way, 'What does she do that you dislike so much?' or 'What makes you say he's creepy?'

Feelings, choices and decisions

- Set a good example in being willing to talk appropriately about feelings, with the boys as well as the girls. For instance, you might agree that a particular video made you sad too, or join in a conversation about the possible motivations of a character in a television programme.
- Take suitable opportunities to explain your own decisions that affect safety. For instance, you might explain, particularly when children ask you the

question, that you were sharp with the person on the other end of the telephone because it was a rude call. Or there might a time to explain, 'I was uneasy about that man in the park, what he was saying seemed very odd. That's why I brought us all away.'

■ Give children a wide range of opportunities to make choices in your setting, with conversation as appropriate about the likely consequences of different options.

■ Help children to develop skills in decision making and problem solving, so that they can view themselves as active and not passive in daily situations.

Rights and responsibilities

■ Children who are treated with respect can learn about the boundaries to personal space and their rights over their own bodies, including a right to say, 'No'.

■ Within a more sensitive conversation, you may talk about 'good' and 'bad' touches or what makes children uncomfortable, 'happy' sitting distances and about 'private' areas of their body.

■ Good practice in physical care, with an appreciation of privacy, is crucial for older children, especially those with disabilities that mean they will need help beyond the age when their friends can manage.

■ Children and young people need ground rules that help them learn consideration of others but not absolutes that put them at risk, such as 'Always be polite to adults' or 'Never yell or hit'.

■ Explain that adults have responsibilities as well, such as not placing children in a difficult position over dubious requests. Adults who behave badly do not deserve courtesy.

■ You will encourage children to deal non-aggressively with their peers (see Chapter 6) but children and young people also need a sensible conversation about when physical self-defence can be an appropriate option. Such an exploration also needs to be kept realistic; there are situations in which the best defence is to run away as fast as possible.

GOOD PRACTICE

Good communication with parents is important to explain what you are doing, and are not trying to do, in terms of supporting children's personal safety. Look for different ways of sharing this information: talking with parents with whom you have contact, open sessions at your setting, letters and other written communication.

Activity   7.12
Prepare and make a short presentation to your team on effective communication with parents and carers.

Be realistic

■ Definitely avoid the trap of focusing on 'stranger danger'. Children and young people are most at risk from adults and other young people whom they know. Sensible precautions should include reactions to strangers and scarcely known adults, but very few children are abducted and hurt by total strangers.

■ Focus on boosting children's confidence and range of strategies to deal with what adults say or do. Stress that it is not a child's responsibility to sort out the 'bad' strangers or less known acquaintances from the 'safe' ones. On the contrary, it is the responsibility of all adults to behave properly towards children.

■ Help children to realise that abusers, for instance paedophiles, look normal, 'just like anybody else'. Encourage children and young people to go by people's behaviour and whether this feels right, now or later on.

Resources

Use of books and stories, leaflets, posters and videos can be a useful support in helping children and young people to talk about and learn strategies in personal safety. However, it is important not to depend completely on media resources. They are no substitute for attentive and personal conversations when children want to share a concern or ask you questions.

Playworkers as people will probably be the most useful support to a child or young person: what you say and do, your willingness to listen and the positive role model that you show in how to deal with uncertain or worrying situations.

Activity   7.13

The NSPCC regularly publishes leaflets about personal safety and related topics. Adults can read and use the information to support younger children. Older children can read the material themselves, especially as part of a conversation with adults who listen to the perspective of the child or young person.

You could contact the NSPCC (see Appendix E for the address) for their most recent material and use the leaflets as a basis for conversations with your setting's users:

■ What is their reaction to the material? Do they feel it is useful for their own daily life?

■ What comments do the children or young people have about putting any advice into practice? What do they experience as easier or harder to do or say? What are the complications from their point of view?

■ What further information would your users like to have?

■ Write up your explorations into a short report.

PROGRESS CHECK

1   Describe two ways in which you could support children and young people to learn about personal safety.
2   Identify two reasons why a strong focus on 'stranger danger' can place children at greater risk.

KEY TERMS

You need to know what these words and phrases mean. Go back through the chapter to make sure that you understand.

Bullying
Child protection procedures
Disclosure
Emotional abuse
Neglect

Paedophile
Personal safety
Physical abuse
Sexual abuse

---

8 PRACTICAL ISSUES OF HEALTH AND SAFETY

> **This chapter covers:**
> - Policy and procedures on safety
> - The health and safety of the children on site
> - Children's safety outside the play environment

Policy and procedures on safety

Sound policies and procedures underpin all good practice in playwork and health and safety is no exception. Without a written policy that has been agreed by staff and management and communicated, where relevant, to parents, carers and children, the maintenance of a safe project can never be guaranteed. Whether it is a local authority policy that is suitable for a number of projects or one specifically designed for your facility it should encompass the key safety factors that relate to:

- the premises
- the outdoor space
- the workers and users
- volunteers, parents and the general public
- the materials and equipment.

It should indicate the standards that are required in any of the given areas and outline the procedures that are necessary to implement and maintain them. It should also state where responsibility rests and what role different people play in ensuring a safe environment. On page 193 is an extract from a policy used by a playground for children with disabilities.

> **Activity** 8.1
>
> Look out the health and safety policy for your project.
> - How does it compare with the sample?
> - Are there clear procedures?
> - Can you see what role you play in putting it into practice?
>
> Put your conclusions into a written summary and make a presentation to your team and/or management committee.

HEALTH AND SAFETY POLICY

SUPERVISION: If the playground is supervised well most accidents can be prevented. Good supervision includes:

CHILDREN NEEDING 1:1 SUPPORT/SUPERVISION: A number of children need continual one-to-one support; they must never be left unattended. If you are working on a 1:1 basis with someone and have to leave them for a short while you must hand over that responsibility clearly to another member of staff before leaving them.

EQUIPMENT: If you get out ANY tools and equipment that are potentially dangerous the responsibility for these MUST be handed over to another member of staff or the tools and equipment must be put away. This can be difficult because we all get called away or distracted, and on every playscheme there are unfortunately times when equipment has not been put away properly. Scissors are the most common problem, but also saws, etc. Everyone who works here is responsible for the safety of the children using the playground; any potentially dangerous activity must be supervised.

Tools must be used properly, both on safety grounds and to be sure they are available for maintenance purposes.

Arts and Crafts materials like face paints, plaster-bandage, etc. should NEVER be left out unsupervised or else our entire playscheme's supply can be wasted in minutes.

INDOORS/OUTDOOR: When the weather is good there is an understandable tendency for people to gravitate outside, or inside if it is raining. We all need to be aware of the need to supervise all areas of the playground, and not have one or two people stuck indoors while the rest of us bathe in the sun.

KITCHEN: Again this must either be supervised or locked. If you are running an activity in the kitchen it should usually be possible to do so without locking the door.

SOFT PLAY ROOM: When this is open it must be supervised; this often needs two workers. Some basic rules: NO FIGHTING, even play-fighting because someone always ends up getting hurt; don't let too many kids in at once; if you get stuck up there and need help or want to come down shout for help! If you are the last to leave the soft play room you must lock both the slide door and the stair door. The slide can get burning hot in hot weather, so cool it down with water, and dry with a towel. SHOES should be left on the shelves outside the toilet area.

LIFT TO SOFT PLAY: is only for use by people who need to use it. It is not to be used as a toy. Don't forget to check the wire before use, it costs about £80 to fix! You will be shown how to use it during the induction.

BIKES: The bikes are potentially dangerous — people fall off them, run over other children, go too fast and lose control. If you are outside try to be aware of potential problems.

WOOD PILE: The wood under the shelter is for structure building and not for the children to use. If you are doing wood work with the kids please use the scrap wood. The wood pile is not a safe place for the kids to play, including the roof.

ROLES AND RESPONSIBILITIES

If you are the senior member of staff you will have the responsibility of ensuring that the project is kept clean and safe and that all hazards are noticed, recorded and dealt with appropriately. It will be your job to keep your line manager or management committee fully informed and to give direction and instruction to workers and volunteers under your guidance. Good teamwork will be essential (see Chapter 9) to ensure that all staff are conversant with the health and safety issues and able to follow the necessary checks and procedures.

KEY POINT

The health, safety and well-being of not only the children, but also of yourself, your colleagues and other adults using or visiting the project is of prime importance. Although in some instances, such as the maintenance of premises, your employer or management committee may have the ultimate responsibility, your role as a playworker will be crucial. You will be the person who, on a day-to-day basis, will be implementing good practice and paying attention to any hazards and recording and reporting them.

THE BUILDING

All buildings need to be kept safe and clean. This includes:
- regular maintenance of the fabric of the building, e.g. walls, floors, doors and windows
- regular cleaning of all rooms and play spaces, particularly floors and surfaces
- keeping all exits and entrances free from obstruction
- maintaining comfortable temperatures throughout the year
- ensuring play areas are well lit
- providing toilet facilities for both sexes and disabled children that ensure privacy but allow access by staff in an emergency
- providing facilities for children to wash and dry their hands.

THE SITE

Outside areas similarly need to be safe and clean for play. On a very basic level you will need to ensure that the environment is clean and free from rubbish and hazardous items through regular checks and procedures.

GOOD PRACTICE

It is important that the users understand the need for health and safety in the play setting. Encourage them to be part of the clearing-up process and involve them in routine maintenance where appropriate. Instructing them in safe and hygienic methods of clearing up, e.g. wearing gloves and safely disposing of hazardous items, is a useful method of raising awareness in health and safety issues.

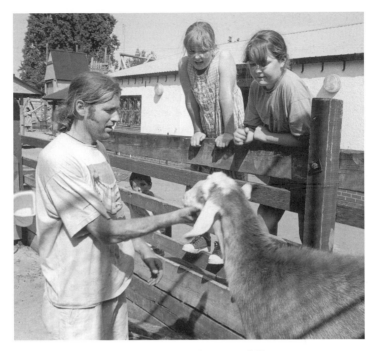

Keeping animals brings additional responsibility

Although the responsibility for maintenance and repair may not be yours, you will need to ensure that any damage or wear to permanent features such as walls, fences, surfaces and out-buildings is recorded and the appropriate person or persons informed.

ADVENTURE PLAYGROUNDS

If you are working on an adventure playground, the extent of your health and safety tasks and responsibilities may well extend beyond the very basic cleaning and maintenance jobs to repairing fences and digging over safety surfaces. One of your primary concerns will be the maintenance of the adventure play structures. You will need to ensure that:

■ the timber is not rotted or cracked
■ ropes and nets are not unduly worn or split
■ other items, such as metal cables and pulleys for aerial runways and tyres for swing seats, are not damaged or worn.

Although adventure play structures are not subject to the same legal standards as is permanent fixed equipment, they must be sound and safe for children to play on. Good practice guidelines on this can be obtained from a number of publications, organisations and agencies. (See Appendices D and E.) Whilst your play structures need to be safe this does not mean they have to be unexciting.

Risk and safety

Children enjoy taking risks and the majority do not take unnecessary risks with their health and well being but rather the step-by-step risks that can gradually extend them. The adventure playground is an ideal setting for this step-by-step approach. By using the facilities regularly a child can gradually go higher on the climbing structures, and faster on the rope swings. She or he can graduate from using a hammer and a few nails to make a camp from scrap wood to using a saw and a chisel to build a play structure from heavier timber. It is a playworker's job to provide the environment that can facilitate gradual risk-taking whilst maintaining the child's safety. A play structure is only inherently unsafe if:

- it does not conform to good practice guidelines, e.g. recommendations on maximum height are ignored
- it is built unsoundly, e.g. poor design, construction or materials
- it is allowed to fall into disrepair.

KEY POINT

Of course, there are occasions where some children will go beyond their risk threshold into a dangerous situation. In the supervised play setting it is the presence of the playworker who can prevent the dangerous situation developing into one which might result in serious injury.

REGULAR CHECKS

Playworkers' regular checks will be slightly different depending on the play setting. The three case studies which follow illustrate the variety.

After-school clubs

The Clydesdale after-school club operates at a purpose-built community centre funded by the local council and run by a local management committee. The centre has an overall health and safety policy, a safety officer and an on-site caretaker. The safety officer and caretaker have overall responsibility for the maintenance and safety of the building and regularly run full health and safety audits.

For the after-school club workers Brenda, David and Raj there only remains the day-to-day checks and the reporting of any hazards noticed or repairs that might be needed. They achieve this through daily routine observation as they prepare for their session. The observation follows a checklist which has been drawn up and agreed by workers and management. On page 199 is an extract from the checklist that the Clydesdale workers use on a daily basis.

Any routine repairs or maintenance work would be carried out on the spot, e.g. replacing a light bulb by either the playworkers or the caretaker. Those requiring more serious attention, e.g. a leaking radiator or a broken table, would be conveyed to the caretaker on a hazard report form for further attention. It might be necessary in such cases to isolate an area or remove a piece of equipment before the children arrive for play and this would be noted on the form.

In respect of their own equipment, which is stored in a large cupboard at the centre, they implement a full maintenance check on all tools and equipment once a month, again following an agreed checklist.

Mobile play facilities

The Fun on the Estates Mobile Play Project operates on several housing estates in an inner London borough. Each time the van with its equipment visits an estate the workers, Gulsen, Mahed and Peter, run through a series of checks and procedures to ensure that the area is safe for children's play. This will include:

- arriving in good time to collect information from the estate superintendent or other link person on the estate
- parking the van away from traffic, not too near residents' flats, away from the estate's rubbish bins, not to block emergency exits and in clear view of the children's normal routes to and from school, etc.
- clearing away any rubbish including broken glass, tin cans and dog excrement.

It is not unusual for them to also find used condoms and needles. This requires them not only to have special tools and equipment, e.g. shovel, trowel, spike, strong refuse bags and safety gloves, but also to follow special procedures for the disposal of the rubbish collected.

What the playworkers have to clear up before they can start a session

CASE STUDY 8.4

Adventure playgrounds

The Willow Tree adventure playground has a brick-built building and an outdoor area comprising a garden area and several timber play structures, including constructions that the children have built themselves. The playground is situated in a park and surrounded by a timber fence and an outer border landscaped with shrubs and bushes. Each day before the session the playworkers run a safety check of the outside site. This will involve:

- checking the children's constructions from the previous session to make sure there are no nails sticking out or sharp edges of protruding wood
- checking the play structures for any damage that might have occurred through vandalism overnight
- clearing any rubbish from the site and surrounding area that might have blown in or accumulated in the surrounding border.

As well as this daily routine there is a monthly check of all the play structures, tools and equipment and a twice annual inspection audit of the whole site, including building, which is carried out by the local play association in

Item	Daily
KITCHENS	
Are floors and surfaces clean and free of spillage?	☐ Visual check
Are all utensils and equipment clean?	☐ Visual check before use
Are cooking facilities clean and in good working order?	☐ Check as required
Are storage facilities clean and free of spillage and vermin?	☐ Visual check
Is fire-fighting equipment in good condition?	☐ Visual check
Are basins or sinks clean?	☐ Visual check
Are taps in good working order?	☐ Test by use
Are waste outlets clear?	☐ Test by use
ACCESS	
Is pedestrian access free of obstruction?	☐ Visual check
Are surfaces in good condition?	☐ Visual check
OUTDOORS	
Is site generally free of debris and hazardous rubbish?	☐ Visual check
Is site free of litter?	☐ Visual check
Is site free of surface water?	☐ Visual check

conjunction with the staff team. Both the monthly check and the bi-annual inspection audit are carried out to written guidelines.

Slides in particular need careful maintenance

Here is an extract from a completed bi-annual inspection on the condition of a playground's outside area:

THE ADVENTURE PLAYGROUND
HEALTH & SAFETY AUDIT SHEET   SITE AND STRUCTURES
                                                    Carried out 8/5/09
Accompanied by Yvonne Gray   Adventure Play worker

Condition	Action required
SITE IN GENERAL: The extractor fan cupboard was broken and open with sharp wire and broken timbers exposed.	Repair and seal off, removing all sharp edges.
There were discarded timbers, metal and various other items of litter on-site.	A thorough clear up needed with all litter and hazardous items discarded off-site.

FENCING, GATES AND ENTRANCES:	
On the gates to the games pitch several panels are damaged with one missing completely. The damage has resulted in sharp edges to wire.	
	Temporary repair needed to make these gates secure and safe. A stronger type of weld mesh panel should be installed in future.
STRUCTURES AND PLAY FEATURES:	
All the main uprights housed in metal tubes are taking and retaining rain-water. As far as one could observe no major rot has set in although some are beginning to show signs of deterioration from damp.	
	These tubes need draining of water and sealing off at the surface. A cover of strong polythene or canvas tacked to the pole would suffice.
One of the shorter pole uprights	
	Monitor at monthly intervals and replace as necessary.
One section of American Swing platform has a broken joist	
	Strip back and replace joist
The climbing net has deteriorated from being left out on-site	
	The net should be removed and inspected for possible repair. All ropes and nets should be fixed in such a way as to allow their removal at the end of a session.

WHO IS RESPONSIBLE?

With permanent provision such as after-school clubs, play centres and adventure playgrounds it is important to establish who is responsible for ensuring that repair work is carried out. Although the on-site staff and, in particular, the senior worker may be responsible for making sure checks take place and information is recorded and passed on, it may not fall to them to put the repair work into action.

On some projects this can be the responsibility of several agencies. For instance the local authority may lease the building to the playground management committee and maintain responsibility for building repairs, the senior playworker may be responsible for ensuring repairs are carried out to the play structures, but it might be the responsibility of the management committee to raise funds to install new safety surfaces.

STORAGE OF MATERIALS AND EQUIPMENT

Ideally you need a strong, lockable storeroom or cupboard of your own. Depending on the size and scope of your project you may well need more than one such space. Alternatively you may have to share the space with another user and even be forced to store some items off-site. On a temporary outdoor play scheme you might find yourself negotiating with a local resident or shopkeeper for use of their garage. Whatever the situation your storage space must be:

- accessible for items you may need during the session
- lockable
- of a suitable size to accommodate its contents
- strong enough to support the weight of heavy items.

CASE STUDY   8.6

When Chris Davis, a National Play Safety Officer, visited the Elm Street Adventure Playground, and asked to see the playground's store room he was appalled by what he saw. Although the playworkers knew that it was not ideal, they had got so used to the store room that they did not realise how inefficient and dangerous it had become. This is what Chris found on his inspection:

1. The door was only lockable by a padlock on a hasp and staple and the padlock was missing.
2. The door was, in fact, loose on its hinges.
3. The floor was awash with paper, bits of material and drinks straws.
4. The shelves, which reached to the ceiling of the room, were bowing in the middle under the weight of the materials and equipment on them.
5. Although it was apparent that some thought had gone into the original design of the storage on the shelves with boxes, compartments and labels supplied, it was clear now that the system had collapsed and it was almost impossible to distinguish between the spaces. Each shelf seemed a mass of different things quickly stuffed into the first available gap. Upon selecting a

ball of wool, Chris found that several paint brushes, paper clips, crayons, buttons, a plastic necklace and a chunk of plasticine also came with it in a tangled mess.

6 A large wooden trunk on the floor housed the tools for carpentry and structure building in a totally indiscriminate manner with small hand tools like pliers and tape measures piled in alongside hammers, saws and electric sanders. None of the blades on knives, chisels or saws were protected.

Questions

The Elm Street store room is an extreme example, but based on real experience. Take a long objective look at your own store room.

1 How would your storage system stand up to scrutiny?
2 How easy is it to find the material or piece of equipment you are looking for?
3 How safely are materials, tools and equipment stored?

Use the following good practice points as a checklist.

Is your store room anything like this?!

Here are some indicators for a safe and efficient storage system:

- The room or cupboard should be of a suitable size, secure and dry.
- Shelving or racking should be constructed for strength and not be overloaded.
- Shelving should be divided up and labelled to facilitate easy access to the different types of materials and equipment.
- Heavy items should be stored on the lower shelves.
- A step ladder should be available to reach higher shelves if necessary.
- All toxic, inflammable and corrosive materials should be stored separately in a lockable and marked cabinet and according to the manufacturers' instructions.
- All sharp edges of tools should be protected with a cover or plastic tape where they are exposed to the touch.
- The storage of hand tools can be made both safe and accessible by the construction of a silhouette board on the wall, i.e. a piece of board that has the outline of the tool painted on and a peg on which to hang the real thing.
- Heavy and power tools should be stored separately in a lockable box or trunk.
- Ropes, nets, canvas and other perishable materials should be stored off the ground to reduce the risk of damp and allow air circulation.

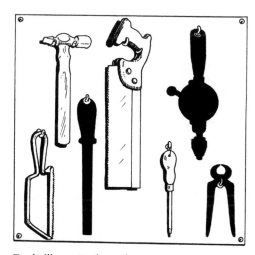

Tool silhouette board

USE OF MATERIALS

Generally speaking the materials used for play activities will not in themselves constitute a risk to children's health and safety – paper, cardboard and water-based paints for example. However, children using them must be of the correct age and employ common sense. A few activities do carry a risk factor in respect of the materials used, e.g. hot wax in the making of candles, hot metal in the making of jewellery, and these will require extra care and supervision by playworkers.

The materials used on the play project for non-play purposes, e.g. cleaning fluids, creosote, gloss paint, etc. should be stored separately in a marked and locked cabinet.

KEY POINT

It would be misleading to say that a playworker should never allow a child or young person to use a material such as gloss paint, or a tool such as an electric drill. Children in the play setting, as at home or at school, can benefit from new and challenging experiences, as long as they are carried out under skilled supervision in a safe situation. The key issues are that:

- the playworker has the appropriate skills and knowledge through experience and/or training
- the child or young person can be trusted to act responsibly under guidance
- the activity is adequately supervised throughout
- there is no conflict with the wishes of the parent or carer.

PROGRESS CHECK

1 What are the key areas that should be covered in a health and safety policy?
2 How will you be involved in the implementation of health and safety policy in your setting?
3 What would make an item of play equipment unsafe for children and young people to use?
4 Name four things to be looking for on a daily check of a play building?
5 If you are an adventure playground worker, what would be the key areas to check in your outside space?
6 Name three good practice points for a safe and efficient storage system.

The health and safety of children on site

ACCIDENTS AND EMERGENCIES

The preceding sections explore the prevention of accidents through the operation of good implementation and monitoring procedures. However, as a playworker you will need to be prepared for the unexpected. In an environment dedicated to children's play it is inevitable that some minor injuries will occur and you may have to deal with the occasional major one.

It is essential for there to be at least one fully-trained first aider on site at all times. It is also essential for all workers to have both a basic grounding in first aid and an understanding of the correct procedures in the event of an accident or emergency occurring. As well as the possibility of injury to the children, you may also find yourself dealing with an injured colleague or member of the public.

In responding to an injury you should be able to assess the situation quickly to determine the nature of the injury and whether you can deal with it yourself or whether you need help. Here is an accident procedure in use by a local authority play centre service:

ACCIDENTS TO CHILDREN
PROCEDURES TO BE FOLLOWED

FOR ALL ACCIDENTS

All accidents, however slight, must be entered in the accident book, stating time of accident, how it occurred, the extent of the injury and how it was treated.

Any witness to the accident should be named.

Playworkers and parents must ensure that all records (address, telephone numbers for work and home, emergency contact person, etc.) are kept up to date.

IN AN EMERGENCY

If the child requires hospital admission, dial 999.

The staff should take all available medical records with them.

Parents must be notified.

If the parents are not available, the emergency contact person should be informed.

N.B. All children attending the scheme must have a completed medical consent form.

On a busy site it will be difficult to deal with an injury that requires treatment without the assistance of your fellow workers, so good communication and teamwork are essential.

Example

One evening at the Downham after-school club, Zoë, one of the assistant play-workers, was supervising a game of football on the pitch outside the building. As the children were playing, one of the boys, Peter, slipped and fell onto his arm. Zoë could see that Peter was in a lot of pain so she stopped the game and went over to assess the injury. Peter's arm did not look distorted and was not badly cut but he was very shaken, so Zoë temporarily halted the game of football and took Peter inside the building.

Once inside, Zoë informed her colleagues of what had happened, took Peter into the office and placed his arm in a sling. After discussion between Zoë and the senior worker, Sally, Zoë telephoned to see if Peter's mum or dad were at home to arrange for one of them to accompany Peter to the local hospital's casualty department. Zoë entered the accident in the play centre accident book and visited Peter's home after closing time to see what the outcome of the hospital visit had been. The X-ray had shown that Peter's arm was not broken and Zoë entered this result in the accident book the next day.

Questions

Zoë was a qualified first aider so she was able to determine the seriousness of Peter's injury and administer some first aid.

1 Do you know who is the qualified first aider in your play setting?

Zoë had to leave the football game to deal with Peter.

2 How easily can you call or have fetched another playworker in your setting?

Proper recording in the accident book is very important.

3 Following an accident would you know how to record the injury in the accident book at your project?

THE ACCIDENT BOOK

All play projects will need to record accidents and injuries either in an accident record book or on forms supplied. There is an example of a completed accident form under 'Recording accidents' in Chapter 5. If Peter's arm had been broken a special form would have been filled out to reflect the seriousness of the injury.

KEY POINT

Under the Health and Safety at Work Act 1974, the Health and Safety Executive require all serious accidents to be notified to the enforcing authority as soon as possible and they provide a form F2508 on which the information can be recorded. Here are the rules which apply regarding these situations:

HSE Health and Safety at Work etc Act 1974
The Reporting of Injuries, Diseases and Dangerous Occurrences Regulations 1995

Report of an injury or dangerous occurrence

Filling in this form
This form must be filled in by an employer or other responsible person.

Part A

About you

1 What is your full name?

2 What is your job title?

3 What is your telephone number?

About your organisation

4 What is the name of your organisation?

5 What is its address and postcode?

6 What type of work does the organisation do?

Part B

About the incident

1 On what date did the incident happen?

2 At what time did the incident happen?
(Please use the 24-hour clock eg 0600)

3 Did the incident happen at the above address?
Yes ☐ Go to question 4
No ☐ Where did the incident happen?
☐ elsewhere in your organisation – give the name, address and postcode
☐ at someone else's premises – give the name, address and postcode
☐ in a public place – give details of where it happened

If you do not know the postcode, what is the name of the local authority?

4 In which department, or where on the premises, did the incident happen?

Part C

About the injured person

If you are reporting a dangerous occurrence, go to Part F. If more than one person was injured in the same incident, please attach the details asked for in Part C and Part D for each injured person.

1 What is their full name?

2 What is their home address and postcode?

3 What is their home phone number?

4 How old are they?

5 Are they
☐ male?
☐ female?

6 What is their job title?

7 Was the injured person (tick only one box)
☐ one of your employees?
☐ on a training scheme? Give details:

☐ on work experience?
☐ employed by someone else? Give details of the employer:

☐ self-employed and at work?
☐ a member of the public?

Part D

About the injury

1 What was the injury? (eg fracture, laceration)

2 What part of the body was injured?

F2508 (05/95)

A specimen F2508 form

The enforcing authority in respect of a play project would normally be the local authority, either through the play officer or Health and Safety officer.

With all injuries other than very minor ones such as a knock on the ankle or graze on the knee, the parent or carer of the child should be informed. This allows for continuity of care after the child has left the project and ensures that the responsibility of the project has been properly discharged.

KEY POINT

Parents can be understanding about minor injuries so long as they are told – either face to face or by a note sent with the child. Parents may be angry, and worried, to find bruises or cuts that are not explained.

THE FIRST AID BOX

A well-stocked first aid box or cabinet is necessary for every play setting. Advice on contents can be obtained from St John's Ambulance, the British Red Cross or your local authority safety officer.

You can express sympathy even when injuries are very minor

Your first aid box or cabinet should be:
- in an accessible place out of the reach of the children, e.g. the office or store room
- clearly marked, e.g. with a green cross
- kept fully stocked
- regularly checked to ensure all the materials and equipment are clean and in good working order.

In dealing with accidents in your play setting you will need:

■ well thought out and agreed procedures in line with your Health and Safety policy
■ an understanding by all workers of what to do in the event of an injury
■ at least one member of staff (normally the senior worker) who is qualified in first aid
■ readily accessible and well-maintained first aid materials and equipment
■ an accident and emergency record book
■ appropriate forms for the recording of serious injuries
■ access to a telephone.

ILLNESS

Some children may turn up at your play setting feeling ill, become ill during the session, or have a continuing health condition. Playworkers are not expected to be able to diagnose what is the matter with an unwell child or young person, but it is good practice to have some basic information of the signs and symptoms of the more common conditions such as mumps and measles. Much of this information is readily available through posters and leaflets from local authority environmental health departments or your area health authority. You can also make this information readily accessible to the parents, carers and children of the project by putting posters on walls and handing out leaflets. Opposite is an Asthma Attack card from Asthma UK, which is designed to remind adults and children with asthma and those around them about what to do during an asthma attack.

Any play setting needs a quiet place available to children who feel unwell so that they can rest quietly and in comfort. You should be able to sit the child down in a comfortable seat whilst they recover or wait for assistance. It is a good idea to keep a cushion and blanket for this purpose. As in dealing with injuries, you will need to have agreed procedures for dealing with illness that all workers know and understand.

If you suspect a child of having an illness or condition that could either threaten their own or other children's health, e.g. a rash, breathing difficulties, serious coughing, feverish temperature, you should:

■ inform your senior worker if appropriate
■ talk to the child and make an assessment of just how serious you think her or his condition is – if you are unsure get a second opinion
■ determine whether:
   i) the child has any medication that they could take, e.g. an inhaler in the case of asthma (see 'Administering medication' on page 212)
  ii) the child should be immediately isolated and/or made to sit or lie down
 iii) you should call an ambulance and contact the child's parent or carer
 iv) you should contact the child's parent or carer to come and collect them
  v) you can leave the child to sit quietly or a worker needs to remain with them until they are collected

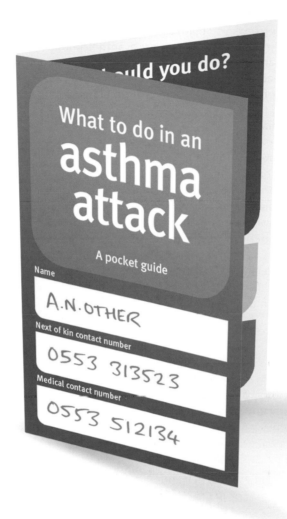

- make out a full report in the accident record book
- notify the child's parent or carer if you haven't already done so
- notify your project manager or the appropriate person on your management committee.

If a child comes to you saying that she or he is feeling unwell the above points will also apply. If you assess the child's condition to be only minor – perhaps she or he has a mild headache, has got too hot running around, or feels a bit sick, you can advise them to rest for a while in a quite place. It may still be important to record what happened in the accident record book and to inform an adult when they are collected.

KEY POINT

On open-access projects you may have a child who has dropped in to play and then feels unwell but is unable to give you a relevant telephone number. Similarly you may have a contact number but are unable to get through on the line. In both cases you will need to be prepared to visit the child's home. It is a good idea to have the names of a couple of people who could help out in times such as these. A parent volunteer, for instance, could either provide temporary cover or accompany an unwell child home.

Administering medication

In some play settings it may be decided by the management committee that the playworkers cannot take responsibility for giving users medication. If you are allowed to take such responsibility make sure you know the correct procedures currently in operation at your project. These will include:

■ obtaining written consent from the parent or carer before any medication is given
■ only administering medicines which are part of a prescribed course of treatment
■ recording each time a dose of medication is given

Children may sometimes be taken ill at your play setting

- ensuring medicine bottles have clear information on their labels, e.g. name of child, name of contents, instructions on use, expiry date
- ensuring safe storage of all medication when not in use.

Activity   **8.7**

Contact your local Social Services or Health Department for information on:
- the minimum periods of exclusion of children suffering from serious diseases
- any diseases which have to be notified.

EMERGENCIES

A play project must be prepared to deal with the sort of emergency which, in the normal day-to-day running of the facility, may seem such an unlikely situation as to be slightly unreal – a fire, a gas explosion, a collapse in the structure of the building.

The key issues are:
- All staff need to be aware of the procedures in force in the event of an emergency situation such as fire.
- The information that children and casual users of the building need to know must be prominently displayed. If your project serves a multi-lingual community you will need translations of the information.
- When an emergency occurs workers should immediately cease what they are doing and assume their designated roles as quickly as possible.
- An emergency evacuation such as a fire drill should be carried out at least three times a year.
- A full report should be made following either a real or a simulated situation.

CASE STUDY   8.8

At the St Dunstan's play centre they organise a fire drill once a term. For the practice, Maureen, the worker in charge, notifies the team that it is time to have another fire drill and, together, they set an evening for it to take place. Maureen then informs the head teacher and caretaker of the school building of the date and the caretaker agrees to set off the alarm at the appropriate time. On the evening in question Maureen, Joseph, Angus and Haki will inform the children at registration that a fire drill will be in operation during the session, but not the exact time of when it will occur. This is to avoid unnecessary fear amongst the children, but, at the same time, to simulate as real a situation as possible. When the alarm sounds the playworkers will follow the evacuation procedures as if it were a real occurrence of fire. Once assembled outside at the grassed area, Maureen will check who has left the play centre by means of the signing-out book and then check off the rest of the children against the register. Once all the children have been accounted for she would inform the school caretaker and the session would re-start. A full written report by Maureen would be made out later.

KEY POINT

Crucial to the whole operation is having the correct procedures in place and making sure that they are well understood and rehearsed on a regular basis.

To think about   8.9

1   What are the emergency procedures at your project?
2   If you work in a play centre setting how do they compare with those in the examples above?
3   If you work in an open-access or other type of setting what are the differences?
4   When did you last have an emergency fire drill?
5   If you had an emergency drill tomorrow would you know what to do?

Check out awareness by asking your colleagues and some of the users.

VISITORS AND STRANGERS

The security of the play setting is a crucially important area of responsibility for the playworker. You need to know who is visiting the facility at all times and their reason for doing so. Any unknown visitors must never be left unchallenged and you will need to be prepared to establish:

- who they are
- why they are visiting the facility
- who they wish to see or speak to.

If you observe an unknown person in your play setting you should follow an approach similar to the one outlined here:

- Enquire whether any of your colleagues know the person.
- If the visitor is known to a colleague, then that person should approach them and find out why they are visiting.
- If the visitor is not known to staff, they should be approached and asked the purpose of their visit.
- If the visitor has no apparent reason to be at the play setting they should be asked to leave – politely but firmly.
- Visitors who are not well known to the playworkers should not be left wunaccompanied.

KEY POINT

Parents and carers must be informed of procedures about visitors to the play setting and asked to cooperate in maintaining safety and security. Most parents will fully understand the need to challenge visitors and will usually be willing to report anything untoward to the playworkers.

SNACKS

As a playworker there are two main aspects of food and drink that you will be involved in:

- The provision of snacks and, sometimes, meals for children.
- The activity of preparing and cooking food with the children which, if successful, will also be readily consumed.

Besides wanting to provide nourishment for the children you will also want to raise the children's awareness of health and hygiene, and of the diversity of foods, drinks and eating habits of other cultures – even if there is little diversity in your project. Over a period of time you can introduce them to new and different foods and drinks both to eat, drink and prepare.

At your project you may have children joining or visiting who have special dietary requirements. It is important to discover this at the earliest opportunity either through word of mouth with the child, their parent or carer, or through a question on the project's registration form.

CASE STUDY 8.10

At the Willow Tree adventure playground there is a canteen that operates during every after-school session and on the school holiday afternoons. It is also operational during the lunch period of school holidays when both workers and children take lunch together. The current team of playworkers, Elroy, Janet, Kieran and Anya, aim to:

- provide healthier snacks and drinks
- raise the children's awareness of healthier foods and drinks
- encourage the parents and carers to be part of the process
- encourage the children to take an active role in running the canteen themselves.

To help them in their aim they also set up a children's 'Food is Fun' group to explore nutrition and food from other countries. The group, with help from Anya who volunteered to service it, soon came up with several ideas they put into action over a period of time:

- Information and awareness posters were put on the play building walls.
- A fun food table was set up once a week with foods and drinks from different countries.
- Parents and carers were encouraged to:
    - i) avoid sending children to the playground with sweets and fizzy drinks
    - ii) provide examples unique to their culture of foods and drinks for the fun food table
    - iii) if possible come and help run the canteen.
- A rota was set up of children who wished to help run the canteen.

The canteen is fully run by the children and volunteers with only minimal help from the playworkers and includes a menu of sugar-free drinks, fruit juices, milk, fresh and dried fruits, raw vegetables, nuts, muesli bars and a range of non-meat

sandwiches. The fun food table continues to be popular on an occasional basis and has featured cous cous, halva, bhajis, bean curd, yams, soda bread, haggis and falafel amongst its delights.

Questions

1 Do you provide snacks for the children using your project? If so, does the menu reflect good nutritional value?
2 In what ways could you involve the users in activities that would raise awareness on:
   i)   healthy eating
   ii) food and drinks from other cultures?
3 As in the case study, could your users run their own canteen?

All play projects have to work within the constraints of their budgets and many are severely limited despite the energy and efforts that may go into their fund-raising activities. The cost of providing alternative foods and drinks that are better for the children's health, however, can be greatly exaggerated. Purchasing from health food shops is, admittedly, more expensive, but the sorts of foods mentioned above for the canteen can be purchased at any large supermarket. Sugar-free drinks are no more expensive and the foods on the fun food table are an occasional purchase which might readily be donated by parents and carers or local shops.

Enlisting the help of the children and their families is crucial and putting information and awareness-raising posters on the walls can stimulate their interest and get them talking to you about food and drink issues.

Cooking with children

Cooking is a very popular activity with children – especially with the attraction of later eating what they have made. Most children enjoy the activity of planning and preparing the food and cooking is an excellent practical way of introducing children to health issues concerned with diet, and to the diversity and variety of foods from other cultures. If you have the use of a kitchen at your project you will be able to run cooking sessions that involve the preparation of hot food. Not having a kitchen, however, shouldn't deter you.

A simple activity such as making a fresh fruit salad can involve you in:

■ discussing how much they can spend and what fruit and fruit juice they would like to buy
■ going to the local shop and buying the fruit and juice
■ preparing for the activity, e.g. setting up a table, making sure that the knives, spoons and bowl are clean, washing their hands
■ washing, peeling and cutting the fruit
■ mixing the fruit with the juice
■ clearing up and washing utensils afterwards.

If you have a kitchen the scope of cooking activity is greatly increased. Of course, with increased facilities there will be extra considerations in terms of health, safety and hygiene. Some of the key factors in cooking with children are as follows:

■ Kitchen areas should be well maintained and clean.
■ All surfaces used for the preparation of food should be washed down before use.
■ The floor should also be washed regularly.

- All kitchen appliances should be clean and in working order.
- Cupboards and other storage spaces should be clean and not over loaded.
- All foods must be kept well off the ground and quickly perishable foods in a fridge.
- All utensils that are not for the children's use (unless perhaps under supervision) must be kept out of their reach, preferably in a locked drawer or cupboard.
- When running a session in the kitchen make sure that:
  i) the activity is appropriate to the children's age and stage of development
  ii) the children can be trusted to act sensibly with equipment and hot food
  iii) the number of children is appropriate to the size of the kitchen space, the demands of the cooking activity and the level of supervision (a ratio of 1:6 is a good guide)
  iv) the children are at no time left without supervision
  v) the children are encouraged to be vigilant about hygiene in the kitchen, e.g. washing hands, rinsing foods, clearing up, keeping surfaces clean.
- There must be adequate equipment for dealing with a fire, e.g. fire blanket and/or dry powder extinguisher.
- The children need to understand what to do in an emergency before the session commences, and this should be reinforced by instructions on the wall.

To think about   8.11

1 Is cooking an activity on your project?
2 If you haven't got a kitchen to cook in, could you still prepare cold foods with the children like fruit salads or dips?
3 In providing food and drinks and running cooking activities are you able to involve the parents and carers of the children?

GOOD PRACTICE IN HYGIENE

Keeping reasonably clean

Children on a play project should be encouraged to develop the same values of personal hygiene as they might at home or in school. Although in the course of play they may naturally get grubby, even very grubby indeed, they should be encouraged to 'clean up' when it is appropriate, e.g. before preparing or eating food as above, after using toilet facilities, before going home.

Toileting

You will need to ensure that toilet and washing facilities are kept clean and well maintained. Toilet paper, soap and towels will need regular checking and re-stocking – more frequently on busy days. You will also need facilities for the girls to dispose of sanitary towels or tampons.

In the event of a user having an accident and soiling herself or himself you will need not only to have some practical measures in place, but also to treat the situation with sensitivity and discretion. On no account should you allow the child to become the victim of ridicule by other children. The practical measures should include:

- having a supply of clean clothes available for the user to change into
- if appropriate, allowing the user to clean and change themselves
- asking the user if she or he would like a parent or carer to be called
- if possible, contacting a parent or carer, to give them the option of coming to the project
- helping them to clean and change if necessary
- if a playworker is to help then he or she should be the same sex as the child
- soiled clothes should be placed in a plastic bag for washing
- the parent or carer should be asked to wash and return the change of clothes to the project.

KEY POINT

Older children sometimes have a toileting accident, either because they have hung on far too long before going to the toilet or because they are ill, perhaps with a stomach upset. On projects working with children with disability there may be a number of children who are either incontinent or experience difficulty in maintaining toilet habits.

CASE STUDY 8.12

The Wooden Tower Playground provides play opportunities for children from 5–15 years of age with severe physical and/or learning disability. It is an adventure playground with a well-equipped building and outdoor provision. There are three permanent workers – Denise, Sejeeven and Ed – and a regular supply of students and volunteers. A small number of children who use the project either wear continence pads or need regular reminders to use the toilet. Of fifty children on site during a holiday-scheme day, four would need changing two or three times a day and six to eight would need reminding every couple of hours.

The playground building is specially equipped with a changing room and all workers undertake this aspect as a regular part of their work. During a change two people would work together, one of whom would be a permanent member of staff. To avoid embarrassment to the child both workers would be of the same gender as her or him. The playground always has a supply of clean pads and soiled ones are disposed of hygienically in plastic bags. If the child's clothes have become soiled the workers would change them for clean clothes that are kept on site. The parents of the children usually provide such a change but the workers also have their own playground supply. As a playground with special provision there is a washing machine to clean the clothes and a shower room if the child is very badly soiled.

Questions

1 What are the procedures regarding toileting in operation at your project?
2 Who is responsible for ensuring that the supply of toilet paper, soap and towels is maintained?
3 Do you keep a supply of clean clothes for changes?
4 Do you have spare sanitary towels for girls whose period starts unexpectedly?

Spillage

The accidental spillage of blood, vomit, urine or faeces must be cleaned up immediately and other people kept away until the task is completed. Make sure that you wear a disposable apron and gloves and discard these, the spillage and any other materials used in clearing up in a tied plastic bag. If you are using a cleaning fluid other than a household detergent, check whether you need to dilute it with water. Make sure you wash your hands afterwards.

PROGRESS CHECK

1 Name three key procedures that you would carry out if a child you were supervising fell and badly hurt their leg.
2 Why is it important to inform parents of all injuries other than very minor ones?
3 What precautions should you take if a parent asks you to give some medicine to her or his child?
4 How often should fire drills be carried out?

Children's safety outside the play environment

The prime responsibility of the playworker is the health and well-being of the child or young person within the play environment itself. However, you can also play an active role in enabling them to be aware of, and take precautions against, some of the dangers they may encounter outside the play setting. These include:

- hazards in the home
- danger from traffic
- drugs and solvent abuse
- hazards in built-up and rural areas.

CASE STUDY 8.13

At the St Dunstan's Play Centre the playworkers work with the children on an on-going project called 'Keeping Safe and Healthy'. Two of the children, Eva and Matt, take keen interest and responsibility, working directly with Joseph who is the key person from within the team. The project operates in several ways:

- A table, display board and bookshelf give information on a variety of issues such as racism, road safety and drugs through posters, leaflets and books.
- Activities are planned that pass on information, stimulate interest and encourage the children to take an active role in their own safety, e.g. board games and videos borrowed from the local authority Social Education Unit.
- Guest speakers are invited, e.g. the council's Road Safety Officer has spoken on traffic danger.

Questions

1 In what ways might you encourage further interest in health and safety amongst your users?
2 Who are the people and agencies that you could call on to help in raising awareness around these issues?

GOOD PRACTICE

Playworkers, in common with other adults, need to encourage children and young people to develop a cautious approach rather than a feeling of continuous worry. It is important to start from where the users are and enable them to think through the issues at their own pace.

Although the methods used in the 'Keeping Safe and Healthy' project can work equally well with young people, particularly the use of film, you may also wish to use research and discussion groups to raise awareness. Close liaison with teachers and youth workers can enable you to have a joint approach and bringing in experts that can not only give a talk but be part of a question and answer session will be helpful. If you have young people within your play setting or know of others who have had first-hand experience of, say, using solvents in the past, they can provide useful and powerful testimony for the group.

City and town dwellers sometimes have a romantic notion of the freedom and adventure of the countryside. In fact there are as many dangers in the countryside as in the city. The rural environment is now less available to children through the extension and protection of farmland, but natural spaces can themselves be potentially dangerous and always have been. If you are working in a rural setting the issues that were indicated in the case study above apply equally forcefully. In some cases they can be of a slightly different nature. For instance:

- It is often the density of traffic that is the issue in the city – in the countryside it can be the absence of pavements and the speed of the cars on the open road.
- In the city children can be tempted to explore building sites, factories and canals – in the country there are cliffs, lakes and chemically-treated farmland.
- Taking and driving cars is an issue in both settings, but in the country there are also tractors and farm machinery to explore and, possibly, try out.

- Although danger from unknown adults may be a concern in urban areas because of the density and anonymity of the population, in the countryside the isolation of the environment can be an equal worry.

If you are a worker in a rural setting your awareness campaign will need to take account of these, and other, issues.

KEY POINT

There is great concern amongst parents about the dangers to their children from unknown adults. However, statistics show that the greatest danger to children is from people they know.

Some of the dangers for children and young people are not just of a social nature but may also bring them into conflict with the law – taking drugs for instance. Once you have established a relationship with other professionals in your locality it will enable you to act quickly and effectively when you recognise that a user is in danger.

There are also relationships with the children's parents and carers. Regular conversations with parents or other relatives will inform you of their general, as well as specific, worries about their children. You can also make families part of the messages you are trying to get across to the users. See also page 188 on helping children and young people to learn about personal safety.

PROGRESS CHECK

1 What are the safety issues for children and young people outside the play environment in urban areas?
2 Are the safety issues different for children and young people in rural areas and, if so, in what ways?
3 How might you involve your users in awareness-raising activities about safety outside the play setting?

TRIPS AND OUTINGS

There are some specific considerations that need to be applied when taking children away from the normal play setting. In particular your communication with parents and carers will not only need to reassure them about the care of the child but also cover you in the event of an emergency occurring. There may be occasions when you can respond to spontaneous requests from the children, for instance arranging a trip to the local park the next day, but you will normally be planning off-site activities well in advance. The special responsibility of caring for children outside the normal play environment means attention to detail and careful procedures.

There are three main types of off-site activity:
- Local trips that can be reached on foot, e.g. another project, local park, library or swimming pool.

- Places of interest outside the locality and requiring transport, e.g. museum, zoo, countryside or monument – these are often a whole-day activity.
- Holiday activities that require sleeping away from home, e.g. camping, residential holiday centre, trip abroad.

During trips, playworkers must ensure that they continue to meet any legislation or requirements that apply to them, such as the EYFS welfare requirements. Appropriate staff ratios must be maintained, and at least one adult must hold a current first aid certificate. The overall ratio of staff to children will depend on the age of children, the nature of the trip and the activities planned. Some settings may ask parents to accompany under fives.

KEY POINT

- Parents and guardians accompanying children should not be required to supervise any children other than their own unless they are already experienced volunteers. In such cases other parents should be informed of the supervisory role taken by volunteers.
- For residential trips of mixed gender, there should be a minimum of two adults, one female and one male, and it is advisable that all supervising adults hold a current first aid certificate.
- If you are planning a camping or residential trip with children, make sure either that you have the appropriate training or experience to carry out any specialist activities safely or that there is skilled supervision at the places you visit. Swimming in the sea, canoeing and climbing all involve risks for the inexperienced – adults or children. Even a walk in an unfamiliar place can hold hidden dangers if you have no map-reading skills and either wander too far or become lost.

Before leaving on a camping trip the supervisors will need to be sure that:
- all the tents and equipment are in good order
- they have an outline of a plan for the week's activities
- they have maps and compasses and any other specialist equipment
- they have adequate supplies of food and drink
- they have a fully-stocked first aid kit
- the bus has been checked and passed as safe and road-worthy
- they have carefully planned the route and a driving rota
- they have received all the signed consent forms.

PROGRESS CHECK

1 Name four safety issues to bear in mind when taking children out:
   i) on a local trip
   ii) on a residential weekend.
2 Explain why obtaining parents' consent for outings is so important.

KEY TERMS

You need to know what these words and phrases mean. Go back through the chapter to make sure that you understand.

Teamwork
Checks and audits
First aider
First aid box

Consent form
Accident book
Fire drill

9 WORKING WELL WITH OTHER ADULTS

> ## This chapter covers:
> - **Teams in playwork**
> - **Communication in the team**
> - **Support and learning**
> - **New team members**
> - **Building relationships with parents**

Teams in playwork

INTERDEPENDENCE

Individual playworkers in any given play setting are interdependent – how one worker behaves in his or her work will affect other team members. This relationship can work positively when everyone is aware of how their areas of responsibility support those of their colleagues. But, of course, it can work as a downward spiral if some members of the playwork team insist on behaving as if what they do has no consequences for the rest of the team. The consequences may be physically dangerous if one playworker skimps on the responsibility to check the safety of large structures, or it may be simply irritating when a playworker fails to check on the stores and an activity cannot go ahead as planned because the materials have run out.

GOOD PRACTICE

Playworkers have responsibilities to each other. It is not a situation in which individuals can claim, 'That's just the way I am – take it or leave it!' The work, even the physical safety, of other playworkers will be affected by the behaviour and standards of their colleagues.

The importance of trust
Trust lies at the heart of good working relationships in an effective team and is built through experience that a colleague can be depended upon. Reliable playworkers are not unrealistically perfect. Part of being dependable is that you are honest about any difficulties and ask for assistance before total panic takes over. Other playworkers will feel reassured if they feel confident that you will admit when you are confused and do not know something rather than muddle through. Of course, for this to work all playworkers, including the centre leader,

have to respond positively to requests for assistance or to questions. A dismissive approach will tell a playworker that, despite all the talk about teamworking, in practice you just have to get on with it and cover up any resulting mistakes.

KEY POINT

Saying that there is a lack of trust in a team is definitely not the same as saying team members are deceitful or dishonest. A low level of trust in practice can mean uncertainty or uneasiness. Past experience leads team members to feel unsure, and this can lead to a pattern of checking up on colleagues that may feel like nagging.

SHARED VALUES AND PRACTICE

Individuals within an effective playwork team will feel enthusiasm and pride in what has been managed together. This excitement about the work and the commitment that takes a team through the bad or frustrating times will be supported by a shared commitment to the key values that underpin all the work.

To think about	9.1

Key values should not change with the weather, but they should be reviewed. In your centre, when was the last team discussion about values and how they are put into practice?

Some key values are developed into public statements of policy for any kind of group or centre. For instance, many centres for children – not only playwork – have a code of practice on commitment to anti-discriminatory practice. A written code of practice demonstrates the commitment of playworkers. It can also help in communication with parents on issues that could be open to misunderstanding.

CASE STUDY 9.2

Bedford leisure centre team wrote into their publicity leaflet the goal of: 'We will encourage all children to participate in all the available activities, whatever the children's level of physical ability or talent.' The team set this goal because of their concern that children and young people were taking on the outlook that it was better to avoid sports unless you were 'good' at them.

The fact that the team had overlooked an entire issue in playwork is highlighted by the arrival of three children with disabilities. The accompanying parents take contrasting approaches to their children's participation. Two parents have been attracted by the leaflet and talk enthusiastically of the empowerment of children with disabilities. Yet the third parent wants to be reassured that his daughter will be protected from physical knocks and any hurtful remarks from other children.

Questions

1 What are the main issues involved here?
2 What should the team do today? What steps should be taken in the longer term?
3 Share your ideas with your colleagues.

Some playwork teams have worked hard to make practice consistent within the regular group of workers and then face dilemmas arising from the behaviour of volunteers or visitors.

To think about 9.3

In the two examples that follow consider these questions:

- What will need to be said, or done? What are the likely consequences if nothing is done?
- It is easy to think, 'well, I'd just tell her ... ', so imagine yourself into these situations as clearly as you can. In each example, what feelings or concerns might hold you back from tackling the problem?
- Discuss your views with other playworkers in your team.

There will always be some paperwork

9.3 contd

1   Downham after-school club have taken a strong line on discouraging
    swearing in the club, especially any bad language based in racist or sexist
    slurs. Playworkers have spent a great deal of time in careful conversation with
    children to explain why they are not willing to have certain words or phrases
    used on the premises. In a recent club meeting several children complain
    about the language of parents, two in particular, and the fact that the
    playworkers do not 'tick them off'.
2   Hummingbird adventure playground has a local management committee,
    chaired by Duncan. He likes to visit the playground regularly but is a heavy
    smoker and continues to light up during his visits. The playworkers have a
    policy, agreed by the committee, of no smoking in the playground. Subtle
    hints have failed to stop Duncan so far.

KEY POINT

Perhaps you feel reticent about telling other people what to do, especially if they
are volunteers who are essentially doing you all a favour. Yet everyone must follow
ground rules and any codes of practice; it is irrelevant whether they are being paid
or not.

PROGRESS CHECK

1 Playwork teams have an interdependent relationship. What does this mean in practice?
2 What can happen if members of a playwork team are unclear about the allocation of responsibilities in the work?
3 Give two reasons why volunteers or visitors should follow the practice of a play setting as closely as the permanent workers.

Communication in the team

COMMUNICATION AS PART OF PLAYWORK

Good playwork depends on communication with the children and young people who use the play setting (see page 68). It also needs good communication between the playworkers themselves.

It is important that playworkers:

- keep each other up to date with what is happening in different parts of the play setting and pass on any information or messages whether this is face-to-face or via a reliable message book system
- can trust other playworkers to support one another and not to undermine colleagues in front of children or parents

Sometimes information from children must be passed on
(Photograph courtesy of Kidsactive; photographer Tilly Odell)

- back each other up in an emergency, including responding quickly to a colleague's call for help
- find time to discuss not only what they will do in a play session, but also to review how a session or a week's schemes worked out
- express any doubts or criticisms in a constructive way
- are as generous with encouragement to colleagues as they should be with the setting's users (see page 148).

COMMUNICATION AND EFFICIENT USE OF RESOURCES

Chapter 4 offers a range of practical suggestions for planning and preparation of activities in your setting. Programmes, schedules or rotas cannot do the work for a playwork team; daily practice depends on good communication and confidence that you can trust your colleagues. Communication within the team, between individuals but also within team meetings, will support efficient use of your resources and flexible forward planning.

Different time scales
Good planning for a play setting works to three broad time scales.
- Short-term planning focuses on your plans for each day within a week. You need to plan activities and check you have all the necessary resources, including enough playworkers (your people resources). There should be some scope for reflection during and after the week for considering how activities unfolded and what the children and the whole team, as involved playworkers, have learned.

- Medium-term planning would usually be for a period of two to three months ahead. You would consider what you hope the children or young people will experience and how their skills could be extended. You would have a draft plan of likely activities and outings so that necessary checks can be made on your stores and to identify any details or bookings that have to be organised in advance.
- Long-term planning can take a perspective up to a year ahead and can include broad-based plans of what you wish to offer to the users of your setting or plans to involve parents and other carers or the local community.

The longer time-scales in planning make sense because of the more detailed planning that your team undertakes closer to the time. However, the weekly plans are more effective because they are part of your longer term perspective on what you want to offer children in their full play experience.

GOOD PRACTICE

Long-term planning is your framework for taking an overall perspective on the range of play and learning experiences you offer. For instance:
- From time to time, you need to stand back as a team and consider whether you are overlooking a whole area of learning and potential enjoyment.
- Consider whether your team may benefit from taking a careful look at basics within the forward planning, such as the balance you create between acceptable levels of safety for children and enough challenge and adventure.
- You may also have to look long term at dealing with the more expensive gaps in your play equipment or changes to how you organise your setting.

Activity 9.4

Supported through conversation with your colleagues and, if possible, also with the children, identify one focus for longer term planning in your setting. You can take any of the areas in the Good Practice above or consider a current issue for your team.

Gather your thoughts about the key issues, the nature of any problems and possible approaches. Prepare and make a short presentation to your team, in order to share your ideas and to invite their views.

Setting useful goals

Definite and realistic goals will support effective team planning. Goals with the following qualities (SMART for short) will help to make your planning and use of resources more clear.
- **S**pecific – phrase your playwork goals so that everyone will be able to tell whether you have reached them or not. Discussion around vague goals, such as 'we need to empower our users' often highlights the very different working definitions of a familiar word or phrase. Communication within the team productively explores, 'We talk about "empowerment" a lot, but what exactly do we mean in practice?'

- **M**easurable – if a goal is worth setting, it is worth your while to observe and perhaps record to what extent you have succeeded. Measurement does not have to be either complicated or tedious.
- **A**chievable – goals must be in areas of your playwork practice where your team has a chance of achieving some change. Enthusiastic playwork teams often have to recognise what they can and cannot influence in children's lives or the local community.
- **R**ealistic – goals need to be possible, given your setting's current resources. By all means have a long-term objective, but ambitious goals, unlikely to be met within weeks, are better redrafted to allow for steps along the way.
- **T**ime-bound – practical goals include attention to 'by when?' Discussion of sensible time limits helps a team to be realistic. You also need time limits, noted down, to ensure goals are reviewed and not forgotten.

Most plans, with their linked goals, need clear organisation and written records about exactly who will do what and how it will be done. All team members need to feel fully involved in their part in the work. Team leaders are responsible for dealing with individual playworkers who appear less than committed to achieving the goals.

KEY POINT

Remember that the whole point of planning and goal setting for your setting is that the team's work has a real impact on the play experience of the children. The whole point of developing skills within your playwork team or expanding your play resources is that these changes have an impact for your users.

DISAGREEMENT AND CONFLICT

Healthy disagreement

There is nothing the matter with differences of opinion within a team. An essentially harmonious team can cope with disagreement, even argument. A great deal depends on how any conflict is handled, which in turn will be affected by the behaviour of all the team members and the pattern set by the team leader. An important part of this pattern is the attempt to communicate with colleagues in the most constructive way possible. Several guidelines will help in this aim. These are:

- Be specific – give details and examples that will illustrate what the difference of opinion appears to be about or how the disagreement has arisen. Sweeping statements about 'you never … ' or 'I'm always the one who has to … ' tend to put people on the defensive.
- Describe what someone has done, or not done. Focus on what you have seen or heard, your concrete observation. Resist the temptation to make judgements about someone's personality.
- Focus on what has happened and not on speculation about why. Discussion can lead to possible reasons, but only when all the information has been considered.

- Be honest about your opinions. Be ready to admit to 'I think ... ' or 'I felt ... ', as an alternative to the pseudo-facts of 'it's obvious that ... ' or 'you made me feel ... '
- Wherever possible, offer a rounded picture. Give credit for what people are doing well; don't put all the discussion energy onto the negatives, or the points on which you disagree.

CASE STUDY 9.5

In the Fun on the Estates play bus, Gulsen and Peter both stress their commitment to the overall aim that, 'We will support the children to learn through their play'.

Peter puts this into practice by standing well back from the activities. If children ask directly for his help, Peter tends to ask them questions until the children come up with their own solution. In contrast, Gulsen makes suggestions on how children might use craft materials and sometimes starts a session by demonstrating the best technique.

Driving to the next location, conversation gets heated when Peter accuses Gulsen with, 'You block the children's self expression. You impose your way on them.' Gulsen retaliates with, 'The point about being a helpful adult is that you share your experience. The last thing these kids need is to re-invent the wheel.'

Questions

1 In what ways are the two playworkers' individual outlooks on children's learning bringing them into conflict?
2 What kind of approach could resolve the issue constructively? What kind of approach could deepen the disagreement?
3 Write up your ideas in a brief report and make applications to your own setting.

Steps in dealing with conflict

Good communication within the playwork team will help to avoid unnecessary conflict by ensuring that confusions or disagreements are aired before people become irritated and the different positions are entrenched. However, some disagreements are longer lasting and some individuals refuse to compromise, especially when their sense of self-esteem or key values are involved.

Every member of the team shares the responsibility for promoting good communication in all the ways described in this chapter. However, sometimes one person within a conflict has to make special efforts to get through the blocks. If communication has become very difficult, then a third team member, who may be more senior, may need to help the process through, ensuring that each person is heard. The following suggestions will be useful whether you are talking individually with a colleague or you are the third person mediating in a situation where two colleagues are unable to listen properly to each other.

The best way to manage differences between people in any work or personal setting is to talk face-to-face about the issues on which you differ and to talk, and listen, without interruption for as long as necessary to reach a breakthrough.

GOOD PRACTICE

It is important to find the time to resolve problems between individuals; persistent disagreements do not go away and are likely to affect other team members. Playworkers who cannot work cooperatively together, or who snipe at each other, are also setting a bad example to the children and young people in your setting. Valuable opportunities can be lost for offering a positive role model.

■ *In brief – the situation as each person sees it*
You need to communicate an assertive view on the problem situation, or help a colleague to take an assertive approach, rather than expressing mainly anger or offended feelings. An assertive statement will include a brief reference to the event or the issue, for instance, 'I believe we need to talk about what happened yesterday afternoon' or 'I don't think we can go on running the craft group together until we sort out our differences'. Sometimes it is appropriate to add your feelings, expressed honestly and not as a criticism of your colleague, for instance, 'I'm now wary about making any comment to you about safety in the garden' or 'I was hurt by what you said and I need to talk more with you'. The other person needs to be invited to put their view as well, but briefly.

■ *Open communication*
You need to listen to what the other person is saying and resist imposing your interpretations or perspective over the top. When colleagues have become very irritated or hurt by past events, a third person can be crucial to act as an 'umpire' to ensure both sides are heard and the conversation stays on a positive track.

■ *Willingness to negotiate*
The whole aim in the conversation is to establish cooperation, of 'us-against-this problem' and 'us both on the side of good playwork practice'. This approach is in contrast to a power battle of 'me-against-you'. You need to work hard, or enable your colleagues to stand back, and to separate the people, and their personalities, from the problem. Avoid arguments about personal foibles or who is most to blame for this situation. Focus on what has happened, the issues that have arisen and what could be done now. It may also be important to recall non-negotiable issues about playwork practice; some options may be professionally unacceptable in your setting. Work to find some common ground and shared values: the disagreement, rather like that of Gulsen and Peter in the case study, may be over methods and not about key values.

■ *Recognise any conciliatory gestures*
In any conflict, it is important to acknowledge gracefully any conciliatory gestures from the other person. The conversation will go sour if one or both individuals are keen to score points with remarks like, 'It would have been better if you'd said that yesterday!'

- *Reach a specific and clear agreement*

  You need an agreement that stands a good chance of avoiding future conflict on this issue. A workable agreement feels balanced, with clear obligations for both sides. What is each playworker committing to do or not do? Most agreements will be verbal, but sometimes it will be appropriate to make brief notes of the agreement. A written record of the conversation will be necessary if the playworkers' conflict has disrupted the work and especially if the clear agreement is necessary to avoid more serious, perhaps disciplinary, action by a senior playworker.

PROBLEM SOLVING

All playwork teams will have to face and resolve problems in their work. It may be how best to deal with a child whose behaviour is disrupting the play setting or the clash between two playworkers with very different styles. Or the problem may be more one of how to deal with outside pressures on the running or finances of the play setting.

The most effective approach to problem solving goes through four steps. These are:

1 What exactly is the problem, in detail?
2 What are alternative ways of looking at the problem?
3 What are the possible ways (preferably more than one) of resolving this problem?
4 Taking everything into account, what seems to be the best way forward?

Successful problem solving – whether in team meetings or supervision sessions – can only emerge if you are willing to step back from how the problem looks at first sight (including whose fault it is!) and from your own favourite solution. This 'stepping back' can be supported by a team leader in supervision and an effective person in the chair for team meetings.

Bringing together a number of people in a group to discuss and resolve a problem should, in theory, be more effective than leaving the thinking and final decision up to one person. You are tapping into more ideas and experience of what could be done and what might be the advantages and drawbacks to possible solutions. However, many people have had the experience of group problem solving that has sunk into argument and personal grandstanding. A very great deal depends on how the group is led, and on how the discussion progresses through the four steps outlined above.

Activity 9.6

Either: Take a previous case study in the book and work through it, using the four steps of problem solving. For instance, you could look at the example of Bedford leisure centre on page 227.

Or: Take this logical step-by-step approach to a problem that you are currently facing in your own play setting.

Present your ideas to a team meeting.

EFFECTIVE MEETINGS

Most play settings will need meetings at some point. Even when the time is short and a great deal has to be done, a well-run meeting will leave the team feeling clearer about what is to be done and satisfied with the time spent.

Why are we meeting?

Everyone needs to be clear at the outset why they are all in the meeting. If it is a regular team meeting that is held at the same time each week, then it is understood that the meeting covers the business of this week and planning for the next. The objectives are to organise and coordinate the work. Playwork teams may sometimes need to come together to resolve a persistent problem in the setting.

An effective meeting is one in which you have all come together because a meeting is the best way to get this piece of work done. Team meetings are not the time for:

- general conversation and catching up with colleagues' interests or concerns
- detailed feedback, praise or criticism of individual team members
- issues that will have to be resolved between just a couple of team members.

Written notes of meetings

Most meetings benefit from a written agenda, which may be made available to the team before the meeting. Agendas will support effective playwork meetings – so long as they list the specific items to be covered and allocate a realistic estimate of how much time will be spent on each.

If it is worth having a meeting, then it's worth having a reliable written account of what went on. These notes, sometimes called the minutes, are not a

Weekly rotas will have been decided in a staff meeting

blow-by-blow account of everything that was said or happened in a given meeting, they are a written record made during the meeting (not afterwards from memory) of:

- Decisions that were taken.
- Ideas that were gathered when no final decision was made.
- Pieces of work that are to be done – what, by whom, where and by when.
- Concerns or problems that have not been resolved and must not be forgotten.

Without written notes, it is all too possible to forget what exactly was decided or to have some confusion. It may be possible to chair a meeting and also be the one to take the notes, but it is probably better if someone else takes this task. If the agenda has been written out clearly, then it may be possible to write key points against each item. Sometimes it makes sense that the person chairing the meeting asks individual playworkers to note down that they have agreed to do something and by when.

Chairing a meeting

A well-run meeting has one person who takes responsibility for chairing the entire process. Team leaders may take the role of chairing, but there are advantages to rotating the task around the individual team members. Everyone then has the opportunity to learn the skills of chairing and to experience, first hand, the hard work of keeping a meeting on track for its objectives and time limits.

The tasks of chairing cover the following:

- Good time keeping, using a watch and not guesswork. Starting and finishing on time. Keeping to the time allocated for the separate agenda items.
- Reminding those present of the objective(s) of the meeting and keeping everyone informed of the move from one agenda item to another.
- Following the agenda – ensuring any new items don't just get shoved in. If you have met to discuss the budget for next year then that is what you do – you don't spend half the meeting on how to deal with the behaviour of one of the children.
- Making sure that key points, ideas and decisions of the meeting are written down on a sheet of paper, a flip chart or board.

GOOD PRACTICE

Meetings are not effective when they are interrupted by telephone calls. Ideally your play setting needs an answerphone. If you cannot afford one yet, then decide on a different team member each time who will take messages.

KEY POINT

When you are the person chairing a meeting, you have to be objective. You will have your own opinions, but your control of the discussion and summing up of the main points must be impartial. If there is a point in the meeting when your colleagues will benefit from your personal view or experience, then hand over the chair for that time.

Some tips for meetings

If you are chairing the meeting of a very vocal team, you may need some tactics to avoid noise overload. You also want to avoid the risk of losing good ideas in the cut and thrust as everybody wants their suggestion to win out.

Here are some ideas that have worked in different groups. Add your own ideas to the end of the list. You will have to judge what is best suited to your team.

1 'Only one person talks at any one time!' Establish this as a ground rule for meetings. The chair must enforce the rule.
2 'Say three good things!' This ground rule can help teams whose approach is too much that of 'Yes, but ... ' Nobody can put their point without voicing three positive comments about the suggestion with which they want to argue.
3 Speakers have to summarise accurately what the last person said before they can say their piece.

Sometimes the problem is more that of long silences. Individuals may approach the team leader later and offer excellent ideas but with 'I didn't like to say in the meeting'. Again, suggestions must be tailored to the group. Some ideas are:

1 Meetings can be fuelled by written suggestions given to the chair or team leader beforehand. Suggestions must be signed.
2 The chair starts off 'round robins' of comments, however brief, in which everyone says something.
3 Specific invitations for silent team members to participate – made before they have been quiet for too long. Bring them in with positive invitations such as, 'Suzie, I know you've done some thinking about why the school pick-up

seems so chaotic,' or, 'Gary, you've worked with children who spoke a different language to you. How do you think we should prepare for the Thai children who are coming next week?'

PROGRESS CHECK

1 List four of the tasks of the person chairing a meeting.
2 What are the risks if nobody takes notes from a meeting?
3 Briefly describe the four steps in effective problem solving.

Support and learning

LEARNING AT WORK

Within your work you may learn successfully through a number of complementary approaches:

- More experienced playworkers may be able to tell you what to do or explain how and why an aspect to the work is organised the way that it is.
- You can extend your understanding through talking and listening in conversations with other playworkers.
- You may read books and articles.
- You may observe other playworkers and follow the pattern they set.
- Experienced playworkers can support and supervise your practice.
- You can be reflecting on your own practice as well as that of your colleagues.
- Your continued learning in your play setting can be complemented by attendance at a course, such as undertaking an NVQ.

LEARNING FROM MISTAKES

An inevitable part of learning will be some level of confusion or actual misunderstanding and some mistakes. Both adults and children benefit from an environment in which mistakes are handled considerately, rather than with irritation. In the play setting you have a good opportunity to show children that adults make mistakes and to model a constructive way of dealing with errors and mishaps.

If you are the playworker who has made the mistake:

- Admit it, even if you feel foolish or annoyed with yourself.
- Give some thinking time to what you can learn here.
- Ask for specific help when you need it.
- Sometimes you may need to talk over your feelings with a colleague.
  If you are the playworker supporting the one who has made the mistake:
- Help him/her to talk about what has happened and his/her feelings. Admitting a mistake has been made is an important first step, but you will have to move on.

- Talk with him/her about what can be learned, what could be avoidable in the future, what he/she needs to know, understand, or now learn how to do.
- Deal with mistakes that perhaps were realistically not avoidable. Some things just happen and cannot be predicted.
- Look at any broader issues that are highlighted. Is there something troublesome about the rota? Has an atmosphere developed in which playworkers resist asking for assistance? Do several playworkers need particular information or training?

GOOD PRACTICE

Simply saying 'we all learn from our mistakes' is not enough. Playworkers need to support each other in standing back to see what can genuinely be learned, for individuals or the whole setting. This means resisting the temptation to blame, to tease and to indulge in the self-satisfaction of 'at least it wasn't me.'

SUPERVISION

KEY POINT

Any play setting will benefit from playworkers who show their own personality and individual styles. Yet all workers must develop their practice in line with the overall approach of the play setting and consistently with the shared values.

Feedback in supervision
An effective supervisor and team leader uses skills of constructive feedback to:
- motivate playworkers, to encourage and support them through the tough times
- guide and improve individual practice, including dealing with poor or doubtful practice.

Sometimes people claim to be giving useful criticism, but they are more accurately taking the opportunity to tell someone off – without any helpful guidance. Giving genuinely constructive feedback is not a complicated technique, but it requires consideration of two key points:

1   What is the basis for what I am saying?
2   How can I make what I say as useful as possible to the other person?

Communication within a supervision session, or in more general conversation can be far more constructive if everyone follows these general guidelines:

- **Be specific.** Nobody can do anything useful with vague feedback, and in the absence of any helpful details it is far too easy to come to the wrong conclusion. So, focus your feedback on what happened and when.

   For example: Zoe is told that she has a 'sloppy' approach to record keeping. She turns this over in her mind and decides she is being criticised for her handwriting and vows to be more careful. In fact, Ian, the centre leader, was more concerned that Zoe does not write up minor accidents promptly in the book and that she leaves children's files open on the table rather than putting them away in the filing cabinet.

■ **Describe what you have observed.** Useful feedback focuses on what someone has done, or not done. The feedback is on their behaviour; it is not an excuse for slapping on labels about someone's personality or style, regardless of whether these labels are overall positive or negative.

   For example: It is of very limited help to criticise with, 'You're offhand. It's not what you say to parents, it's the way that you say it.' The other person needs definite examples of what you or reliable colleagues have seen or heard in this playworker's approach to named parents.

■ **What and not why.** The value of feedback is in the description of what you have observed. You do not know people's reasoning, their motivations or their worries. Playworkers' reasons for their actions, or inaction, may be important in the conversation that follows your feedback, but they have to come from the other person

   For example: Comments such as, 'But I expect you were thinking that … ' or, 'I'm sure what you meant to do … ' are only guesswork on your part and these attempts at mind reading will muddle up your feedback.

■ **Opinions are given honestly – not disguised as facts.** If you have been alert to the other person's practice, then you will have some opinions. The important issue is to keep a clear distinction between factual feedback and the opinion that you are giving. Your perspective or feelings should be honestly given as an 'I think … because' or 'I see it this way … let me explain'.

   For example: It is Denise's opinion to claim, 'Ed, you've got the wind up after that unpleasantness with Gemma's mother. You scarcely talk to any parents any more.' More constructive feedback from Denise would be, 'Ed, I want to talk some more with you about the incident with Gemma's mother. I'm concerned that the experience has made you wary about the more argumentative parents.'

■ **Balance positives and negatives.** Although a brief conversation may focus on just one aspect of someone's work, useful feedback in supervision has to acknowledge the rounded picture. Feedback should include details of what is going well and the improvements that a playworker has made as well as identify areas that need attention through constructive criticism.

   For example: Especially in a sit-down conversation about someone's overall work, you should give time, and detail, to, 'I've noticed how much better you handle … ' or, 'I think your new approach to teasing from the boys is paying off … '

GOOD PRACTICE

If a playworker's feelings about your feedback become more prominent than the discussion of the detail of what you are saying, then it is best to allow the other person to express those feelings. Listen and attempt to understand what has led to this situation in which the feelings are running high.

To think about   9.7

Read through the following two examples of feedback to playworkers. In what ways is the feedback unconstructive? How might the point be better made? Discuss your ideas with a colleague.

1   The St Dunstan's records show that Haki has been late at least twice a week for the last month. Maureen, the centre leader, has been tackled by other playworkers who complain that they have to cover for Haki in all the preparations before the children arrive. Maureen catches Haki and says, 'You keep being late. You've got to be here on time, Haki – you're upsetting everybody.'

2   The other playworkers welcome the liveliness that Bill brings, but are irritated that he doesn't seem to know when to stop – either with the more energetic play or with teasing the children. Anthea loses her patience one day when she has to calm down a group of children. 'You're an insensitive clod, Bill! You never think! You just walked away from the kids when they were totally wound up and left me to sort it out.'

KEY POINT

Feedback should be helpful to the person on the receiving end. The content of the feedback may not always be welcome, it may be critical, but it must be given in such a way that it can be used.

RECEIVING FEEDBACK

The playworkers giving feedback can do their best to make what they say as constructive as possible. However, in any team, some responsibility also lies with the person on the receiving end.

When you are receiving feedback – in a short exchange or through supervision – you can learn the most from what you hear if you:

- Listen carefully to what is said, without interrupting or disagreeing.
- You may or may not agree, but do you understand? You can check your understanding of the feedback if you summarise the comments using your own words.
- Ask questions and ask for examples if the feedback is vague.
- Think it over and allow for the fact that a colleague may have a point, even if you felt uncomfortable about hearing it.
- Accept compliments gracefully. Some people react to positive feedback in such an offhand way that the giver can come to regret having said anything at all. A simple thanks is fine.

KEY POINT

It can be easier to see the flaws in other people's feedback because you know how you felt when you heard their comments. So, it is important to review honestly how you give feedback and listen carefully if your words are not well received.

GOOD PRACTICE

You can never be sure for certain that somebody to whom you are giving feedback will not go on the defensive. Workers' reactions are also affected by their previous experience of feedback, which may not have been very constructive. In your play setting it may take time to build playworkers' confidence that the feedback and the wish to develop workers' skills are a genuine objective. This is as true of feedback between playworkers as it is for the supervision relationship between a team leader and individual workers.

COACHING

In any playwork team it is very possible that different playworkers will have a varied base of skills and so could help colleagues to learn. The term 'coaching' is used here to describe this working relationship, when one playworker is more experienced than another – overall or on specific skills – but the relationship is not one of more formal teaching.

In order to coach another playworker, you have to continue to reflect on your own practice:

- What are your reasons for doing it this way?
- What steps did you go through in learning? Is there any logical progression to follow?
- When your colleague seems confused or unable to do something that you

find easy, then put yourself in your colleague's shoes. Recapture that feeling of what it was like when you didn't know, when it did not come automatically.

What may seem so obvious to you now is far from obvious whilst someone is learning. You often have to take apart your skills and knowledge in order to share them through coaching. Adults, like children, need manageable steps, a chance to practise, encouragement with constructive feedback and enough challenge without anxiety.

PROGRESS CHECK

1   Describe at least four characteristics of constructive feedback.
2   Why would it be just as important to have examples when feedback is generally positive as those times when it is more negative?
3   How might you deal with mistakes when you are coaching a colleague?

New team members

A playwork team will need new members from time to time. There are several aspects to good practice in this area of your work:
■   planning ahead for how many and what kind of new playworkers you need
■   fair and safe systems in recruitment and selection
■   induction of new workers or volunteers into their job role.

PLANNING AHEAD

The team as a whole needs to anticipate when new staff will be needed. Some possibilities include:
■   A current team member is about to leave, either permanently or on parental leave. Alternatively, personal circumstances might mean that a worker has asked for less hours or to try for a job share.
■   You run half-term or holiday playschemes for which you need temporary playworkers for the duration of the scheme.
■   The setting is developing a new part to the work or activities and additional team members are needed.

If you run regular holiday playschemes then good records of previous playworkers can be your starting point for this temporary team. If you and the children are fortunate, you may well have some playworkers returning for subsequent playschemes, but you will always need at least some new workers.

Job and person specification
All playworkers should have a written job description that covers the details of their responsibilities. The existing job descriptions will be a guide in seeking new workers. However, you may also properly look at the current skills balance

within the team and consider whether, ideally, you would like to bring in a new colleague with specific skills and background.

GOOD PRACTICE

Any job description has be specific enough that workers understand what is expected of them, but good practice will always need further discussion about, for instance, what 'promoting children's rights' means in practice in this setting. Recruiting voluntary helpers is likely to be a less formal system, but care should still be taken to plan ahead and communicate your team's expectations clearly to any potential volunteers.

RECRUITMENT

Advertising and the short-list

All playwork settings need to follow a consistent process in seeking new staff. Procedures are in place to ensure fairness in recruitment but also the safety of users as a result of proper checks on new staff. You will have to advertise in publications likely to be read by playworkers, but also think about a broad enough spread to ensure anti-discriminatory practice when inviting applications.

You have to think about the job that is vacant and the qualities and experience that you seek. However, there are some legal restraints about specifying the kind of worker you would ideally like. For instance, neither a senior playleader nor the management committee can decide arbitrarily to employ a female, or a male playworker (against the Sex Discrimination Act 1976) or to employ a playworker only from a certain racial group (against the Race Relations Act 1976). You can seek a new worker with specific linguistic skills or cultural background, but only if the job and person specification demonstrates that certain qualities are essential for this post. Otherwise your team is in the position of weighing up the qualities and experience of those individuals who reply to the advertisement. Team discussion can be important to air and perhaps de-bunk untested assumptions along the lines of, 'We need more men in this team because then we'll be able to...' or 'An Asian colleague would definitely contribute...'.

Be ready with any written material to send out to applicants and decide whether you are happy for people to visit the setting before their interview. Follow up the references for all your shortlisted candidates.

INTERVIEWING AND ASSESSMENT

Ensure that everyone involved in the interviewing process is clear about the qualities and experience you need in your potential team member. During the interview and in discussion in the team afterwards, you should compare individuals against the job and not against each other. Your setting needs a playworker suitable for the role and not just the best of a mediocre shortlist.

Within your team, perhaps in cooperation with your management committee:

- Prepare a list of the questions you will ask every applicant and any further queries that are specific to individuals. For instance, perhaps one candidate has a special area of expertise about which you would like to know more. Another candidate looks promising but has never stayed longer than six months in any job – are there reasons for this short-term approach?
- Decide whether one person will interview all the candidates or whether there will be a panel, and then who will lead? Facing a panel can be more daunting for interviewees but is more effective than, for instance, a series of interviews with each member of a management committee. Will there be one or two setting users on the interviewing panel?
- Identify the ways in which you will involve children and young people in this whole process. Even your youngest users will have suggestions and opinions and they will all become more experienced in decision making and interview skills, if you involve them appropriately.
- Let the applicants know in advance what will be involved in the interviewing process as well as the timing. For instance, do you want them to give a short presentation about their experience or a playwork issue?
- Organise a realistic schedule for a chance for applicants to look round your setting, a time for the formal interview and for any group discussion or task that is part of the process.
- Organise a quiet space for interviews, where you will not be interrupted, and arrange the room so that everyone can sit comfortably and see each other.

KEY POINT

Of course candidates want to present themselves in a positive light, but they are also gaining an impression of the existing team and your setting. Chaotic organisation of interviews or mismanagement of candidates' expectations may dissuade good playworkers from joining your team.

Interviewing skills

Effective interviews use the range of good communication skills that are important in other aspects of your playwork, but your aim in interviewing is to find out facts and to draw out the candidate. So, more control of the conversation properly stays with the person doing the interviewing – in contrast to running a supervision session or helping a young person to talk through a problem.

- *The pattern of the interview*
  An effective sequence in a selection interview is to start with questions about candidates' general qualifications and experience, then move on to this area of work and their most recent jobs or relevant voluntary experience. You would then explore candidates' reasons for wanting to join your setting or playscheme and ask further questions to assess their capability for the work. Finally, you should offer candidates time to ask their own questions.

- *Using questions and summaries*
  Your communication in the interview should follow a sequence of asking a question, listening to the answer and often summarising what you have heard. The point of frequent and brief summaries is to check that you have understood what the candidates said and to give them an opportunity to extend or modify their answers.

  The best pattern is usually to ask more open-ended questions early in the interview and then later you ask more focused questions. For instance, you might ask everyone a 'What if...' question, such as 'We have a no-smoking policy in the play setting. How would you approach a group of twelve-year-olds who you find smoking behind the garden hut?' If you involve children in the interview process, they can often prepare some good 'What if...' questions, for instance, 'In this adventure playground we're expected to tell you about bullying. But suppose we don't want to grass up a friend? How will you handle that?'

  Some detailed questions would be appropriate to individual candidates, for example, 'You say on your application that you worked with refugee children. What do you believe is most important in that kind of playwork?' Or you may need to explore gaps in this person's experience with, 'You've never worked with disabled children. We sometimes have children with severe learning and physical disabilities. How do you think you will cope?'

- *Listen and note*
  Good interviewers do not interrupt but you will need to intervene courteously if a candidate is continuing with a long answer. Someone needs to note down the candidate's replies, otherwise there is the risk that details will become muddled if you interview several people one after another. The

notes will also help the discussion that will follow the end of the interviewing process when the playwork team, and ideally also the users, weigh up who will be the best person to join the setting.

Finally, you would offer the job to your preferred candidates, subject to police checks necessary for the safety of children.

Activity 9.10

Explore and plan for ways in which you could involve the children and young people in the process of finding and choosing new playworkers. You could consider an upcoming interview process or look back over the most recent time you found new workers.

- In what ways could you involve, or better involve, the users of your play setting?
- Discuss within the team, and with your current users, possibilities within each part of the process.
- Ensure that you are honest with the children about the ways in which they can influence the choice and about those decisions that will remain with the playwork team.
- Write up your plans in a short report and then later add comments about how the process went in practice.

INDUCTION

New workers and volunteers deserve a warm welcome and guidance about what is expected of them from experienced staff. A useful induction process will usually stretch over several weeks so that new colleagues do not feel pressure to understand their responsibilities within a few days and then just get on with the work. An induction can be well organised and yet still feel friendly and informal. The pattern should include the following:

- An unhurried conversation, ideally on the first day of work, with a senior playworker who explains the work and answers any questions.
- Access to your written material on policies and procedures, with opportunities later to talk about the issues and ask any questions.
- A named playworker whom the new colleague can consult even over minor issues. This experienced worker, sometimes called a mentor, may support the new member of staff for as long as several months.
- A clear role for children and young people in helping the settling process. You obviously have to be aware that some users may delight in testing and winding up a new worker. However, at least some of the children like to be able to offer positive support.

Volunteers

Some play settings depend on volunteers, but unpaid workers are sometimes left out of the induction process. Yet a regular parent-helper or an interested student volunteer needs to understand what should be done in the work and how, just as much as paid staff.

PROGRESS CHECK

1 Describe two ways in which anti-discriminatory practice should underpin your choices and decisions in seeking new playworkers.
2 Offer two advantages to involving children and young people in the selection and interviewing process.
3 Pinpoint four ways in which you might prepare the setting and candidates for the day of the interview.

Building relationships with parents

Parents are important in the playwork relationship because they:
■ have the long-term responsibility for their children
■ have knowledge and unique experience of their own children and young people
■ are, in some settings, users of the service along with their children
■ will have knowledge and skills which they may be pleased to share with the play setting
■ may be a member of the voluntary management committee of a play setting.

Playworkers may be very important in part of the lives of children and young people, but it is only one part and the responsibility taken for users is specific to particular times and places. Certainly no playworkers should ever take children on trips or make decisions for them that are outside the remit of the setting. Even

when there is serious concern that children or young people may be at risk from their families, good practice is to make contact with parents sooner rather than later. (See page 29 in Chapter 1 and page 177 in Chapter 7.)

KEY POINT

It is very important that every individual in the playwork team takes an equally courteous approach to parents, since the offhand manner of one playworker can rebound on other members of the team.

CONTACT WITH PARENTS

In play settings where children are picked up, playworkers may be able to build relationships with parents through the daily contact. But often the contact may be as much with other carers or relatives, perhaps older brothers and sisters. In some of the open-access settings or mobile facilities, playworkers may have little or no contact with anyone in the family except the child or young person who attends.

A friendly relationship

Playworkers should aim to make parents welcome when they come to the play setting whether this is on a daily basis or very infrequently. Playworkers will be trying for a friendly working relationship with parents. There may not be long conversations each day – this would be utterly impossible in some busy play settings – but the possibility for friendly contact needs to be created. Parents need to be able to feel that they could approach playworkers.

Play settings vary in how well you are likely to get to know parents. In some adventure playgrounds you may scarcely see parents and some after-school clubs find that many parents are in a hurry when they pick up their children. In contrast, some open-access schemes find that parents can become quite regular visitors, bringing their children and perhaps staying for coffee and conversation.

GOOD PRACTICE

Some play settings take specific responsibility for children between fixed hours and there is effectively a sharing of the care of children after school and in the holidays. The channels of communication between home and play setting need to be open for this to work well and for important information to be passed from one to another.

Parents' names

You will have the same considerations to bear in mind for learning and using parents' names as have been outlined for children's names on page 65. Perhaps you may only have very limited opportunities to introduce yourself to some parents and to learn their names. On the few occasions you do meet, you may get by with a friendly 'Hello', or with 'Andy, your dad's here today.' On the other hand, when there is the chance of a longer term relationship, then it is courteous to learn parents' names. Introduce yourself in the way that you are known to the children; this will almost certainly be by your first name. Many parents may be pleased to give their first name in return. If they say, 'I'm Mr … ' or 'Mrs … ', then follow their preference. If your introduction does not produce any name then ask, 'What may I call you?'

SHARING INFORMATION

Parents need information on the play setting that is accurate, clear, up to date and appropriately expressed so that they can make choices where possible, feel involved and give their informed consent or refusal where appropriate.

Good practice in a relationship with parents is that playworkers should:

- Explain to parents initially how the play setting operates and give them an opportunity to ask questions. In an open-access facility playworkers may not see parents, but opportunities can be taken to put up posters or send home leaflets with the users.
- Parents who visit should be given copies of any leaflet about the play setting and any policies. It is considerate to have copies made in the languages spoken in the neighbourhood.
- Take the opportunity to run an open day, if that may be the best method to communicate with parents, and the local community.
- Involve parents in the gathering of information about a child or young person that will enable the play setting to work well and safely with this individual. (See page 113.)

- Make available any records of a parent's own son or daughter, if parents request. Ease of access is good practice with written records, but if you keep information on a computer, it is a legal obligation to make it available under the Data Protection Act 1998.

CONSULTING AND ASKING PERMISSIONS

Play settings vary and some may have very limited opportunities to consult with parents of users – most of the consultation will be with the children and young people themselves. However, some settings may be able to canvas for parents' views on some issues, either through conversation or by sending round a letter.

Individual consultation may be important when issues arise about which playworkers are uncertain. The need to talk may especially arise if playworkers wish to take appropriate account of the family's culture or religious beliefs and feel that they do not know enough to make a proper decision.

GOOD PRACTICE

It is essential that playworkers ask permission of parents for any trips outside the usual play activities and give enough information that parents can make an informed decision. (See page 123.)

SETTING THE BOUNDARIES

In some cases playworkers may need to be very clear about the boundaries between home and play setting and the pattern of responsibilities of playworkers and parents. Misunderstandings and disagreements can arise, for example, when parents:
- have expectations of the play setting that are not realistic, even though sometimes playworkers may have inadvertently encouraged them
- wish to intervene in events in the play setting, for instance, by coming into a play scheme to confront a user, or group of users, who they believe is troubling their child.

Such disagreements have to be dealt with courteously, although very firmly on occasion.

GOOD PRACTICE

Parents are owed respect and consideration of their views, but they have obligations in turn and one of these is not to disrupt the play setting. A playworker has the right to ask parents to leave if they are verbally or physically aggressive, and to call for help from colleagues.

Downham after-school club started with a goal; 'To offer a service that is flexible to parents' needs and expressed wishes'. This particular goal was set because of playworkers' concern about setting up an equal relationship with parents in which the club did not in effect say 'This is the service – take it or leave it!'

However, the request from some parents that the club should make a quiet area for children to do their homework has led to unexpected difficulties. One mother blamed Zoe for not ensuring that her daughter had actually completed her homework and a father came in to berate Ian, who had offered help to his son on maths, but had got some answers wrong.

Questions

1 What has happened here? Answer from the perspective of the club and from the perspective of the parents.
2 How could the playwork team sort out exactly where the responsibility of the playworkers ends and that of parents begins on the homework issue or on any other issue?
3 What else might need to be clarified about 'flexibility'?
4 Discuss the issues in your team and consider potential confusions in your setting.

COMPLAINTS AND PROBLEMS

Sometimes playworkers will be facing parents who come with complaints or issues about which they feel strongly. You have an obligation to deal promptly and courteously with any problems or disagreements, but the discussion has to be honest over the ground rules and any codes of practice of the play setting. On some occasions, the result of this kind of conversation will be a realisation that the playwork team has made a mistake, or failed to notice what is going on in the setting. It will then be very important to share this new information with colleagues and raise any general issues about practice with the whole team.

GOOD PRACTICE

All playworkers should know the official complaints procedure for their setting. Only a minority of disagreements with parents will go this far, but every member of the team must know what should be done, and at what point an irate parent should be passed on to the most senior playworker.

Sometimes, playworkers will be the ones to contact parents. The playworkers may be concerned about a child or young person's well-being – perhaps she or he seems unhappy or has confided problems (see for example the case study of bullying on page 186). On other occasions a user's behaviour may be so unacceptable that he or she is likely to be banned from the play setting.

In any conversation with a parent over a concern, it will be important that the playworker:

■ expresses the issues or serious concerns in a descriptive way and tries to avoid implying that the parent is in some way to blame or should have realised what was happening
■ explains what has been done so far to deal with the situation and the reason that it has been decided to call in the parent
■ leaves as much room for discussion as is realistically possible if a child's behaviour is unacceptable, but is honest about what needs to happen from the play setting's perspective.

GOOD PRACTICE

A complaint from a parent or a meeting called by playworkers with a parent should be written up clearly – recording what was discussed and what emerged as a result.

To think about   9.12
Consider any recent examples in your play setting when you needed to talk with parents.
1   How did the conversation go?
2   If it went well, what do you think was most important in making that happen?
3   If the conversation did not go as well as you hoped, can you think now of ways that you could have made the exchange more constructive? (Look back at page 232 on constructive feedback.)
4   Write up your reflections and discuss them with a colleague.

If playworkers suspect child abuse there is likely to be a code of practice on the pattern of contact that should be followed. It may be that, under certain circumstances, playworkers should contact the local child protection team before talking with parents. All playworkers should be aware of the code of practice in their setting. (See also page 174.)

PROGRESS CHECK

1   Give two reasons why every play setting should make efforts to establish contact with parents.
2   Describe three basic points to bear in mind when dealing with a parent's complaint.

KEY TERMS

You need to know what these words and phrases mean. Go back through the chapter to make sure that you understand.

Teams
Interdependence
Teamwork
Trust
Values
Rota
Problem solving
Agenda
Minutes of a meeting

Chairing a meeting
Supervision
Constructive feedback
Coaching
Feedback
Goals
Job specification
Induction

10 DEVELOPING AND PROMOTING YOUR PLAYWORK SERVICE

> **This chapter covers:**
> ■ **Knowing your community**
> ■ **Promoting your service**
> ■ **Effective working relationships with others**
> ■ **Developing joint initiatives**

Knowing your community

To be effective a play project must know who the people and organisations are within its community. There are two principal reasons for this. Firstly, to be successful the play project must be striving to offer play opportunities to all sections of the community and, secondly, to maintain growth and development the project needs to be promoting its good quality and effectiveness.

The term 'community' is a catch-all word which can mean different things to different people. For the purpose of this chapter we are defining community as:
■ the children, parents and carers who use the play project
■ the children, parents and carers who live in the area
■ the shops and businesses within the immediate vicinity of the play project
■ the services within the immediate vicinity of the play project, e.g. town hall, leisure centre, youth club
■ the shops, businesses and services within the wider reaches of the play project.

THE CHILDREN, PARENTS AND CARERS WHO USE THE PLAY PROJECT

All play projects have a core of users – the children and their parents and carers who visit the playground on a regular basis. Knowing this core should be the easiest part of 'knowing your community' and these relationships have been explored in earlier chapters of this book. In particular, your interaction with the children and young people who use the project on a very regular, often daily, basis will enable you to get to know them quickly. If both you and they remain in the community for a prolonged period of time, you will get to know them in some depth. This will be true, to a greater or lesser degree, for all settings. For the playworker with a mobile play project you may be getting to know several groups of regular users. For the temporary holiday playscheme worker, although you may only be interacting with the children for a short period it is likely to be intensive and the scheme may well be a regular service to the area and you will meet the same children each year.

The same may well be true of your interaction with the parents and carers, but this will naturally have a different perspective. In some settings you may have a very strong relationship with parents and carers. In voluntary managed projects, parents and carers not only visit the project but may also sit on the management committee. In all settings, they often play a part as volunteer helpers. With care settings the interaction with parents and carers at registration and picking up time can facilitate an opportunity to share information about the child and for some social exchange between playworker and parent. In open-access settings, parents and carers will also spend time chatting if they drop off or collect their child and in some settings, adventure playgrounds in particular, they may well drop in during the session for a cup of tea and talk with you and other parents.

Spending some time considering how well you know the adults in the children's lives, however, is important. For what underpins that importance is the question of how well the parent or carer knows the project. Can you be certain that all the parents and carers know what the project offers, how often it operates and what opportunities there are for them to be involved? Do they really understand what you do and why stimulating play opportunities are so important for their children's development? If the playground got into difficulties would you be able to count on them for their support?

For although you may have a very good relationship with some, perhaps many, of your regular users' parents and carers, there may be others whom you seldom or never see. In open-access projects, by their very nature, the children walk to and from the project and some adults may have little interaction with you. In care schemes the children may be dropped off by a friend or a relative and you may seldom meet the actual parent or parents.

Activity   10.1

With a colleague, or in your team, take a sample group of your regular users. You may wish to take a small number across a number of age ranges: 4–6, 7–9, 10–12, 13–16, or a larger number from just one or two age groups to start with. Identify how often you have met the parent and/or carer of each child in the past month and what the nature of that interaction was. Was it just a quick hello and goodbye at registration time or did you spend twenty minutes speaking at a recent open day? Then pose the questions, 'How much do I think this mum, dad or carer knows about the project?' and 'How much do I think they understand about the importance of play and what we do?'

If you have access to a computer, you could devise a simple method of recording the above information and include a graph to show the degree of contact with each age group.

The outcome of this activity might well be that you identify a strong need to publicise the project and send an invitation for parents and carers to visit for further information.

It is important for playworkers to make time to speak to parents and carers. In a busy project it may be necessary to take a planned approach to this and nominate a worker or workers to be on hand for this kind of exchange, particularly at opening up and closing down times. Registration is an ideal opportunity, but it will probably need more than one member of staff as the process of actually registering the children in requires concentration. Parents and carers also may not have the time at registration as they could be on their way to jobs or study. Picking up time may well be a better opportunity for a chat.

THE CHILDREN, PARENTS AND CARERS WHO LIVE IN THE AREA

As well as your core users and their families, there will be other children, parents and carers who either only use the project infrequently or perhaps never use it at all. There may be people, often 'communities' within the community, who you will need to spend time researching in order to determine what approach to take in order to promote and publicise the project. Researching your community can provide a useful opportunity for a joint initiative with another group or organisation and we will be exploring this later in the chapter. The reasons why some children only use the project infrequently may be very straightforward but nonetheless worthy of attention. Perhaps they live too far away to be able to visit frequently, but if you run a pick-up and drop-off service near to their home or school, do they know about it? Perhaps the parent or carer has a very busy work or study schedule and is unaware that your project runs a before-school as well as an after-school service.

There may, however, be other more substantial reasons why children either use the playground infrequently or not at all. It could be that in some areas of your community they are literally unaware that the project exists. This can be particularly prevalent if the project doesn't occupy a prominent position in the area and is therefore 'invisible' to those who do not, in the normal course of events, pass by. It could be that the project is in a sparsely populated rural area and some families are too distant to be on the informal communication network. Or, conversely, it could be that the project is situated in a densely populated urban area but because of busy roads and a 'hostile' environment parts of the community do not stray far from home and, in particular, do not allow their children to do so.

In some areas there will be parts of the community who are of a different ethnic or cultural group. These people may either experience the project as being 'not for them' by nature of its image and activity or even hostile to their own culture and needs. There will also be other needs that groups or, for that matter, individuals may have which they perceive the project as not providing for. This may be a misapprehension as, for instance, a parent may have a child with a disability and think the project will not be able to accommodate their child. A family may not speak English and be unaware that the project has a specialist interpreting service that provides someone to help new children settle into the project. It is only through research and then promotion and publicity that the true nature of the project can be communicated.

KEY POINT

Although the above aspects are of particular relevance to the project that is permanently located in one place, mobile projects and holiday play schemes also need to know the nature and needs of the community they are providing a service for. It is rare for a mobile play project, for instance, to just 'turn up' at a location. It will be important for the organisers to discover what the nature of that community is and what action needs to be taken before visiting. Leafleting of a housing estate, for example, will give the parents and carers of the children information about the project and what it offers. This publicity will need to be in a style and language that suits the community in question.

SHOPS, BUSINESSES AND SERVICES WITHIN THE IMMEDIATE VICINITY OF THE PLAY PROJECT

Shops and businesses

As described in earlier chapters, local shops and businesses can have an important part to play in the life of a project. They can offer:

■ financial help
■ materials and equipment
■ a means by which to publicise the project – word of mouth, posters and fliers
■ assistance on the management group
■ a friendly face, help and support.

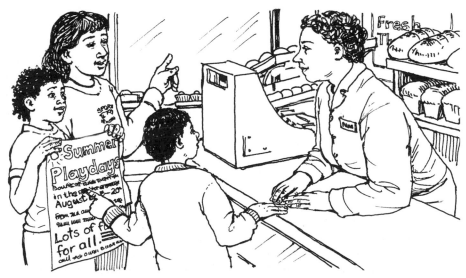

Local shops can help to publicise events at the play project

It is important therefore to maintain a good relationship and keep them informed of the project and its work.

Local services
Local services also have an important and useful part to play. There will be the services that have similar aims and activities to your own, for instance other play projects, youth clubs and community centres. A relationship with schools, in particular, can be an essential part of establishing and maintaining links between the different kinds of provision for the same children. Good working relationships of this kind may be crucial in some circumstances for a child's safety. An example would be the effective transfer of responsibility between a primary school and the pick-up arrangements of an after-school club.

There will be those services that can provide an opportunity for a play activity or outing that the children have chosen to do, swimming, a museum trip or library visit, for example. Other services will provide an opportunity to maintain the profile, continuity and professional development of your project. Keeping councillors on the town hall leisure and recreation committee informed and up to date on the success of your project will be advantageous when spending cuts are being considered. Ensuring your local Learning and Skills Council is aware of your activities in the community will stand you in good stead for applications for staff training and qualifications.

SHOPS, BUSINESSES AND SERVICES WITHIN THE WIDER REACHES OF THE PLAY PROJECT

All of the above may apply equally to shops, services and businesses that are further afield. There are two determining factors:

- the degree to which these organisations do, could or should play a part in the life of the play project themselves – for instance, your town hall or local Learning and Skills Council may, in fact, be some miles from your project but have a crucial role to play in supporting the project
- whether through promotion, publicity and co-operative working arrangements you might reach out to potential children, parents and carers who would benefit from your play project – for instance, by placing posters in shops and businesses outside of your normal catchment area publicising your forthcoming summer playscheme or by circulating information leaflets through day care centres to parents and carers of children with disabilities or special learning needs.

GOOD PRACTICE

A play setting should have names and addresses of important contacts in an easily accessible form, most likely a file that is available to all the playworkers. You might also like to make space in the team's file for the contact addresses and information on national organisations, for instance, on playwork, children with disabilities, health issues and so on. Appendix E will give you a start on this.

SOME EXAMPLES OF USEFUL SERVICES IN THE COMMUNITY

Local play associations and resource banks

A local play association may be able to offer activity packs and specialist equipment, for example, a badge machine, jewellery making kits and materials that would be hard or uneconomical for you to obtain yourself. Associations may also have sessional staff who, with warning, could run activities for you.

A resource centre or scrap bank will have a variety of materials such as paper, cardboard, cloth, buttons and often a myriad of other scrap materials for craft activities. They may also, rather like the play association, produce activity packs and instruction sheets and have specialist equipment available for loan. Such centres may make a small charge or run a system of membership and you will find this out by exploring your own locality.

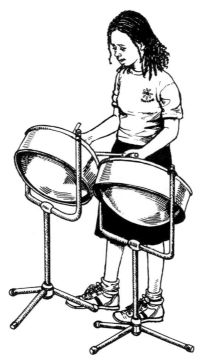

Local contacts may help you with equipment that you do not have in the play setting

Libraries

There has been considerably more published on play and the under-5s than for the age range of 5–15. However, you will find ideas by delving into books written for schools, and on sporting activities, home recreation, crafts and hobbies. Your local play association may have a library and national organisations, such as the National Play Information Centre and the National Children's Bureau, can be a good source of leaflets and reading suggestions. Appendix D has a list of suggested publications and Appendix E a list of useful national organisations.

Museums
Temporary exhibitions and more permanent museums have changed considerably in recent years and the vast majority are inviting, hands-on places. Apart from being enjoyable to visit with the children, museums can also be another source of ideas, often supported by written material designed specifically for easy use with children of different ages.

GOOD PRACTICE

If you open up contacts with local business and services, you may find a new range of possible activities, and at the same time, in some cases, communicate a positive image of your play provision. This type of friendly relationship may take a little time to build up well, but can then be a source of ideas and visits.

Groups of children can be taken, with prior warning, to local shops or for visits behind the scenes in your fast-food establishments. The emergency services of fire, ambulance and police may be able to offer opportunities to visit as well as someone to come and talk to the children about their work.

Any of these visits – of your group to elsewhere, or of visitors to your play setting – will benefit from careful prior planning. You will need to confirm details of timing and contents of visits as well as any necessary preparation of the children. If at all possible, you should have a detailed conversation with anyone who is willing to come and talk with the group. Ideally you want someone whom you have heard talk before, or someone recommended by a fellow playworker as being able to give an interesting presentation. Any possible touchy areas, for instance, that some users of the play setting have a less than positive view of the local police, will need to be considered with care before a speaker talks to the group.

Activity   10.2
Start a file of information on the resources that you have available to you locally. You can include names and addresses and leaflets. An A4 ring binder with both paper and a store of plastic pockets will keep material in good condition. If you have access to a computer, you could create the file electronically which can make it much easier to keep your information updated. You may still want to print out a hard copy for reference.

Promoting your service

There are two principal reasons for promoting your service in the community:
- to inform people of what you offer and increase the numbers of children using the project

- to raise awareness about the quality and importance of what you do.

The two reasons are, of course, inter-related but one may take precedence over the other and each may involve reaching a very different audience. Before embarking on work to promote your project, you need to be sure why you are doing it, who you are speaking to, what messages you are going to impart and what methods are going to be most effective. Handing out leaflets at local schools where parents and carers can see and speak to you, for instance, will be far more effective than just posting them through letter boxes even though it may take a lot longer to reach everyone. Inviting local councillors to an open day where they can see playwork in action will often be far more effective than just writing letters or lobbying the town hall.

Below are two case studies outlining two very different approaches to promotion.

CASE STUDY 10.3

Brenda, David and Raj are the workers at the Clydesdale after-school club. They are concerned that, although they run an integrated service, few children with disability or special learning needs are using the project. They take this issue to the management committee and it is agreed to plan and implement some special action to encourage increased use.

First the team draw up a list of ways of reaching the children and their families. This includes contacting the council education department for schools that cater for disabled children and the social services department for statutory and voluntary services providing care.

They then decide what the important messages are that they wish to convey and decide on the following:

- the values of the project, e.g. equal opportunities, safety, a caring and friendly attitude
- the quality of the play experiences, e.g. stimulating, creative, adventurous
- the project's commitment to a policy of integration
- the project's place in the community, e.g. local provision, able to network with other services.

After this they plan their course of action. They decide that initially they will do three things. Firstly, Brenda and Raj will design a colourful leaflet that they can get printed cheaply locally to circulate to schools and, where possible, direct to families through care agencies. Secondly, David and Raj will arrange with some of the schools to make a special visit both to play with children during the school break and to talk to parents and carers at picking up time. This will also provide an opportunity to give out the leaflets. Thirdly, all the team with help from the management committee plan an open evening where children, with members of their family, can visit the club and try out the facilities alongside the regular children.

It is agreed that this promotional activity will take about two months to complete and the team, with the committee, will review progress after this time. If the action plan has been successful the review will also need to evaluate just how well the team is coping with the new users and whether any new training or staff development needs have been identified.

CASE STUDY   10.4

The staff and voluntary management committee at the Hummingbird Adventure Playground are very concerned that the local council which provides their annual grant is going to have to make substantial cuts in next year's leisure budget. The playground has just completed a very successful summer holiday scheme and the team think that this would be a good time to promote the value of the project to the local authority.

Initially Michelle, the senior worker, talks this over with the Chair of the committee, Duncan. They agree that they should set up a small working group of committee members, parents, older children and staff to plan a presentation that they can take to a meeting of the Early Years Development and Childcare Partnership (EYDCP) in the autumn.

During the summer they have taken lots of photographs of the children using the playground and the working group decide that they should get these made into a slide show as part of their presentation. It is agreed that Michelle and Angus, with Duncan and Katie, one of the older children, will make the presentation.

The messages they want to give are that the playground, in providing a valuable service to children and their parents and carers, meets many of the aspirations of the council itself. These are:

- social inclusion
- children's development through informal education
- a safe environment for play and care
- employment for local people
- helping to combat children and young people's involvement in vandalism, crime and drug abuse
- links to other services.

Duncan writes to the chair and lead officer of the EYDCP and he and Michelle follow the letters up with phone calls. They are given 10 minutes at a meeting in October. It's not very long, so the group have to work hard to make the most of the available time. They decide on an outline of what the playground does with the slide show from the summer by Michelle and Duncan. Katie will then say what the playground offers her as a user and Angus, whose own daughter uses the playground, will give a parent's perspective. Duncan will end the presentation by giving out a special leaflet and highlighting the key points.

Questions
1 What do you think of the strategies employed in these two case studies?
2 Will the play projects achieve their aims?
3 What would you have done in similar cirumstances?

Leafleting at local schools is an effective way of promoting the project and meeting parents

There are many ways of promoting your service in the community and each will have its own purpose depending on whom you want to reach and what you want to say. These are summarised in the table below.

Ways of promoting service and their key purposes

Type of promotion	Key purposes
Open day	■ Good for involving local people. ■ More time to speak to parents and carers. ■ Can be a fun day with a family atmosphere. ■ Opportunity to show people around the project. ■ Can provide a good photo opportunity for local councillors and MPs.
Newsletter	■ Can provide regular information about the project. ■ Can be used to convey an image of the project in its style and content. ■ Children and young people can participate in its content and production.
Leaflet or flier	■ Good for one-off events. ■ Can be produced cheaply and quickly if kept to a simple format. ■ Can be made colourful with photographs or children's paintings. ■ They can be distributed by hand, mail and through the letter box. *contd*

Type of promotion	Key purposes
Poster	■ Expensive if done properly but can be very powerful and eye-catching. ■ Good for special events such as open days or play days. ■ Posters are useful to display information over a period of time in shops and businesses in the area.
Presentation	■ Good for getting your message across to funders and other organisations or groups you wish to influence. ■ Information can be put across in a direct and 'entertaining' way using overhead projections, slides and video. ■ Making a presentation requires the confidence of public speaking and some training may be needed.
Special project	■ Can be a useful tool in promoting your service to sections of the community in an interactive way. A junk modelling project with a local school for instance can be interesting and educational for the children and demonstrate your skills and knowledge to teachers.
Canvassing	■ Can be useful if you need to reach a lot of people in a short time and you can keep the information short and to the point. ■ A useful lobbying tool with the local community if you need to gather support in a time of crisis. Needs following up with a meeting or special event.
Special event	■ As well as open days and play days which have been referred to above, special events such as meetings, conferences and demonstration projects can provide an opportunity to communicate to a larger and/or wider audience your good practice and issues about play and the playground.
Visits, e.g. schools and youth clubs	■ Visits to talk to children and young people about your project can be a very direct way of recruiting new users. It is also an opportunity to talk to other professionals, parents and carers.

PROGRESS CHECK

1 Why is it important to research who lives and works in your community?
2 Identify three areas of benefit for your project in maintaining good relations with local shops and businesses.
3 How might you increase the use of your project by children with a disability?
4 Describe three methods of promoting the play project and its work.

Effective working relationships with others

In the preceding sections of this chapter and in Chapter 9, we have described some of the principles and practice of establishing good working relationships with parents and carers and other groupings in the community. In this section we are going to look at some of the broader issues around networking.

WHY NETWORK?

No play project can exist in isolation from other organisations and individuals in its community. The children and young people you work with interact with a large number of other people and institutions in the community. These will include:

- teachers
- youth workers
- doctors
- other playworkers
- shopkeepers
- leisure and sports centre workers
- health care workers.

As a service your project can be affected by or impact on other professional organisations such as:

- the local authority, in particular departments for:
  - leisure and recreation
  - education
  - social services
  - housing

Supervised outings give children the opportunity to interact with many people in the community

- economic development
- housing
- early years
- sure start programmes
- pre-schools
- children's centres
- nurseries
- churches, mosques and temples
- day care centres
- schools
- voluntary or private organisations with similar aims to yours
- libraries
- resource centres
- the police
- park staff and patrols.

As a provision which will benefit from support, advice and guidance for its own growth and development, particularly in respect of staff development and fulfilment, you will want to maintain knowledge of and good relationships with:

- other play projects
- youth clubs
- schools
- early years childcare and education providers
- support organisations such as local and national play associations
- training agencies at national, regional and local level.

Of course, your interaction with the above will be of a different degree depending on the nature of the relationship. If the education department in the local authority is your principal source of funding, you will need to have an in-depth and frequent interaction with your grants or monitoring officer. Your contact with the local health centre, on the other hand, may be very infrequent, but it is advisable to make initial contact and have their details logged at the play setting.

Activity   10.5

A good way to understand and make priorities in networking is through a simple exercise. With your colleagues take a large sheet of paper and at the centre put the playground. Using the heading 'Who do the children interact with in the community?' draw in all the contact points they have, beginning with an inner circle of the people and places they will visit most and working outwards to those they will visit least, as in the example on page 269.

Having done this ask yourselves the following questions:

- Which of these people or places do we already have contact with?
- Which should we have contact with?
- Which do we need only to make ourselves known?
- How many do we already have logged at the project on a database or contacts list?

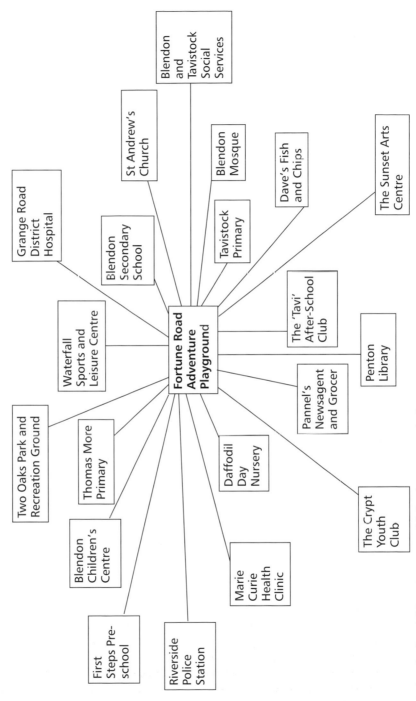

Grange Road District Hospital

Blendon Secondary School

St Andrew's Church

Blendon and Tavistock Social Services

Blendon Mosque

Tavistock Primary

Dave's Fish and Chips

The Sunset Arts Centre

Waterfall Sports and Leisure Centre

Fortune Road Adventure Playground

The 'Tavi' After-School Club

Penton Library

Pannel's Newsagent and Grocer

Two Oaks Park and Recreation Ground

Thomas More Primary

Daffodil Day Nursery

Blendon Children's Centre

Marie Curie Health Clinic

The Crypt Youth Club

First Steps Pre-school

Riverside Police Station

Who do the children interact with in the community?

Activity contd   10.5 contd

Repeat the exercise and questions with the headings: 'Which people and organisations is the playground affected by or could make an impact upon?' and 'Which people and organisations could the project and its staff benefit from in terms of its professional development?'

A networking strategy

Once you have completed the exercise above, you can work together to draw up a strategy for contacting those people and organisations you have discovered you should have more contact with. This will involve examining the nature of the relationship and the degree of depth and frequency that relationship should have. Inevitably your contact will involve promoting your service to raise awareness about play and playwork and describing your policies and working practice. In this you can employ the methods described in the sections above as appropriate.

KEY POINT

It is important when engaging in a networking exercise to recognise that you can only describe what you already know. Before going on to devising a strategy, you will need to examine the make up and cultural diversity of your community. If you have children from ethnic minorities, for instance, do you actually know the places and people they might interact with, e.g. cultural centres, places of religious worship?

Initial contact

Irrespective of whether you are going to have a frequent or infrequent relationship with an individual or organisation, you will still have to make that initial contact. First impressions may not necessarily be lasting, but it will be to your great advantage to get it right first time if you can. Initial contact usually takes one of the following forms:

- a letter and/or flier introducing the contact to your project with a request for a contact person and telephone number, fax and/or e-mail address for further communication
- a letter with perhaps a flier or information pack introducing yourself and your project and requesting a meeting
- a telephone call to introduce yourself and your project and request further contact probably through a meeting
- an informal meeting at another meeting, training event or conference that you are attending
- a request by mail or telephone for further information on the organisation you are contacting.

In all your communications, it is vital that your project be presented in a way that is professional, competent and consistent with the policies and principles of the organisation. Getting it right is not something you can do in isolation; you will need feedback and scrutiny. If you are sending a letter or flier, consult with your colleagues on its content and make sure that someone else proof-reads it for mistakes and inaccuracies before you send it out. As thorough as you may think you are, you can still miss something which is very obvious to someone else. Check how you sound on the telephone. Sometimes people are too polite to tell us that we speak too quietly or too quickly.

Further contact

Meetings, formal or informal, are the principal way in which we develop contact and communication with others on a regular basis. Again, first impressions count. Whether your other team members are involved in the meetings or not, it will help to consult with them in preparation for the meeting. Being prepared is essential. Some key points in making a good first impression are as follows.

- Be on time – if you are going to be late, ring and let them know either directly or through a colleague.
- Dress appropriately – it's always essential to look professional, but for some meetings you may need to be dressed more formally than for others.
- Make sure you have the information you need for the meeting, including your own contact details for them to get back to you.
- Take any information sheets or fliers about your project to hand out.
- Make sure you *listen* as well as speak, but get your points across in a confident and assertive manner.

Contact lists

Good networking depends on cultivating a comprehensive and up-to-date list of people and organisations you are in contact with. If your project has a computer, you may be able to collate the information on a database and merge the contact names and addresses for mail outs. If not, you can keep lists on paper or in a book. If you have contacts who receive regular mailings, you can generate a mailing list by hand using a template that fits address labels. This will save you the chore of addressing lots of envelopes each time.

Make sure you group your contacts under appropriate headings for easy reference.

GOOD PRACTICE

It is important to review your networking strategy and contacts list on a regular basis to check whether you are maintaining the appropriate relationship and whether the details you hold are accurate and up to date. It is useful occasionally to carry out the networking exercise again to see if the people and organisations in your community have changed or whether a different kind of relationship is needed.

There are often changes at national and local government level, for instance, that will require you to re-evaluate your contact and communication with agencies and services in your community.

Developing joint initiatives

A joint initiative with another organisation can be a powerful mechanism towards:
- forging stronger relationships
- effectively meeting a child's needs
- promoting your project
- raising awareness about play and playwork
- extending the service to users and their families.

This will enable you to meet new challenges and develop new areas of skills and knowledge. The idea of a joint initiative may originate with you, a member of your team or the partner organisation. Whichever, it is important to be clear from the outset why you want to carry it out and what the benefits are going to be for the play project and for the partner organisation. Before embarking on a joint initiative you will need to be confident that both the initiative itself and the organisation and people you are working with are compatible with the aims and policies of your own project. Check on this at the outset.

By its very nature, a joint initiative will involve you in either working with new people or working with people in a new way. There is therefore more uncertainty involved and more reason to plan carefully and be clear about roles and responsibilities and lines of communication. If you are the only member of your team engaging in a joint piece of work, it is important to keep your colleagues informed about what is involved and how it is going. There may be occasions when you will need their support and they are much more likely to be sympathetic if they fully understand and appreciate the work in hand.

Once you have decided on what the joint initiative is going to be and have a rough idea of what might be involved, it is essential for you and your colleague or colleagues from the partner organisation to get together for some well thought out planning. A useful tool you might employ is the SMART method by applying the following headings to your objectives:
- **S**pecific – do the objectives clearly state what you need to do?
- **M**easurable – will you be able to measure your achievements?
- **A**chievable – will the task be challenging but not over-difficult?
- **R**ealistic – can you achieve your objectives within the resources available?
- **T**ime-bound – can you achieve your objectives within a given time?

In your plan make sure you have clearly identified:
- which person will be carrying out each task
- how you will monitor and evaluate its success
- how you will communicate with each other and with your respective colleagues
- who you will go to if you encounter difficulties along the way.

If all this seems like hard work, don't be put off – planning is key to the success of any piece of work be it large or small. Many play settings that cater for children as young as four are now beginning to work more closely with other providers delivering the Early Years Foundation Stage. This is particularly beneficial for the children who attend more than setting, as well as for the playworkers. Good networking is important to ensure that those involved are clear about their responsibilities – such as which setting will be completing the child's Early Years Foundation Stage Profile.

CASE STUDY 10.6

At the Downham after-school club several of the children in the 11–13 age range have been showing an interest in drama and Zoë has been helping them. At least once a week they have use of the art room to improvise, act out favourite television programmes, face paint and make costumes. Zoë has also, as part of her own development, been visiting a local arts centre to improve her skills in media and creative arts. In conversation with Roger, the head of media studies, he mentions that he has a couple of students who would like to make a video of people in the local community. Zoë suggests that they could make a film with her and her drama group at the after-school club. This would be an exciting project for the children and they could show the video to the committee and parents at the club's AGM. Roger is interested and thinks it would be a challenging piece of work for his students. He agrees to speak to them on the next available occasion.

The students Shazia and Gareth are interested and they first make an informal visit to the club to meet the children and Zoë's colleagues, Ian, Mike and Suzie. Of course, they take a camera with them and have some fun doing some impromptu filming.

The next step for Zoë is to explain to the rest of the team what she has in mind and what it might mean for them and the other children at the club. They all think it is a great idea, although as the art room would be needed more often for filming there would need to be some compensatory benefit for the other children. Zoë suggests a visit to the arts centre mid-way in the schedule.

With the go-ahead from the team Zoë, Shazia and Gareth get together for an in-depth planning session where they map out what they want to achieve and how they are going to realise it. Shazia and Gareth have a small budget from the arts centre and Zoë some funding from the after-school club which they pool together. The rehearsing and filming will take ten to twelve weeks to complete and Shazia and Gareth will edit the film and make some copies ready for the AGM in October.

Questions

1 What do Zoë, Shazia and Gareth need to bear in mind most to make this project a success?
2 What are the key points that Zoë would need to discuss with her team?
3 If you have you been involved in a similar initiative, compare your experience with the case study.

To think about 10.7

The making, and showing, of the video went very well overall with several benefits for both the after-school club and the arts centre. However, a number of difficulties arose during the project:

- One of the boys in the drama group got a crush on Shazia and became very inhibited when asked to improvise.
- Three weeks into the project Gareth's wallet went missing from his jacket when filming at the club.

- Six weeks into the project and Suzie and Mike were getting a bit fed up with keeping the other children away from the art room as they were increasingly curious about what was going on.
- Towards the end of the filming period the children got more interested in being behind the camera than in front of it.
- Zoë was not happy about the initial editing of the video and questioned her role in the process.

On reflection, do you think these difficulties could have been avoided and if so, how? If not, how would you as the playworker have dealt with them? Discuss this in your team.

GOOD PRACTICE

Permission in writing must always be sought from parents and carers when children are to appear on film or in a photograph. A letter or other document should clearly state to what purpose the video or photograph is to be used and should be signed by a senior member of staff and the parent or carer concerned. A copy must be kept on record.

The above case study illustrates a joint initiative based on a quite practical task involving the users – the making of a video – and, as a worker involved with children and young people and their activities, you may find that such is the case for you.

Here are some examples of other such joint initiatives that play projects have been involved in:

- junk modelling with children in a local school
- camping trip to the countryside with the youth club
- playday activities with other local play projects
- children from the local school visiting an adventure playground for environmental studies
- visits to the project by local police officers to discuss their work in the community.

Activity   10.8

Taking each of the above initiatives in turn, with a colleague, list what the benefits of each might be to:

- the children using the project
- your play project
- the partner organisation
- the raising of the awareness of the importance of play
- the raising of the status of playwork
- your own personal development.

As well as the above more practical examples, there are, of course, many other joint initiatives that may not involve the children at all and may be of a more theoretical or 'political' nature. They are, nevertheless, just as important and beneficial to the development of the play project. For example:

- the development of a local association of playworkers working in partnership with other colleagues in the region
- attendance at a residential training weekend with representatives from other organisations doing similar work, e.g. health, social services, teaching, coaching, probation and youth work
- running training sessions with the local FE college for teachers on play and playwork
- running workshops for councillors from the education committee on the fun and learning of play in partnership with early years workers.

In all of the above, the benefits both for the project and for your own development will be enormous. They will require a certain degree of knowledge and confidence that you may not feel you have enough of at the moment, but that shouldn't deter you from enquiring of your line manager how, through gradual experience and training, you might acquire such skills and confidence.

PROGRESS CHECK

1   Name six of the organisations and institutions in your community that your users visit on a regular basis.
2   What are the key points in making contact with new people?
3   What does SMART stand for, and why is it useful?
4   Identify three factors why planning is so important.
5   What might be a good joint initiative to undertake involving the children from your project?
6   What might be a good joint initiative to undertake that would raise the awareness of play and playwork?

KEY TERMS

You need to know what these words and phrases mean. Go back through the chapter to make sure that you understand.

Informal communication network	Presentation
Leafleting	Canvassing
Local Learning and Skills Council	Networking
Early Years Development and Childcare Partnership (EYDCP)	SMART method

APPENDIX A: THE S/NVQ AWARD AND PORTFOLIO BUILDING

> **This appendix covers:**
> - **How you obtain the qualification**
> - **Portfolio building**

Note: In Scotland the National Vocational Qualification is called the Scottish Vocational Qualification. To cover both titles we are using the term S/NVQ throughout this appendix.

How you obtain the qualification

S/NVQs are achieved through a process of assessment. A candidate works with an assessor to plan how they are going to produce the evidence required to prove competence. At some point this means a candidate must register with an approved assessment centre. Before this, however, a prospective candidate might wish to access a training programme which is S/NVQ linked, or a pre-S/NVQ induction programme. In both cases, depending on what exactly is offered, you will be able to:
- raise awareness around S/NVQs
- think through the process
- determine which levels and units to start with
- develop knowledge and understanding underpinning the standards of competence
- begin planning for assessment
- gain workplace practice
- make contact with an assessment centre.

It is only through registering with an assessment centre that you will be able to work towards S/NVQ qualification. Once you have made contact with your assessment centre you will link up with your assessor and begin the process of identifying and collecting evidence. You will be given a candidate book which will outline the standards at your chosen level, give you general guidance on achieving your award and provide the paperwork necessary for recording your competence. The latter includes observation record sheets, for instance, which will be signed by yourself, your assessor and the internal verifier of the assessment centre. Your assessor will also provide you with the other sheets and forms you will need to help you through the process.

UNIT CERTIFICATION OR WHOLE AWARD?

You have a choice as to whether you want to gain certification for your units as you complete them or whether you want to wait until you have them all and gain the whole award. Your assessor will advise you. Whichever method you choose you will need to begin compiling a portfolio of evidence.

Portfolio building

For the purpose of achieving an S/NVQ a portfolio is a collection of evidence that proves your competence in your chosen occupational area – in this case playwork. It enables you to organise your evidence as you collect it.

Although the term portfolio conjures up an image of a hard-backed folder containing lots of sheets of paper it is also a 'catch-all' term used to describe a variety of evidence including photographs, audio and visual tapes and even, in some circumstances, artefacts such as craft work made with the children. The hard-backed folder with sheets of paper, however, will, for the majority of people, be the principal means by which the core of evidence is collected.

When looking at your portfolio your assessor will be applying a checklist of terms when making a judgement about competence of evidence and you can use them also. It will help you decide not only 'what' evidence but also 'how much'. This is the checklist:

- **Validity** – does the evidence match the specified standards?
  An assessor will need to be able to make a direct match between pieces of evidence and the performance criteria and range statements. Evidence which doesn't match cannot be assessed and, in fact, can be unhelpful to the process of assessment.
- **Authenticity** – is it clear that the evidence relates to the candidate?
  Records of meetings or projects, for example, will need to clearly show the part the candidate played and witness testimonies will need to be signed and dated and describe the status of the witness, e.g. parent, user, colleague, line manager.
- **Currency** – does the evidence relate to current competence?
  The issue of currency is particularly important with evidence that may have been gathered in a previous job or training situation, or just some time ago. Is the evidence still up to date with current practice within playwork?
- **Sufficiency** – is there enough evidence of the right quality?
  Across a whole unit an assessor will need to see evidence that will fully cover the performance criteria and range for each element. You will also need to show evidence that you have sufficient knowledge and understanding of the unit's tasks and activities. Your assessor can assist you with this evidence through questioning and 'what if' scenarios, if necessary.

SOME TIPS ON PORTFOLIO BUILDING

Your portfolio will be a collection of all kinds of written materials, of which your assessment plans and a record of the observations your assessor carried out will be of prime importance. It may also include minutes from meetings, diary sheets, playworker reports, health and safety records, witness testimonies and play programmes. Accompanying the portfolio could be photograph albums, and audio and visual tapes. How are you going to make sense of it all and, perhaps more important, how is your assessor going to find her or his way through it? Portfolios are personal items and each one will look different. The final decision on how it is organised and presented will rest with you. However, there are some guiding principles, that can help you.

Be systematic in your collection of materials
Although it's good advice not to throw anything away if you're unsure whether it might be useful as evidence or not, the more focused you can be at the outset the less time you will need in the final organisation of your evidence. Of course this means being as familiar as possible with the requirements of the standards. If you are working to an assessment plan devised with your assessor this will be easier, but, at the same time, you want to make the best use of naturally occurring evidence. It is essential therefore to:

- Read the standards thoroughly at the level you have chosen and think through the evidence that is required. Your assessor will be able to supply you with self assessment forms which will help you identify what you already have in the form of evidence and what you still need to achieve.
- Make the most of every collecting opportunity. In the normal course of a day's work there may be a number of occasions where, with a planned approach, you could collect some evidence. For instance if you are running a play activity with a colleague you could ask for feedback on your performance afterwards, record it and ask your colleague to sign it.
- Similarly, whenever you decide to keep a piece of evidence make sure that you date it and, if necessary, say with a report or collaborative piece of work, have it signed by the colleague, manager or trainer.
- Make up plastic folders with labels for at least the different units and, if possible, the different elements so that you can immediately begin organising your evidence.

Be systematic in organising your portfolio
As often as possible collate your evidence into the format of your portfolio. Again, the earlier you devise the system for the organisation of your evidence the better. It may feel a bit of a chore at the beginning but it will be even more so if you leave it all until the end when you will have a mass of materials to make sense of. What system you decide on will, of course, be up to you, but the following are some tips to help you, based on the experience of S/NVQ candidates so far.

1 First of all decide on whether you are going to have one or more hard-backed folders to contain all your evidence in sections covering your whole

award or whether you are going to have an individual folder for each unit. S/NVQ candidates have so far successfully employed both methods

2 Whichever method you choose, your portfolio will have divisions based on the units, elements and performance criteria of the standards.

Let's take a unit and look at a layout which can be repeated throughout. The unit section should start with the unit title and a contents list of the various elements in the unit. For example:

Unit PA2: Prepare for children's play
Element PA2.1: Support the safety of the play setting
Element PA2.2: Help to organise a setting for children's play

Each element can then follow in numerical sequence. Within each element division there should be the following:

- The full element as it appears in the standards.
- A brief overview of each element which can include your action plans devised with your assessor and will indicate what evidence you are presenting for which performance criterion and where it is located within the element section (i.e. page number).
- The evidence itself titled and page-numbered, e.g. observation record, session programme, meeting minutes, etc.

You can see by the example on page 280 that some items of evidence are not contained within the element section itself but that clear indication is given of what they are and where they can be found.

As well as these unit and element divisions you will need some paperwork to co-ordinate your whole award or, at least, to put the various sections into a whole context. These can include, for example:

- Something about yourself. A sheet stating your name, job title, work place, contact telephone number, S/NVQ assessment centre, assessor, S/NVQ level.
- An overall contents list with page numbers.
- A cross-reference guide listing the evidence that has more than one application and to which performance criteria it relates.

Whether you choose to collate your evidence in one or more folders, you will want at some point to have all your evidence collected together to give a full account of your S/NVQ achievement. This will, in any event, be necessary for the purposes of internal and external verification. In the case of the external verifier it will probably be the first time that she or he has seen your portfolio and she/he will need to be able to access it quickly and efficiently. This process undertaken for the external verifier is a useful way for you to take an overview and make a summary on what has been described above. The external verifier should be able to:

- identify straight away who the portfolio belongs to and what S/NVQ level it relates to – *from the sheet about yourself*
- obtain an overview of the totality of evidence and where it is located in the portfolio – *from the contents list*
- obtain an overview of how much evidence has been cross-referenced and use this overview when verifying the portfolio – *from the cross reference guide*

- be able to track the evidence in a logical sequence – *from a layout in unit sections*
- be able to match the performance criteria with the evidence presented – *from a layout in elements with an overview and location list*
- be able to verify the evidence as competent – *validity, authenticity, currency, sufficiency*
- be able to verify that candidate and assessor have agreed competence – *from a signed candidate book or evidence summary sheets.*

When you reach this point you will have a comprehensive and accessible portfolio documenting your achievement of an S/NVQ in Playwork.

Below is an extract from the overview to Element PC14.1 from the Unit PC14 'Promote and maintain the health and safety of children' that might feature in a candidate's portfolio'.

ELEMENT PC14.1

Maintain children's safety during play

PC14.1.1 During the normal course of a session we have a rota that ensures a member of staff is always present in either the main hall space or in the outside playground to keep a watching eye on the children. The other member or members of staff are then able to focus on a particular activity with a small group of children. Sometimes we need to vary this. For instance, a particular activity might need two or even three staff to facilitate it, which could mean closing down a space whilst the activity is in progress. Sometimes we are too busy to do more than supervise the centre while free play is going on.
* See Observation Record 10/8/09
* See Staff Rotas March–September 2009

PC14.1.2 I always encourage the children to be mindful of their own safety and how their behaviour might affect others. I have a number of posters around the main hall that, in a humorous way, encourage the children to be careful not to rush around crashing into each other. I always ask a child about safety issues rather than just telling them.
* See Observation Record 10/8/09
* See Witness Testimony: Mrs Marley, Parent 15/7/09

PC14.1.3 I recently had to take a stick away from a boy as he was brandishing it in a way that might have caused an injury to another child.
* See extract from Daily Log Book 6/10/09
* See Observation Record 10/8/09

APPENDIX B: USING THE BOOK TO SUPPORT THE NVQ UNITS AND KEY SKILLS

NVQ units

If you are following a course of study that is guided by the NVQ units, you may wish to identify the parts of the book that are especially relevant to particular units. The matrix below gives all the units within levels 2 and 3, and indicates those chapters that will be of most direct help to you.

STUDY MATRIX

Chapters Units	1	2	3	4	5	6	7	8	9	10
A27					*					
A319									*	*
A320									*	
A321									*	
B226										*
B227					*			*		*
B228				*						*
PW6	*	*		*	*		*			*
PW7		*		*	*		*	*		
PW8	*	*	*			*			*	*
PW9	*	*	*	*	*					
PW10									*	*
PW11									*	*
PW12							*			
PW13		*	*	*		*	*	*		
PW14									*	*
PW15	*				*					*
PW24	*			*						
PW25									*	

Chapters / Units	1	2	3	4	5	6	7	8	9	10
PW26	*	*		*						
PW27									*	*
PW28	*			*						
PW29									*	
PW30	*	*								
PW31	*				*					
PW32				*						*
PW33		*	*						*	
PW34	*	*	*	*						
PW35	*									
PW36					*	*	*	*		

KEY TO CHAPTERS

Chapter 1 The tradition of playwork
Chapter 2 Working with children and young people
Chapter 3 Positive relationships with children and young people
Chapter 4 Planning for play
Chapter 5 The daily running of play facilities
Chapter 6 Responding positively to children's behaviour
Chapter 7 Helping to keep children safe
Chapter 8 Practical issues of health and safety
Chapter 9 Working well with other adults
Chapter 10 Developing and promoting your playwork service

KEY TO UNITS

Level 2
Mandatory units:
PW33 Support relationships in the play environment
PW34 Work with children and young people to create play spaces and support freely chosen, self-directed play
PW35 Contribute to the health, safety, security and welfare of children and young people using the play environment
PW36 Help to improve your own practice and the work of your playwork team

Optional units:
PW25 Contribute to providing food and drink in the play environment

PW26 Facilitate a specific play opportunity at children or young people's request

PW27 Support the development of playwork opportunities in the community

PW28 Contribute to supporting disabled children and young people in the play environment

PW29 Support work with parents and carers in the play environment

PW30 Carry out playwork in a school setting

PW31 Contribute to the administration of the play environment

PW32 Support the travel of children and young people outside the play environment

Level 3

Mandatory units:

PW6 Contribute to an organisational framework that reflects the needs and protects the rights of children and young people

PW7 Develop and maintain a healthy, safe and secure environment for children

PW8 Develop and promote positive relationships

PW9 Plan and support self-directed play

PW10 Reflect on and develop practice

Optional units:

PW11 Work with colleagues in a team

PW12 Respond to concerns about possible child abuse

PW13 Contribute to children's health and well-being

PW14 Work with parents and carers

PW15 Administer playwork provision

PW24 Inclusive play, working with disabled children and young people

B226 Promote your organisation in the community

B227 Contribute to evaluating, developing and promoting services

B228 Organise and supervise travel

A27 Manage a budget

A319 Recruit, select and keep colleagues

A321 Provide learning opportunities for colleagues

A320 Allocate and monitor the progress and quality of work in your area of responsibility

Key and Core skills

The Activities, Case Studies and To Think About points in this book can be mapped to the Key and Core Skills, so you may like to use your work in some of these sections as evidence. For instance, Activity 2.3 (page 36) links with Communication.

APPENDIX C: GLOSSARY OF TERMS

Each of the following words or phrases has been listed at the end of one of the chapters in the book. This glossary gives you an explanation of each term that can have a specific meaning within playwork practice.

Admissions procedure
The process administered by 'closed-door' play settings which requires children to be registered with the facility and signed in and out of the play session.

Anti-discriminatory practice
An approach to children, young people and their families that works to redress any inequalities that exist and to develop a service that actively promotes equal opportunities for the future. The approach is relevant to racial and cultural origins (including linguistic background and religious faith), social background, gender and for children and young people with disabilities.

Anti-racism
A conscious attempt to counteract the results of racism, perhaps within a particular setting or service and to promote an anti-racist outlook and approach for the future.

Anti-sexism
A deliberate attempt to counteract the results of sexist attitudes and behaviour, perhaps within a particular setting or service, and to promote an anti-sexist outlook and approach for the future.

Banning
The exclusion of a child or young person from a play setting for reasons of his or her unacceptable behaviour. Banning should not normally be without prior warning and would usually be for a fixed period of time.

Bullying
Ill-treatment, verbal or physical, between children and young people. The actions of the bullies are unwarranted by what the target child has done and the

perpetrators do not stop even when it is clear that the child is distressed or scared.

Canvassing
As in political canvassing, door-to-door contact with the local community on particular subjects of interest and importance.

Child abuse
Ill-treatment of a child or young person by adults in a position of trust or responsibility for the child. Abusive actions may be those of direct harm to the child or harm can follow the lack of appropriate action by the responsible adult. Abusive actions are categorised into one or more of four types: physical abuse, neglect, emotional abuse and sexual abuse.

Child centred
Policy and practice that starts with the child's needs as the principal consideration. Because play settings attract young people as well as children, this book has used the term user-centred.

Child protection
The system of policies and detailed procedures developed to prevent child abuse and to stop abuse when the facts become clear. Local child protection systems have to meet the requirements of the relevant legislation within the different countries of the UK.

Commercial sector play provision
Play activities run by individuals or companies on a fee-paying basis. Commercial enterprises may work under contract to a local authority or a private employer in the provision of holiday playschemes.

Consent form
A form signed by a parent or guardian which gives permission for a child or young person to go on an outing and/or engage in a special activity.

Consultation
A form of communication that seeks to encourage ideas and opinions from others – for example, from children, young people or parents. Consultation might be achieved by talking with individuals or in a meeting.

Culture
The patterns of behaviour and associated beliefs which are shared by individuals within a given cultural group. Some aspects of culture have their origins in religious beliefs.

Daily diary – see log book

Disclosure
Communication from a child or young person that she or he is experiencing abuse or bullying. A child may tell in words or through other forms of communication, including body language.

Early Years Development and Childcare Partnerships (EYDCPs)
The partnership groupings in England within the 150 local authority and district council structures charged with overseeing the development of the National Childcare Strategy. Each partnership has an elected chair and a lead officer from within the council and each year submits plans to the Department for Education and Employment.

Empowerment
Conferring power to an individual through an enabling or facilitating process.

Facilitator
Someone who gives guidance and support without taking control.

Free play
The play of children that is determined spontaneously and solely by them and is not guided in any way by adults, although the adults may have made play materials available.

Gender differences
The differences between males and females that unfold because of social or cultural expectations set for the two sexes. Gender as a term refers to the social identity of being male or female and not to variation that can be attributed to the biological sex difference.

Local Learning and Skills Councils
To replace Training and Enterprise Councils in April 2001, these local councils will take a strategic approach to the learning and skills needs in their regions. Like TECs, they will be a source of funding for local training initiatives.

Log book or diary
A book in which to record information on the running of the project on a regular basis including special events and incidents.

Modelling
Adults' conscious attempts to behave in a way that they would like children and young people to copy.

National Occupational Standards
The tasks that a worker carries out in an occupational area to show that she or

he is competent. Devised by analysing workers' performance in a given occupation, the standards also define the range of contexts in which the worker must operate to be fully competent.

National Vocational Qualification (NVQ)
A qualification that can be achieved in an occupational area by providing evidence of competence. The competence in any area is determined by meeting the requirements of the National Occupational Standards.

Networking
A term used to describe the establishment of contact and communication with people and organisations relevant to a project or piece of work. The 'net' often extends beyond the immediate community and requires some proactive work by the playworker.

Paedophile
An adult, most usually male, who is sexually attracted only to children below the age of consent. Paedophiles often spend considerable time gaining access to children and developing their trust before making any sexual move.

Playcare
Play settings that provide a direct service to parents and carers by ensuring that children remain on the premises until collected.

Playwork S/NVQ
The National and Scottish Vocational Qualification for the Playwork Sector. There are currently three awards at Levels 2, 3 and 4 (Development). Work is currently in progress for a new Level 4 award in Management for both the Playwork and the Early Years sectors. This award is being developed by the Early Years NTO and SPRITO and will share the same core and optional units.

Play programme
The details of what will be offered to children and young people in a given play setting. The overall aim is to be properly prepared, to offer a range of activities and to leave flexibility for users' interests and spontaneous play.

Positive management of behaviour
An approach in which adults are prepared to intervene and to guide the behaviour of children and young people. The focus is on encouragement of children and an awareness of adults' own behaviour.

Presentation
The use of speech, visual images, written data and participative activities to communicate information on an important topic. It is usually delivered to a group

of people, and the emphasis is on getting the salient points across in as direct and interesting way as possible. The use of video, slides and overhead projections are often employed.

Race
A term that can raise difficulties because of the association with unjustified genetic claims. It is used to cover a number of visible differences between groups, including physical characteristics such as skin colour, broad differences in racial origin and cultural variation.

Racism
A pattern of attitudes and behaviour grounded in the belief that one group of people, defined by racial or cultural identity, is naturally superior to others. Language or behaviour would be racist if offensive words or discriminatory actions were directed at an individual or group because of their racial or cultural origins.

Reflective practitioner
The orientation within playwork, and other areas of work with children and young people, of a willingness to think and discuss, not only focus on actions. Reflection also includes allowing for the perspective of other people within a situation.

Shared-use environment
Play settings that share the site and premises with other users – play centres in schools and community centres for instance.

SMART
A method to aid planning that focuses attention on key objectives and helps the thinking through of the whole task. Uses the following headings: **S**pecific, **M**easurable, **A**chievable, **R**ealistic, **T**ime-bound.

Statutory sector play provision
Play settings run by the local authority and funded through the budget of the relevant department – play, leisure and recreation or education for instance. Normally run with direct-line management from the play officer and often with support groups of parents and carers.

Stereotypes
A relatively fixed belief about the characteristics or capabilities of individuals, applied because they are seen as belonging to a particular group. Stereotypes can be held about individuals of a particular racial or cultural group, on the basis of sex or because an individual has disabilities.

Supervision
Part of the working relationship when one person is responsible for meeting

regularly with another in order to discuss and review the first person's work and to resolve any problems or concerns.

Unacceptable behaviour
Ways of behaving – by a child, young person or adult – that cannot be ignored because the actions impose unreasonably on others, are very unsafe or go directly against the ground rules of a play setting.

User centred
An approach to running a play setting and planning activities that keeps children and young people to the fore in all aspects.

Vetting procedure
A procedure carried out by the police and co-ordinated by local authorities to ascertain whether a person has any previous criminal convictions which might prohibit them from working with children and young people.

Voluntary sector play provision
Play settings or play organisations that are run by voluntary groups and funded by grant aid and voluntary donations. Many seek charitable status and local projects often involve parents and carers as volunteer managers and workers.

APPENDIX D: FURTHER READING

Books and booklets

4children, *Early Years Foundation Stage – It's child's play*

4children, *Getting Started: Developing childcare in and around schools*

4children, *Holiday Play Schemes Activity Guide*

4children, *Policy into Practice no. 5: Linking with schools...to deliver extended services*

4children, *Policy into Practice no.7: Holiday provision for older children and young people*

4children, *The Early Years Foundation Stage and out of school provision*

Bee, Helen, *The Developing Child*, Allyn & Bacon, 12th Edition, 2009.

Brandreth, Gyles, *Children's Games: Over 300 Indoor and Outdoor Games for Children of All Ages*, Chancellor Press, 1992.

Briggs, Freda, *Developing Personal Safety Skills in Children with Disabilities*, Jessica Kingsley, 1995.

Brown, Fraser, *Foundations of Playwork*, Open University Press, 2008.

Brown, Fraser, *Playwork – Theory & Practice*, Open University Press, 2002.

Carter, Margaret, *You and Your Child in Hospital*, Methuen, 1989.

Children's Play Council and the Children's Society, *The New Charter for Children's Play*, 1998.

Cohen, David, *The Development of Play*, 3rd Edition, Routledge, 2002.

Elliott, Michele, *Bullying: A Practical Guide to Coping in Schools*, Longman/Kidscape, 1991.

Elliott, Michele, *Keeping Safe: A Practical Guide to Talking with Children*, Hodder & Stoughton, 1994.

Elliott, Michele, *Teenscape: A Personal Safety Programme for Teenagers*, 3rd Edition, Kidscape, 2002.

Fenwick, Elizabeth and Smith, Tony, *Adolescence: The Survival Guide for Parents and Teenagers*, 2nd Edition, Dorling Kindersley, 1998.

Garvey, Catherine, *Play*, Fontana Press, 1991.

Gill, Tim, *No Fear: Growing Up in a Risk Averse Society*, Calouste Gulbenkian Foundation, 2007.

Harrison, Jean, *Children's Rights: Safety*, Save the Children with Evan Brothers Ltd, 2004.

Hobart, Christine et al, *Good Practice in Safeguarding Children*, 3rd Edition, Nelson Thornes, 2009.

Hobart, Christine et al, *A Practical Guide to Activities for Young Children*, 4th Edition, Nelson Thornes, 2009.

Jeffree, Dorothy and Cheseldine, Sally, *Let's Join In*, Human Horizons series, Souvenir Press, 1984.

Kindlon, Dan and Thompson, Michael, *Raising Cain: Protecting the Emotional Life of Boys*, Ballantine Books, 2000.

Konner, Melvin, *Childhood*, Little Brown & Company/Channel 4 publications, 1993.

Lindon, Jennie, *Safeguarding Children and Young People*, 2nd Edition, Hodder Arnold, 2008.

Lindon, Jennie, *Child Development from Birth to Eight Years*, Open University Press, 2007.

Lindon, Jennie, *Equality in Early Childhood*, Hodder Arnold, 2006.

Lindon, Jennie, *Growing Up: From Eight Years to Young Adulthood*, National Children's Bureau, 1996.

MacDonald, Simon, *The Little Book of Playground Games*: Little Books with Big Ideas, Featherstone Education Ltd, 2004.

Malik, Hyacinth and Walker, Miranda *A Practical Guide to Equal Opportunities*, 3rd Edition, Nelson Thornes, 2009.

Meynell Games on… Parachute Play, Meynell Games Publications, 1993.

Moore, Robin, C., *Childhood's Domain*, Mig Communications, 1990.

Moyles, Janet, R., *The Excellence of Play*, 2nd Edition, Open University Press, 2005.

Pearson, Jane, *Why do we have rules?* (Living, Learning and Playing Together), Heinemann Library, 2006.

Petrie, Pat, *Play and Care, Out-of-School*, HMSO, 1994.

Plant, Martin and Plant, Moira, *Risk-takers: Alcohol, Drugs, Sex and Youth*, Tavistock/Routledge, 1992.

Playlink, *Open Access Play and the Children Act*, Playlink, 1992.

Quilliam, Susan, *Child Watching: A Parent's Guide to Children's Body Language*, Ward Lock, 1994.

Rosen, Michael, *The Penguin Book of Childhood*, Viking, 1994.

Schaffer, H. Rudolph, *Making Decisions about Children: Psychological Questions and Answers*, 2nd Edition, Basil Blackwell, 1998.

Sutherland, John, *Mrs Humphry Ward – Eminent Victorian, Pre-eminent Edwardian*, Oxford University Press, 1990.

Walker, Miranda, *A Practical Guide to Activities for Older Children*, 2nd Edition, Nelson Thornes, 2009.

Weatherill, Cat, *Primary Playground Games*, Scholastic, 2003.

Weller, Barbara, *Helping Sick Children Play*, Baillière Tindall, 1980.

Whaite, Anne and Ellis, Judy, *From Me to You: Advice for Parents of Children with Special Needs*, Williams & Wilkins, 1987.

Magazines and journals

You will find some useful articles in the following publications (relevant addresses are given in Appendix E, if not below). The journals and magazines are relevant to children and young people, not exclusively about playwork.

Child Care (from newsagents)
Children Now (National Children's Bureau)

Childright (Children's Legal Centre)
Early Years Educator (EYE, from newsagents)
ISPAL Ezine (The Institute for Sport, Parks and Leisure)
Journal of the National Association of Hospital Play Staff (from 30 Guildford Street, Staines, Middlesex TW18 2EQ, written communication only)
National Occupational Standards (www.skillsactive.com/playwork/nos)
Nursery World (from newsagents and book shops)
Play Scotland News (Play Scotland, Edinburgh)
Play Today (Play England)
Play Words (www.commonthreads.org.uk)
Play Wales News (Play Wales)

APPENDIX E: USEFUL ADDRESSES

4Children
City Reach
5 Greenwich View Place
London E14 9NN
Tel: 020 7512 2112
Fax: 020 7537 6012
E-mail: Info@4Children.org.uk
Website: www.4children.org.uk
Works with Government, local authorities, primary care trusts, children's service providers, and children and parents to ensure joined up support for all children and young people in their local community.

Action for Sick Children
Unit 6, High Lane Business Court
Rear of 32 Buxton Road High Lane
Stockport SK6 8BH
Tel: 01663 763 004
Supports sick children and their families, whether they are being nursed at home or in hospital. Works to ensure that health services are appropriate and responsive to children and parents.

Association of Play Industries
Federation House
National Agriculture Centre
Stonleigh Park
Warwickshire CV8 2RF
Tel: 02476 414999
Fax: 02476 414990
Website: www.api-play.org
Promotes quality and safety in playgrounds. All members have to comply with relevant British and other European standards.

Child Accident Prevention Trust (CAPT)
Canterbury Court (1.09), 1–3 Brixton Road
London SW9 6DE
Tel: 020 7608 3828
Fax: 020 7608 3674
Website: www.capt.org.uk
Provides information about the nature and prevention of accidents to children, and works to promote safe practice in the UK.

Children in Scotland (Clann An Alba)
Prince's House
5 Shandwick Place
Edinburgh EH2 4RG
Tel: 0131 228 8484
Fax: 0131 228 8585
E-mail: info@childreninscotland.org.uk
Website: www.childreninscotland.org.uk-children
Brings together statutory and voluntary organisations and professionals working with children and their families in Scotland.

Children in Wales (Plant yng Nghymru)
25 Windsor Place
Cardiff CF1 3BZ
Tel: 02920 342434
Fax: 02920 343134
E-mail: info@childreninwales.org.uk
Website: www.childreninwales.org.uk
Brings together organisations and professionals working with children and their families in Wales.

Children's Legal Centre
University of Essex
Wivenhoe Park
Colchester
Essex CO4 3SQ
Tel: 01206 877910
Offers information and advice on issues and legislation relevant to children and young people.

Child Rights Information Network (CRIN)
East Studio
2 Pontypool Place
London SE1 8QF
Tel: 020 401 2257
Website: http://www.crin.org/
A global network of organisations supporting effective information exchange about children and their rights, in general and under the UN Convention on the Rights of the Child.

Council for Disabled Children
8 Wakley Street
London EC1V 7QE
Tel: 020 7843 6061
Fax: 020 7278 9512
E-mail: cdc@ncb.org.uk
Website: www.ncb.org.uk
A source of information, research and advice on issues relevant to children and young people with disabilities and their families.

Daycare Trust
21 St George's Road
London SE1 6ES
Tel: 020 7840 3350
Fax: 020 7840 3355
E-mail: info@daycaretrust.org.uk
Provides information for parents and a consultancy service for local authorities and organisations, promoting quality in child care services.

Fair Play for Children
32 Longford Road
Bognor Regis
PO21 1AG
Tel: 08453 307635
E-mail: fairplay@arunet.co.uk
Website: www.fairplayforchildren.org
Campaigns for children's right to play and for greater quantity and safety in play facilities and services.

FIT
2d Woodstock Studios
36 Woodstock Grove
London W12 8LE
Tel: 020 8735 3380
Fax: 020 8735 3397
E-mail: info@fieldsintrust.org
Website: www.npfa.co.uk
Aims to improve recreational facilities and play space for children and young people, and the general community.

Joint National Committee on Training for Playwork (JNCTP)
E-mail: contact@jnctp.org.uk
Website: www.jnctp.org.uk
An independent, national organisation for people involvement in playwork, relevant education or in training.

Kids
49 Mecklenburgh Square,
London WC1N 2NY
Tel: 020 7520 0405
www.kids.org.uk
Promotes play and opportunities for children and young people with physical
and learning disabilities.

Kidscape
2 Grosvenor Gardens
London SW1W 0DH
Tel: 020 7730 3300
Fax: 020 7730 7081
Website: kidscape.org.uk
Publishes books and runs training on children's personal safety and dealing with
bullying.

Local Government Management Board (LGMB)
Layden House
76–86 Turnmill Street
London EC1M 5QU
Tel: 020 7296 6600
The Industry Training Organisation for the statutory sector and supplier of the
occupational standards in sport and recreation, including playwork.

National Association of Hospital Play Staff
c/o Sue Simpson
50 Illtyd Avenue
Llantwit Major
Vale of Glamorgan CF61 1TH
Organises training and experience to anyone who wishes to specialise in playwork with children in hospital.

National Association of Toy and Leisure Libraries
1A Harmood Street
London NW1 8DN
Tel: 020 7428 2280
Fax: 020 7428 2281
Website: www.natll.org.uk
Will loan toys to families with young children, including those with special
needs.

National Centres for Playwork Education

- *Cheltenham and the South West*
  University of Gloucestershire, Oxstalls Campus
  Oxstalls Lane
  Gloucester, Gloucestershire
  GL2 9HW
  Tel: 01242 714603
  E-mail: swplay@skillsactive.com
- *London*
  Professional Development Centre
  Laylock Street
  Islington
  London N1 1TH
  Tel: 020 7457 5824
  E-mail: londonplay@skillsactive.com
- *North East*
  Kielder House
  University of Northumbria
  Coach Lane Campus
  Benton
  Newcastle-upon-Tyne NE7 7XA
  Tel: 0191 215 6279
  E-mail: neplay@skillsactive.com
- *West Midlands*
  PO Box14762
  Birmingham B45 5DB
  E-mail: wmplay@skillsactive.com
  Developing education, training and qualifications for the playwork field.

National Early Years Network
77 Holloway Road
London N7 8JZ
Tel: 020 7607 9573
Fax: 020 7770 1105
Offers training, information and publications relevant to children and their families: care, education, welfare and good practice within services.

National Society for the Prevention of Cruelty to Children (NSPCC)
42 Curtain Road
London EC2A 3NH
Tel: 020 7825 2500
Fax: 020 7825 2525
E-mail: help@nspcc.org.uk
Website: www.nspcc.org.uk
A national organisation that works to protect children and promote their welfare. Local branches are likely to work closely with the local authority Child Protection Team.

Playboard
59–65 York Street
Belfast BT15 1AA
Tel: 028 9080 3380
Fax: 028 9080 3381
E-mail: info@playboard.co.uk
Focuses on play for children and young people in Northern Ireland.

Play England
8 Wakley Street
London
EC1V 7QE
Advice line: 020 7843 6300
www.playengland.org.uk
Play England provides advice and support to promote good practice, and works to ensure that the importance of play is recognised by policy makers, planners and the public.

Playlink
72 Albert Place Mansions
Lurline Gardens
London SW11 4DQ
Tel: 020 7720 2452
E-mail: info@playlink.org.uk
Website: www.playlink.org.uk
Brings experience of adventure playgrounds together with general issues and policy affecting children's play in any facilities.

Play Scotland
Midlothian Innovation Centre
Pentlandfield
Roslin
Midlothian EH25 9RE
Tel: 0131 440 9070
Website: www.playscotland.org
The policy and coordinating body for play in Scotland.

Play-Train
The Post Office Building
149–153 Alcester Road
Moseley B13 8JW
Tel: 0121 449 6665
Fax: 0121 449 8221
E-mail: team@playtrain.org.uk
Website: www.playtrain.org.uk
Aims to increase the number and quality of creative play opportunities for chil-

dren. Operates the Article 31 Action Network which promotes children's rights under the UN Convention.

Play Wales
Baltic House
Mount Stuart Square
Cardiff CF10 5FH
Tel: 02920 486050
The national organisation for play and playwork in Wales.

Rights 4 Me
Office of the Children's Rights Director
Ofsted
33 Kingsway
London
WC2B 6SE
Tel: 0800 528 0731
Website: www.rights4me.org

Working Group Against Racism in Children's Resources (WGARCR)
Unit 34 Eurolink Business Centre
49 Effra Road
London SW2 1BZ
Tel: 020 7501 9992
Website: www.wgarcr.org.uk
A source of information and publications on good quality play resources, especially for younger children and for an anti-racist approach.

INDEX

R

racism, anti-racism 60–2, 285, 288, 289
range of users 145–7
ratios, children to adults 22, 223
realistic expectations 59, 145–7, 190
Reasonable Practometer 19–20
reasoning 44–7
records
    accidents 123, 125, 207–9
    children 113–25
    income and expenditure 138
    legislation factors 23, 26
    procedures in daily running 113–28
    staff 126–7
    volunteer workers 126–7
recruitment 245–9
reflective practitioners, x 58–9, 288
registration/register of children 9, 11,
    22–9, 63, 113–23, 129
regular safety checks 196–201
relationships 151–2, 228–39
    colleagues 228–39
    community 256–75
    and feelings, children and young
        people 47–52
    parents 112, 116–24, 126, 249–54
    see also positive relationships
religion 24, 48, 60, 62, 66, 159
reports 175
residential holidays 15
resources
    for childcarers 28–9
    personal safety 190
    resource banks 261
    use of 230–2
responsibilities
    children and young people 189
    safety 194–205
reviews
    materials 135
    play programmes 84, 86–8, 91, 98,
        105–8
rewards and incentives 151
ridiculing 158, 170
rights of children and young people 3,
    29–30, 33, 90–1, 189, 245
risk
    assessments 19–20, 62, 65, 85, 100–2,
        106–8
    safety 19, 81, 196
    see also child abuse
role of playworkers 66–7, 164, 184–6,
    194–205

rotas 230, 236–7, 240
rural areas and play 14–15, 220–2, 258

S

safety 192–224
    adventure playgrounds 195–6, 198,
        200–1
    buildings 194, 199
    checks 196–201
    equipment 202–4
    hygiene 215, 218–20
    illness 210–14
    keeping children safe 164–91
    legislation factors 22
    materials 202–5
    outdoor sites 131–3, 194–6, 197–201
    outside the play environment 220–3
    personal safety 188–91
    planning play programmes 97
    policy and procedures 192–205
    regular checks 196–201
    risk 196
    roles and responsibilities 194–205
    sites 194–6, 197–201, 205–20
    snacks 215–18
    storing materials and equipment
        202–4
    strangers 97, 190–1, 214, 227
    trips and outings 222–3
    visitors 97, 190–1, 214, 227
    see also accidents; health and safety
school play centres 11–12
scrap stores 15
seasonal playschemes 13–14
security 214
self-confidence 102–3
self-esteem 50
self-help skills 52–5
self-reliance 52–5, 96–7, 243–4
settings of playwork 9–15
settlement movement 4–6
sexism, antisexism 37, 59–60, 285
sexual abuse 171–3
sexual behaviour 161–3
sexual overtones in bulling 183, 186–7
shared-use environments 11, 289
shops involvement in play services
    259–62
short playschemes 64–5
sign language 43, 73, 160–1
site safety 194–6, 197–201, 205–20
SMART method 231–2, 272, 288
snacks 97, 215–18